Human Beings

EDITED BY

David Cockburn

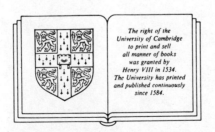

CAMBRIDGE UNIVERSITY PRESS

CAMBRIDGE
NEW YORK   PORT CHESTER   MELBOURNE   SYDNEY

Published by the Press Syndicate of the University of Cambridge
The Pitt Building, Trumpington Street, Cambridge, CB2 1RP
40 West 20th Street, New York, NY 10011-4211, USA
10 Stamford Road, Oakleigh, Melbourne 3166, Australia

A catalogue record for this book is available
from the British Library

ISBN 0 521 42245 0 (paperback)

Library of Congress Cataloguing in Publication Data
Data applied for

Origination by Michael Heath Ltd, Reigate, Surrey
Printed in Great Britain by the University Press, Cambridge

Contents

Contents

Introduction

DAVID COCKBURN

The papers in this volume, or earlier versions of them, were delivered at the Royal Institute of Philosophy conference on 'Human Beings' which was held at St David's University College, Lampeter in July 1990. It was hoped that this theme would provide a focus for discussion of a range of philosophical issues—in particular in the philosophy of mind and ethics—which, while deeply connected, are often treated in relative isolation from each other. Linked with this hope was the idea that the notion of a 'human being' is not one that has, in recent philosophy, been given the attention that it deserves. The relation of each of these papers to that theme creates a number of strong threads running through the volume. This is combined, however, with some radical divergences of views. In this introduction I will try to bring out both the continuities of theme and the differences in approach.

A number of the contributors to this volume are united in thinking that the notion of a human being *is* of crucial importance in our thought. This marks their views off from ways of thinking which have a strong hold in much contemporary philosophy. It is, for example, sometimes argued that to give the notion of a human being a fundamental position in our moral thought is to be guilty of a bias which is closely akin to racial prejudice. Again, it is suggested that there is no difficulty in supposing that an artificially created being—a being not born of human parents—should be a 'person', having the capacity for the full mental life of a normal human being. Finally, it is assumed that my thinking is only clear in so far as it is unconditioned by the fact that I live the life of a human being. In challenging these three, closely linked, ideas the papers by Cora Diamond, Christopher Cherry and Raimond Gaita insist that the notion of a human being is of fundamental importance. The responses, by David McNaughton and Oswald Hanfling, to the first two of these papers call for some qualification of that claim. The papers by Geoffrey Madell and Stephen Clark, on the other hand, call for an outright rejection of it.

The character of the relationships between the notion of a 'person', the notion of a 'human being', and the notion of an 'animal of the species homo sapiens' is of central importance to these issues. A series of particularly striking contrasts in approach to this can be seen in a number of the papers. In taking it to be clear that I am something other

1

David Cockburn

than the extended, tangible being in the publicly observable world, the views of Madell and Clark stand in sharp contrast to those of Diamond, Lowe and Snowdon. Yet the contrasts between the views of the latter three contributors are in some ways just as striking. While he believes that there are objections which still need to be answered, Snowdon is inclined to say that a person is an animal of a certain kind. Diamond and Lowe both reject that view. A crucial difference in the *way* in which they do so emerges, however, in their radically different understandings of the importance of the fact that something is a human being.

It is quite widely thought that Christianity is clearly incompatible with the suggestion that the notion of a human being is of fundamental importance in that it is incompatible with any picture of ourselves as essentially embodied beings. The papers by Fergus Kerr and John Haldane examine this suggestion. Both argue, though in rather different ways, that, far from requiring the Cartesian picture of a person as an entity quite distinct from the human being, Christianity provides the resources for a fundamental critique of such views.

The topic of 'personal identity' has had an important place in the philosophy of mind of the last twenty or thirty years. The papers by Snowdon, Madell, Hertzberg, Clark, Wilkes and Dilman are linked in one way or another with this issue. (Though it is important to recognize that significantly different issues may be being raised under that head.) Two general themes which run through this group of papers deserve to be highlighted. First, Madell, Clark and Dilman all stand in opposition to the strongly third person approach which characterizes much recent philosophy of mind; there are, however, fundamental differences in the *kind* of priority which they give to the first person point of view. Second, Snowdon, Madell and Hertzberg all give a central place to a theme raised in a recent book by Kathleen Wilkes: that of the role which thought experiments can play in a philosophical investigation of the kind of beings that we are.

*   *   *

We normally draw a fairly fundamental distinction between human beings and all other beings, animate or inanimate. No doubt it is pretty well universally agreed that certain kinds of sensation, belief and emotion can be ascribed to all but the very lowest forms of animal life, and, with this, that certain of the obligations which we owe to other human beings we owe, at least in some form, to non-human species. Nevertheless, we draw some fundamental distinctions. We do not hold funerals for sheep; indeed, many of us eat them. Looking in a rather different direction, while some may speak without any sense of incongruity of computers as 'thinking', few, I suppose, are tempted to ascribe, say,

2

depression to their personal computer in quite the way in which they do to other human beings. Now it is often suggested that the existence of such distinctions in our thought stands in need of rational defence; or, alternatively, that certain developments could undermine them. Two of the symposia explore such challenges to the distinctive place which the notion of a human being now has in our thought.

Christopher Cherry and Oswald Hanfling consider the question of whether we could ascribe sentience to, and describe as a 'person', an artificially produced being that was not made of flesh and blood. Both suggest, in opposition to certain strong currents in much philosophy of mind, that the possibility of doing so would depend on the fact that the being we are dealing with has the human bodily form and behaves as human beings do. Cherry, however, argues that this is clearly not enough, that we would be strongly pulled in opposite directions in our reaction to such artificially produced beings, and that if we did speak of them as 'persons' this would represent a massive, and grotesque, shift in our thought. Hanfling argues in opposition to this that facts about the origin and internal materials of these beings would be no reason for thinking of them differently, and that we would, in fact, find it impossible *not* to treat them as people. In defending his position Hanfling suggests that there is a crucial contrast to be drawn between the notion of a human being in the biological sense and that of a being 'who looks and behaves like a human being, engages our sympathy, respect and resentment, is held responsible for what he says and does, and so forth'.

It has been argued, for example by Michael Tooley, that the notion of a 'human being' is responsible for serious confusion in our moral thought in that it has two faces.[1] On the one hand, it serves to identify something as a member of a particular biological species; on the other, it carries the suggestion that a being demands a certain kind of respect from us. Since there is no reason to hold that these go together we should, if we wish to avoid confusion, use the term 'human being' exclusively in the biological sense and employ the term 'person' when we want to indicate that a being has a certain moral status. Some of those who argue in this way would place 'having the human form' in the 'merely biological' category. In stressing the importance which the human form has in our relations with others Hanfling distances himself from suggestions of that kind. He does, however, speak of the particular origin that we have as a 'biological', hence not morally significant, feature of us.

In insisting that the notion of a human being is of fundamental importance in ethics, Cora Diamond is making a more radical break

---

[1] See, for example, Michael Tooley, 'Abortion and Infanticide', in Peter Singer (ed.) *Applied Ethics* (Oxford: Oxford University Press, 1986), 60–62.

with the tradition represented by Tooley. One of her principal targets is the idea that we must draw a contrast between the biological properties of human beings, which it is claimed cannot possibly be of moral relevance, and non-biological properties, such as our capacity for reasoning or self-consciousness, which, while they may be morally relevant, are not found in all human beings and could be found in members of non-human species. Diamond points out that such an approach may conflict violently with our understanding of how, for example, the mentally retarded are to be thought of and treated. She challenges the thinking behind the contrast appealed to here by suggesting that the notion of the human which is relevant in this context must be understood, as she puts it, 'not in a biological sense, but imaginatively'.

While not disputing Diamond's suggestion that the notion of a human being is important in ethics, McNaughton defends a very different view of the *kind* of importance that it has. Diamond insists that we do not need a ground for, say, treating the severely retarded human being quite differently from the chimpanzee. By contrast, McNaughton argues that we *do* need such a ground, and, further, that the ground can be provided. The *justification* for giving the special treatment that we do to the severely retarded human being is found in the fact that he or she has suffered a terrible loss: the loss of distinctively human capacities. This justification, McNaughton points out, appeals ultimately to the *biological* fact that the individual belongs to a certain species. He insists, however, that this need have none of the unacceptable moral implications which have worried some.

In his contribution E. J. Lowe defends the view that a person is a 'psychological substance': a concrete individual thing which is distinct from the biological substance that is his or her body, and yet which does have corporeal characteristics. In defending this view Lowe criticizes two currently popular rival accounts of what a person is. The first is the view that persons are a kind of animal; the second the view that a person is in some sense 'constituted by mental states'. The suggestion that persons are a kind of animal, Lowe argues, runs into very serious difficulties unless we hold that human beings are the only persons that there could be; and *that* claim, he suggests, is 'not only morally repugnant and dangerously arrogant, but also symptomatic of a philosophically inadequate imagination'. Lowe argues further that what is crucial to being a person is the possession of certian psychological characteristics and that there is no reason why these characteristics should not be associated with an inorganic or wholly artefactual body.

These strands in Lowe's discussion link his paper strongly with the two preceding symposia. In particular, his worry about anthropocentrism can be contrasted with Diamond's insistence that the notion of a human being is of crucial significance within moral thought, and with Cherry's suggestion that if we come to speak of human-like artefacts as 'persons' then our use of that term will have 'massively—and in my view grotesquely and deplorably—shifted'. Yet, while it is clear that there are serious tensions between these contributions, the relationships between the three approaches are complex. For, on the one hand, Lowe's version of the thesis that a person is a 'psychological substance' is, as he insists, quite consistent with the claim that the person is the being in the world that can be seen and touched by others; and, on the other, Diamond insists that there is a crucial distinction between the notion of a human being and that of a biological organism of a certain structure.

Lowe's argument against the claim that persons are a kind of animal turns in part on the following suggestion: the circumstances in which we could say that a particular *person* has survived some change are not the same as those in which we could say that this particular *animal*—this member of the species *homo sapiens*—has done so. P. F. Snowdon is sympathetic to 'animalism' but acknowledges that there may be difficulties at this point. His paper is an examination of what he takes to be the most serious of these difficulties. It is widely assumed that it is in principle possible for a person's brain to be transplanted into another body and that if this was done 'the subject (or self) would go with the brain'. Since we clearly cannot say that the animal goes with the brain, we must distinguish between the person and the animal. Snowdon considers a number of possible replies to this argument, focusing in particular on recent attempts by Mark Johnston and Kathleen Wilkes to show that this *method* of argument—that which appeals to thought experiments—is misguided. While concluding that none of these arguments succeeds, he closes with a sketch of another possible line of defence for the animalist.

The acceptability of arguments which appeal to thought experiments is also central to the symposium between Geoffrey Madell and Lars Hertzberg. Madell's paper is a defence of the claim that no view which identifies the person with some 'item in the objective world' can possibly be correct. We will fail to see this, Madell argues, if we focus exclusively on the third person point of view. For it is the first person perspective which creates the following two difficulties for such views. First, there are things that I can imagine for myself—for example, I can imagine having been born earlier or later—which would be unintelligible if I were a certain kind of object in the public world. Second, there is no possible answer to the question: what is it for something which is *merely* an item in the objective world to be me? Madell concludes that the idea that the notion of a human being should be central to our thought about persons is radically flawed, or, as he also expresses it, 'there is no way of entertaining the possibility, that "I" and its objective setting are anything but contingently connected'.

Madell suggests (in ways which partially converge with Snowdon's treatment of this point) that Johnston's and Wilkes' objections to arguments which appeal to thought experiments are misconceived. In his response to Madell's paper Lars Hertzberg offers other grounds for doubt about this method of argument. While not denying that I can imagine, for example, having been born in a different time and place, with quite different characteristics, and so on, Hertzberg suggests that this fact cannot be used in a philosophical argument to establish conclusions about what a person is. For a particular exercise of the imagination is something that takes place against a particular background of concern. (In this case, for example, it might be connected with a feeling of gratitude.) There is no answer, in the abstract, to the question 'Can this be imagined?' and so no room, in abstraction from a particular background of concern, for claims of the form 'I could have been born at a different time and place'. Hertzberg goes on to suggest that we should distinguish arguments which appeal to the imagination in this way from the appeal to 'thought experiments': the idea that considering how we would speak of the identity of people if our lives were very different in certain respects can show us something about 'our concept of personal identity'. This idea also, however, involves a confusion since it is an illusion to think that there is a 'definite answer to the question what, in a different set of circumstances, would constitute going on using our expressions with their present meaning'.

In his discussion of thought experiments Snowdon writes: 'The normal view about language is that we have conferred upon its terms an interpretation in such a way that determines them as true of or false of certain merely possible (but non-actual) situations.' This is what Hertzberg is rejecting when he suggests that 'The structure we take ourselves to be exploring by the aid of thought experiments is one I have been arguing does not exist.' If Hertzberg's arguments are accepted they would appear to have important implications not only for Madell's paper but also for those by Snowdon, Lowe, Cherry and Hanfling; and, further, for most of the recent literature on personal identity (and, perhaps, considerably more besides.)

Hertzberg's approach to these questions is, as he notes, closely linked with what Raimond Gaita, in his paper, calls 'the possession of sense'. The notion of a human being does, however, enter Gaita's argument at a point different from that stressed in most of the previous papers. (Though Gaita's concerns are directly linked with a question addressed by McNaughton: 'Is the moral point of view essentially a human point of view?') The emphasis in Gaita's discussion is not, as with Hertzberg, on the way in which a certain form of argument can *lead* to particular conclusions about what I am, but, rather, on the way in which a certain form of argument, in particular, that which Descartes employs in the *Meditations*, can *reflect* a view of what I am. We see the picture that is at work here in the way in which Descartes asks us to take seriously suggestions—such as the suggestion that I may be dreaming—which would *not* be seriously entertained by anyone of sense. The possession of 'sense'—which is linked with the fact that we are beings of a certain bodily form and have a certain way of life—is, then, being represented by Descartes as external to our nature as thinking beings. Thus, Descartes is asking us to suppose that it is accidental to our nature as thinking beings that we are 'beings who live a particular kind of life, in our case, the life of human beings'.

Why is it that the Cartesian picture of the thinking subject as 'a purely rational, disengaged and timeless entity', only contingently linked with the world of extended and tangible things, has the hold that it does on our imagination? Fergus Kerr's paper opens with an examination of Heidegger's answer to this question. Heidegger argues that it is the influence of Christian conceptions of God, and of our relationship with Him, which are responsible. Kerr suggests, however, that the 'conceptions' (if any) at work here might have been *mis*conceptions and that the philosophical anthropology with which Heidegger replaces the Cartesian myth contains strongly Christian themes. Kerr emphasizes in particular the Christian notion of being *in* this world but not *of* it: a notion which he links with the New Testament sense 'of how the things of this world *matter* to human beings'.

John Haldane is also concerned to show that Christian doctrines need not lead to the confusions of Cartesian dualism. Having spelled out the difficulties which he sees in current approaches within the philosophy of mind, Haldane argues that reflection on the doctrine that, in the person of Jesus Christ, God became a man may open up new ways of understanding the kind of beings that *we* are. If we are to make any sense of this doctrine we must think in terms of a *single* subject of Divine and Human attributes. Applying this 'one person/two natures' formula within the philosophy of mind will lead to a view which avoids both Cartesianism and the idea that the existence of a particular person depends upon his being human. Taking as a model the way in which *Christ's* existence was not dependent on *his* being a man we can 'explain how a created person could be at one time a rational animal incarnate in an empirical medium, and at some later stage possibly be transfigured into a different mode of being'.

The final three papers in the volume discuss the notion of 'the self' within the context of cases in which there is a doubt whether the face which an individual presents to the world, and to himself, 'really is him'. In the first part of his paper Stephen Clark expresses scepticism about many of the claimed cases of individuals with multiple personalities. Quite apart from *that* scepticism, however, he has serious doubts about the suggestion that we should link the notion of 'the self' closely with that of 'the personality' and so conclude that in such cases, if they do exist, we should think in terms of several selves successively occupying a single human being. (His discussion here has close links with Lowe's treatment of the view that a person is a 'psychological mode'.) Now this claim would be consistent with a view which maintained that the person should be identified with the human being. Clark, however, goes on to argue that it is quite clear that this will not do and to offer an alternative, Plotinian, account. Central to Clark's worry here is his suggestion that no view which gives the fundamental position to the notion of a human being can leave room for the idea of the value of the individual person which is so important in our thinking. The reason it cannot is that, as Clark expresses it, 'there are no such things' as human beings: the class of 'human beings' is dependent on the values that *we have given* to particular portions of the world. (This step in Clark's thought should be placed alongside Kerr's observation that 'initially and normally—"proximally"—others are disclosed, as Heidegger says, "in concernful solicitude"'; and with the Appendix of Diamond's paper: for example, with her suggestion that 'what it is that we are talking about is shown in how we talk about it, and in how that talk enters our lives, the shape—the "face"—that life containing such talk has.')

In her response to Clark's paper Kathleen Wilkes argues that Clark's question—'How many selves make me?'—is misguided; for the notion of a 'self' has no useful role to play in philosophical discussions of these issues. We can describe (supposed) cases of multiple personalities entirely in terms of the notion of a 'person'. (But, it should be noted, Wilkes' discussion of this point involves an implicit appeal to a contrast between the notion of a 'person' and that of a 'human being'.) Wilkes allows that if suppositions of the kind discussed by Madell and Hertzberg—'I might have lived in the eighteenth century'—made sense, we would have to think in terms of a 'self-spark'; but we do not have compelling grounds for thinking that they do.

In his contribution İlham Dilman discusses Sartre's treatment of the notion of 'being oneself'. Dilman's approach is marked off from that of Wilkes in that he argues that the notion of 'the self' *does* have a crucial role to play in discussions of these issues. His understanding of what that role is is, however, quite different from that presented in Clark's paper. There is a question 'Who am I?' which may be asked, not by an amnesiac, but by a person who is 'trying to find himself'. Dilman rejects attempts to capture the sense of this question in terms of the notion of a 'self' conceived as an entity waiting to be found—as my lost watch is waiting to be found. The significance of this contrast is seen in the way in which the question 'Who am I?' is necessarily asked in the first person. To try to find oneself is to try to *make* of one's life something more genuine; not to try to locate something which is *given* to me independently of what I make of it. Thus Dilman argues that there is a crucial insight in Sartre's contrast between the idea of what makes a *person* the person he is and that of what makes an *object* the individual thing that it is. He also argues, however, that this insight becomes seriously distorted in Sartre's conclusion that a person can *never* be himself.

The language in which Dilman discusses these issues is, in many ways, close to that in which Madell speaks of 'personal identity'. Either, for example, might write: We cannot think of the self in purely objective, third person terms. But while those words, as written by Madell, would serve to indicate a fundamental disagreement with those contributors who give a central place to the notion of a human being, that cannot, I think, be said of the point that Dilman would be making. As with many of the papers in this volume, surface similarities or differences in verbal formulation may disguise the real relationships which hold between the views expressed.

Machines as Persons?

CHRISTOPHER CHERRY

I

I begin, as I shall end, with fictions.

In a well-known tale, *The Sandman*,[1] Hoffmann has a student, Nathaniel, fall in love with a beautiful doll, Olympia, whom he has spied upon as she sits at a window across the street from his lodgings. We are meant to suppose that Nathaniel mistakes an automaton for a human being (and so a person). The mistake is the result of an elaborate but obscure deception on the part of the doll's designer, Professor Spalanzani. Nathaniel is disabused quite by accident when he overhears a quarrel between Spalanzani, who made Olympia's clockwork, and the sinister Coppelius, who contributed the eyes (real eyes, it seems).

His fellow students are not sure what to make of Olympia. They find her behaviour oddly disturbing, it is true; but it is far from clear that they are not likewise duped. Siegmund remarks that

> [S]he has appeared to us in a strange way rigid and soulless . . . She might be called beautiful if her eyes were not so completely lifeless. I could even say sightless. She walks with a curiously measured gait; every movement seems as if controlled by clockwork. When she plays and sings it is with the unpleasant soulless regularity of a machine, and she dances in the same way. We have come to find this Olympia quite uncanny; we would like to have nothing to do with her; it seems to us that she is only acting like a living creature, and yet there is some reason for that which we cannot fathom.[2]

[1] E. T. A. Hoffmann, *Tales of Hoffmann* (London: Penguin 1988).

[2] Hoffmann, ibid. 116. Grotesquely inappropriate transactions between human beings and artifacts are a significant theme in Fantastic and Surrealist literature and painting, and (like the present case) seem to be special applications of the idea of the inanimate *becoming* animate which is found everywhere in myth and fairytale. The audience attunes to the business with an unerring sense of epistemic pitch that baffled and enraged Rousseau. Discussing, in *Emile*, La Fontaine and Aesop, Rousseau wonders how we can possibly expect children to so much as grasp the idea of talking things: it's bad enough with animals. Worse still, the dish and the spoon speak the same language, and the same language as the cow.

Christopher Cherry

Well, is the situation uncanny? And if it is what makes it so? In his essay on the subject,[3] Freud addresses himself to these questions. Jentsch, to whom Freud refers, identifies as situations peculiarly likely to excite impressions of uncanniness those which illustrate 'doubts whether an apparently animate being is really alive; or conversely whether a lifeless object might not be in fact animate'. Freud develops this observation in all manner of brilliant (though reckless) ways; but its application to *The Sandman* leaves him cold: '. . . Jentsch's point of an intellectual uncertainty has nothing to do with the effect. Uncertainty whether an object is living or inanimate, which admittedly applied to the doll Olympia, is quite irrelevant . . .'[4]

Up to a point Freud is right, at any rate about the source of uncanniness in this story (his own proposals are by the way). Yet he is careless. He shows only that 'intellectual uncertainty' is unnecessary for exciting a sense of the uncanny. For all he says it might here—and elsewhere—suffice. And whom does Freud take to be uncertain? It cannot be Nathaniel, so perhaps it is Siegmund. More to the point, why on earth should Freud call uncertainties—and, presumably, certainties—of such an order 'intellectual'? Isn't this just what they are not? What they are is, of course, conclusively *resolved* in the tale. The issue is settled once and for all the moment Nathaniel discovers that Olympia is not a thing of flesh and blood but an artifact made of wood: an *imitation*. One certitude replaces another.

No doubt it was the availability of such a straightforward, conclusive resolution that led Freud to focus, dismissively, on the 'intellectual' dimension. If so, he was over-hasty. For it is, rather, their easy resolution that makes Nathaniel's initial certitudes at once evidently pathological and philosophically untroublesome. (He is thus both like and unlike Sack's visual agnosiac who famously mistook his wife for a hat.[5]) Quite generally, resolution stifles a sense of the uncanny. For such a sense demands that doubts of the sort Jentsch identifies will *never* be satisfactorily resolved; that one will forever remain unsure if one's attitude and conduct towards the suspect entity are appropriate . . . or grotesquely inappropriate. This means, of course, that no coherent posture will be assumed since higher-order anxieties will colour and subvert every transaction. Nothing of this sort is suggested in *The Sandman*.

[3] 'The "Uncanny"', *Art and Literature* (London: Penguin, 1985).
[4] Freud, ibid. 351.
[5] Oliver Sacks, *The Man Who Mistook his Wife for a Hat* (London: Pan, 1986). Sacks says (p. 20) that his patient had special difficulty with the animate, which he so 'so absurdly misperceived'.

12

So a degree of uncertainty whether something is living or inanimate must persist indefinitely. And yet it cannot be perceived as *irresolvable*. If it were, the suspicion that one might be mistaking the inanimate for the animate (and vice versa) would begin to look empty, and a contrast between what, on any existing conception, is appropriate and inappropriate to each would cease to have any clear sense. For it to be uncanny the uncertainty must be chronic; but it must also be accidental rather then essential.[6]

Fictions of another genre show us what it is like, and what our responses are like, when it is made essential. They deal in things which belong nowhere because they belong simultaneously to both animate and inanimate worlds, and move easily between the two; or—which is not so very different—deal in apparently animate objects brought into existence by impossible means.[7] They do so by conjoining in their

---

[6] Here we move into encounters not with inanimate things behaving in suggestively animate ways but with kinds which are unnatural because impossible: unthinkable human derivatives, the assorted *undead*. They belong nowhere, have no world to call theirs. Yet any description of their nature and capacities must begin by borrowing from the human. (See Anne Price, *Interview with the Vampire* (London: Futura, 1977); and Joseph Margolis, *Dracula the Man: An Essay on the Logic of Individuation*.)

[7] The best and decidedly uncanny example I know of the apparent 'manufacture' of the animate is in U. Eco's *Foucault's Pendulum* (London: Secker and Warburg, 1989), 347:

> Among tropical plants were six glass ampules in the shape of pears—or tears—hermetically sealed, filled with a pale-blue liquid. Inside each vessel floated a creature about twenty centimetres high: we recognized the gray-haired king, the queen, the Moor, the warrior, and the two adolescents crowned with laurel, one blue and one pink . . . They swayed with a graceful swimming motion, as if water were their element.
>
> It was hard to determine whether they were models made of plastic or wax, or whether they were living beings, and the slight opacity of the liquid made it impossible to tell if the faint pulse that animated them was an optical illusion or reality.

I do not wish to deny that the uncanny can also be constructed in other ways which contrast what seems to be with what is:

> He observed this court with fascination: how different it was from the one that he had left in Florence! It radiated a sense of brute force that both attracted and repelled him. Through the smoke, he saw powerful jaws, with several teeth missing, vociferating, laughing and devouring; hands covered with lace and jewels, but greasy and scarred, closing over viands or other hands; ardent, but witless eyes resting on him with cruel insistence. Were these creatures entirely men, or were they all more or less the products of matings with bears, wolves, or some

Christopher Cherry

subjects and their subjects' worlds features which we accept as unproblematically animate (and perhaps sentient) with ones which are just as unproblematically neither. The rules of this game make resolution *between* the animate and the inanimate unthinkable, and discourage us from seeking any. Instead, they propose new categories and so stimulate fantasies about categorially *novel* responses which are sure to be as hybrid and incoherent as their impossible fictional objects.

Tracking these species of reactive uncertainty—the resolved, the forever unresolved but resolvable, and the necessarily unresolvable— let us recall that Nathaniel was mistaken about what Olympia was made of and how and why she came about, and so saw her and what she did in a certain light. When obliged to acknowledge that she was a wooden imitation he saw things very differently—which does *not* mean that initial assumptions of some sort which he worked from turned out to be premature; for he neither needed nor made any. It will probably be said that nothing like this could happen with a doll. Perhaps not. But it is easy to think of things with respect to which it could. We need only imagine Nathaniel meeting Rachel and Pris, Nexus-6 robots engineered by the Rosen Corporation.[8] By comparison, Olympia is laughably inert. Unlike her, they do not seem to move 'as if controlled by clockwork' but appear to act in every respect like human beings. And by this I do not (yet) mean what Siegmund means, that they *only act like* living creatures. They look exactly like us, too, seeming to possess the mobility, the 'variability', demanded for distinguishing between posture and physiognomy on the one side and anatomy on the other.[9] The

[8] The brain-children of Philip K. Dick in *Blade Runner* (London: Grafton, 1987). For present purposes I take them to be made of stuff such as silicon or cellulose. But Dick is neither clear nor consistent on this point, or again on how it bears upon, and ought to bear upon, our perception and account of them. Sometimes he says they are dead, sometimes alive; sometimes insensate, sometimes merely affectless, psychopathic; and this inconsistency is what one would expect in the circumstances.

[9] See Wittgenstein, *Remarks on the Philosophy of Psychology*, II (Oxford: Blackwell, 1980), 358, 627. There is no *logical* absurdity in the supposition that machines should be contrived to display such features. The idea that we could always tell that they *were* machines when we encountered them gains some of its force from Wittgenstein's disposition

other beasts of the forests of the Vendée? Foxes' eyes, wild boars' muzzles, badgers' heads, hairy chests hung about with golden chains and pectoral crosses, a hundred surprising details—flared nostrils, pointed ears that could be made to move, and the squeals, wails and hisses that replaced words and laughter as the night wore on—yes, everything about that ball suggested animal brutality and innocence. (M. Tournier, *Gilles and Jeanne* (London: Minerva, 1988), 79.)

14

conceit is familiar and I shall not elaborate further. (The difficulty lies elsewhere; to describe without prejudice.)

How might we expect Nathaniel to respond when he learns that Rachel and Pris are not made of flesh and blood, are *facta non genita*, and are *imitations*? Not, I suspect, as he did when he learned the truth about Olympia. (For one thing, though I do not take it to be central, we need no longer imagine malicious deception.) But Nathaniel, being mad, does not set the best example. How would *we* react? The question is not an extravagant one since some people already see mobile expert systems as primitive versions of Rachel and Pris, and most anticipate the fully-fledged variety within the next few decades. Let me suggest three possible ways. The first corresponds more or less with Nathaniel's reaction when he discovered what Olympia was. The second corresponds with Siegmund's as Hoffmann describes it. The third corresponds with that we direct towards the impossible entities of the kind I identified.

Implicit in these sorts of reaction are three views about sentience. In respect of the first, doubts about whether an object is sentient or insentient (as I shall henceforth make the contrast) are *always resolved* by determining what it is made of, and/or how it was made, and/or whether it is an imitation, a representation, of an 'original'. I have more to say about these things, and in particular the last, below. In respect of the second doubts about whether an object is sentient or insentient are not always resolved by appeal to such features. In the case of the things I have talked about they persist, even if in an episodic and shadowy way. Yet, though unresolved they must be resolvable. In respect of the third, doubts about whether an object is sentient or insentient are not always *resolvable* because our humanity instructs us in contrary—and contradictory—ways. In the most substantial possible sense we must, and fairly urgently, learn to live with them, doubts and objects alike. From now on I shall focus mainly on the third reaction and the doubts which inform it.

II

What lies beneath the third kind of reaction, with its sense of irresolvable uncertainty? At root, a certain sort of divided vision. But we must

---

to take inert dolls and the like as paradigms of the inanimate and insentient, and from his assumption (like Hoffmann's) that machine behaviour must somehow *look* 'mechanical': 'A dog is more like a human being than a being endowed with a human form, but which behaved mechanically' (p. 623).

start, higher up, by noticing a pull, from opposing quarters, to say with respect to the things I have been discussing both that they are and that they are not animate, sentient. This pull on us in opposite directions may result in a compulsion to attribute sentience to the activity and insentience to its author, in an effort to do justice both to what is seen to go on and to what it is which makes it go on. So a readiness to acknowledge the inanimateness of something because it is a manufactured imitation of (say) a human being *need* not set its behaviour in a wholly different light. The impression that what we are witnessing is animate (or at any rate not inanimate) behaviour *need* not be dispelled in any consistent or lasting way, irrespective of what we think of the status of its source. (Of the other two reactions I mentioned, the first either does not experience the contradictory pull, or else resolves it by bringing into accord its vision of author and activity; while the second distances itself by suspending judgment, hoping perhaps for developments in biochemistry or neurophysiology.)

So the third reaction categorially divorces author and activity, and feels driven to allow behaviour to take on a life of its own. (A good case of life imitating art.) 'Well, there is at any rate flesh-and-blood *behaviour*', it would seem to declare. Now certainly we can sometimes think of real flesh-and-blood behaviour as having a will quite its own without any ascribable orchestrating agency. See how Plato, towards the end of the *Timaeus*, talks of parts of the body as if each were itself its own, independent actor; certain bones contain little soul or intelligence 'in their marrow', he remarks. But here, of course, there *is* flesh and blood. None the less, there is a level on which it is easy enough to see what prompts and informs this third reaction, and why. Complex behaviours of the kind I am now supposing machines to reproduce have—until recently, anyway—always been associated with humans and certain animals, and the connection is easily misread as internal. (Remember, the different connection between humans and animals and sentient *agency* is not, now, in dispute.) Again, behaviour is bound to strike everyone on occasion as independently expressive—expressive under its own steam, so to say, like a sign-post which guides, or an inscription in a dead language which no one knows any more. Yet again, we have for the most part none but intentional modes for characterizing behaviour of the order in question. (It will be said that I am ignoring the uses of metaphor in the last two remarks. But some metaphors are dead, or near death. And in any case, I am seeking not to justify but to explain the sense some have that behaviour has its own life.) Finally, there are endeavours which categorially mismatch in the reverse direction; so why not in this? At a time of great distress, Rousseau sought to see the behaviour of those around him as mere movements, which 'I could only calculate . . . according to the laws of motion'.[10]

[10] Rousseau, *Reveries of the Solitary Walker* (Aylesbury: Penguin, 1981), 129.

However, there is a deeper level on which to come to grips with the reaction. For on one view, certain sorts of behaviour just *are* constitutive of animateness, sentience. This will be the view taken (I do not say 'held') by one who reacts in the way I've described. The machines to which he reacts reproduce the appropriate sorts, and so their behaviour is animate, sentient. But does not this mean—indeed presuppose—that *they* must be? Well, it certainly ought to. But he just cannot see them in this light. As Radford points out: 'It would seem that a machine's duplicating the behaviour of a sentient creature is not enough to lead us to say that it is sentient. It may duplicate behaviour which is, *qua physical movements*, indistinguishable from "animate" behaviour, but we do not see it as animate'.[11]

Our subject's problem is that he is unable to see machine-actors as other than inanimate, yet at the same time unable to see machine activity as other than animate. Different lights illumine each and permit no resolution. This is the nature of his incertitude. Of course the posture is incoherent, but then it was never presented as other. Thus, must not animate behaviour derive its animation from its author? And if it presupposes then it cannot possibly constitute animate authorship. So one route to resolution is blocked off: he cannot hope to pass from the former to the latter to make them accord with one another. In any case, the point, as we have already noted, is that he simply cannot *see* machine-actors as animate. But on the other hand, he cannot move in the reverse direction, since he cannot in any sustained way see machine activity as anything *but* animate. So it is useless to point out that there is all the difference in the world between behaviour which has an author of a kind to confer animation upon it and behaviour which has not. At the epistemic level on which he places himself the two behaviours *are*, unlike their respective authors, indistinguishable. This is what leads him to feel as he does about machine behaviour.

But why cannot he give machine-actors the same treatment as he gives their behaviour? Why is he driven to attribute animation to the one and withhold it from the other? After all, from his point of view the machine ought to be as indistinguishable from a human being as its behaviour is indistinguishable from human behaviour. Any answer is really little more than a redescription of his selective, and as such incoherent, vision. He sees animateness, sentience in the human being but can see neither in the machine. Wittgenstein writes:

[11] Colin Radford, 'Life, Flesh and Animate Behaviour: A Reappraisal of the Argument from Analogy', *Philosophical Investigations, 4*, No. 4 (Fall 1981), 59–60. It must not be thought that Radford and I necessarily agree on what conclusions to draw.

'We *see* emotion'.—As opposed to what?—We do not see facial contortions and *make the inference* that he is feeling joy, grief, boredom. We describe a face immediately as sad, radiant, bored, even when we are unable to give any other description of the features.—Grief, one would like to say, is personified in the face.[12]

Now, it is all right to describe our seeing sentience (or better, sentient states) in human beings—and many other creatures—as (say) having an attitude to a soul so long as this way of talking is not taken to further *explain* anything, and in particular to go substitute for the inference Wittgenstein is anxious to block. For either it is an attitude towards what is already seen as a sentient thing, in which case it would come too late to explain the possibility of seeing sentience; or else it is one towards certain sorts of physical movements, in which case it would have to be identically productive in both sorts of case: men and the machines which so perfectly represent them. And so it is unless we already know, or until we discover, that there *are* both kinds. But with the machines which so trouble those with chronic (and irresolvable) doubts about animateness or otherwise we cannot know, or discover, this by *seeing*; and I shall take it that no one wants to talk of intuition. That is, we know, or learn, by *independent* means that the thing is an imitation manufactured out of some material we are not made of; and this knowledge renders one kind of seeing impossible, or no longer possible, and a different kind inescapable, or inescapable now. At all events, such was Nathaniel's experience. It is not, however, the chronic doubters', especially those who see no hope of resolution. For them knowing, regardless of whether it is sooner or later, simply does not operate in so clear and total a fashion upon their vision. Above all, it does not incline them to stop talking about *behavioural resemblances* between machines and human beings—and, by the very nature of their case, over-whelmingly impressive resemblances. Yet at the same time what they *know* pulls them in the opposite direction, making it impossible for them to see animateness, sentience, in machine actors. The result is impossible objects and incertitudes to which no resolution seems thinkable.

I am far from clear why knowing their provenance and composition should work so dramatically on how many people see them, and why some people should be immune, or selectively immune. Nor am I clear that they should, or should not, or even that this is a proper question to put. I say something further about these topics a little later. However, what the foregoing does help to clarify is a peculiar weirdness which

---

[12] Wittgenstein, *Philosophy of Psychology*, II, 570. I do not examine the grounds of Wittgenstein's hostility to inference in contexts such as these. I agree with what I take to be his position.

pervades the—so to say—phenomenological aspect of the debate about human (and other) beings and machines. Putative resemblances, to the point of identical similarities, between the two are often marshalled with a view to establishing, or at least predisposing towards, an attribution of sentient states in the latter. But such undertakings are perfectly question-begging. Resemblance is *relevant* resemblance, and may be canvassed as such only if the issue is already settled in favour of machines; but then, of course, it is just not needed. If the matter is unsettled, then precisely what is unsettled is whether resemblance has relevance to the undertaking, so we are returned to square one. Resemblance starts work only once the fine print is reached, when the issues are comparative ones about degrees of sentience in creatures already acknowledged to be so non-problematically, or else to be of kinds which might be so non-problematically. Nevertheless, resemblances have such a habit of reminding us of their existence that for some, as we have seen, they assume one of their own.

One way of putting this is to say that animateness and sentience (and their contraries) are not, or are not like other, enumerable properties, even complex and supervenient properties, of things. (And for this reason I am uncertain what Wittgenstein intends when he remarks that he is 'inclined to speak of a lifeless thing as lacking something', and that he sees 'life as definitely a plus, as something added to a lifeless thing'. But he adds in parentheses 'Psychological atmosphere', which suggests that he may want merely to characterize a feeling. Rather the same impression is excited by contrasting an electrically-powered machine with one driven by clockwork.[13]) Another way to make the point is to imagine someone insisting that with machines which imitate humans we have to work harder, plumb deeper, to uncover animateness, sentience: we have to make inferences based upon a wealth of (identical) behavioural similarities to ourselves—procedures he claims are either otiose or second nature in our own case. Well, if such machines were like us *in the respects* he seeks to establish, the only 'grounds' he would need (and could use) would be those needed and used by ourselves in connection with ourselves: he would, ordinarily, *see* the states he trawls for. That he is driven to look for 'abundant behavioural similarities' and the rest reveals that whatever he claims to uncover cannot possibly be what he set out to find. Such items could be pressed into service only if and once they were not needed. But suppose he does come up with claims of successful inference. How would what he infers to connect with what he infers from? Evidently not in the fashion sentience connects with human behaviour. But if so, what leads him to suppose he has inferred to anything, or at least to any thing of the sort *we*

---

[13] Wittgenstein, *Zettel* (Oxford: Blackwell, 1967), 128.

possess? And if he says he can now see machine behaviour as expressive of animateness, sentience, as a result of his 'inferences', the response must be that if this *is* what he sees it was there to be seen before he started. Furthermore, how does he know that the behaviour is expressive of what he believes he inferred to? What kind of 'match' is he looking for, and what encourages him to suppose he has found it? And so on, in the same vein.

What he would actually have done is to posit a wildly contingent (not to say fortuitous) connection between what such machines do and what *in their case* he is pleased to call 'sentience'. This amounts to something like the following: machines may after all be animate, sentient, but these things stand in *no particular relation* to what they do. And this means they may express and display their sentience in any way they choose, including in no way. Far from yielding the conclusion he set out to reach this logic is a *reductio* of the thesis with which he started: a 'for-all-we-could-ever-know' reductio. I have to add that most cosmogonies are in the end similarly vulnerable, not least Plato's in his beautiful story of the creation of humankind in the *Timaeus*, which deserves quoting at some length:

> They copied the shape of the universe and fastened the two divine orbits of the soul into a spherical body, which we now call the head, the divinest part of us which controls all the rest; they then put together the body as a whole to serve the head, knowing that it would be endowed with all the varieties of motion there were to be. And to prevent the head from rolling about on the earth, unable to get over or out of its many heights and hollows, they provided that the body should act as a convenient vehicle. It was therefore given height and grew four limbs which could bend and stretch, and with which it could take hold of things and support itself, and so by god's contrivance move in all directions carrying on top of it the seat of our divinest and holiest part. That is the reason why we all have arms and legs. And as the gods hold that the front is more honourable and commanding than the back, they made us move, for the most part, forwards. So it was necessary to distinguish the front of man's body and make it different from the back; and to do this they placed the face on this side of the sphere of the head, and fixed in it organs for the soul's forethought, and arranged that this our natural front should take the lead.[14]

In his radically dualist fashion, Plato is limning creatures, ourselves, who in essence belong not here but elsewhere. What *we* are like is totally other than what our bodies and hence our bodies' behavioural displays

[14] Plato, *Timaeus* (Middlesex: Penguin, 1965), 60–1.

20

27

are like. This conception encourages us to personify the last, and to see it as driven by principles remote from the first and from everything we might incline to say about it. Plato is perhaps writing to please himself; but the same drive to divorce and personify behaviour, under pressures Plato could scarcely have imagined, is bound in with the sense of irresolvable uncertainty about what is and is not animate.

It is significant, too, that Plato depicts the sublunary creatures we are as fairly botched constructions, much modified copies of pre-existent originals. Hybrid assemblages, we are in a manner of speaking *imitations*. The machines I have been considering are in every manner of speaking imitations; and this is a feature far more important than what they are made of. It causes and inflames many of the problems I have discussed, but at the same time it suggests how some of them might be resolved. This I shall now try to show.

III

I said above that I am unsure if it makes a lot of sense to ask how we *ought to* respond to imitation human beings like Rachel and Pris, not to say Olympia. Partly this is because people cannot choose their responses—which, I have said, does not mean that they would respond identically. Now, the claim that they cannot choose their responses may be voiced in more than one tone. It may intend to emphasise the primitiveness of differential human response to on the one side machines and on the other human beings (and some animals): we see animateness and sentience in the latter, and do not see them in the former. (The seeing and not seeing are not the *causes*, or *grounds*, of the respective responses. It would be better to say that they *are* the responses; and better still that there are as many responses as there are sentient states responded to.) But this would be only partly true. For some people do sometimes seem to see them in the former, or would do if they did not know or had not learned certain things about them; and some of these wonder whether they should or should not, and bog down in incertitudes. So these people are asking how they should respond.

Made in another tone of voice, the claim that they are not subject to our will means to imply that our differential responses are for this reason inadequate or irrelevant as courts of appeal when we try to answer the question: How should we *treat* imitation human beings? Recall the person who sought to infer to sentience in machines. He might, less incoherently, have declared that we do not see it not because it needs winkling out but because we have not been trained to. (He might say we have been trained not to, but this sounds less plausible. Neither, incidentally, commits him to holding that we have been trained to see *one another* as sentient.) And he could add that this form of 'sentience-discrimination' is superstitious and reactionary, and that we must develop new and superior practices: if we make a start the epistemological and phenomenological clutter will then sort itself out. The following remarks have this ring to them:

> [W]hat we should be arguing about is not the possibility of machine souls or machine minds, but whether robots could ever join human society. The requirement that must be met by a robot is that people are prepared to treat it as a person. If they are, they will also be prepared to attribute to it whatever inner qualities they believe a person must have. If a future culture takes a sufficiently permissive attitude to robots, they may come to be accepted as persons without a fundamental change in the concept of a person.[15]

There are so many oddities on so many levels in this passage, with its brisk no-nonsense all-doors-open approach. What can it mean to talk of machines 'join[ing] human society', being 'treated', 'accepted', as persons, and so forth? Dolby thinks we should start (not end) by awarding colours. We can then, but only if we feel the need, hang on them sentient 'qualities'—in my words, see sentient states in them. Here there are vulgar parallels with the theologian's injunction: act in order to believe, and believe in order to understand. At the best of times this is puzzling advice: on this occasion it is unappealing as well, intimating that our very humanity is a metaphysical fancy to be indulged.

Whatever is being urged, it cannot have to do with persons and personhood. One reason why, and I shan't elaborate it here, is most clearly shown in something Dolby has earlier said to the effect that many people already advocate treating machines as persons in limited contexts and for specialist purposes. This strikes them (and him) as an anticipation of what it will be like to treat them as persons *unrestrictedly*: it will be just like this but all the time instead of only sometimes. But to treat entities now and again 'as persons' is precisely not, now and again, to treat them *as persons*. The other reason returns us to the matter of choice. No matter what Dolby and others think, there *is* a deep incoherence in asking in respect of machines which imitate human beings whether or not it might be appropriate to respond to and treat them as we respond to and treat beings like ourselves. It is not just that responses of this order are not of a nature to be cozened and cudgelled, channelled and re-channelled, in this direction or that, though this is true enough. It is also, and more importantly, that the question is itself

---

[15] R. G. A. Dolby, 'The Possibility of Computers Becoming Persons', *Social Epistemology, 3*, No. 4 (Dec. 1989), 321–36. My reply to Dolby is in the same issue.

a confused proclamation that the alternatives it specifies are obsolete and will not cover the novel case in hand, but must be superseded. The answer is in one respect very simple. The way to respond to imitation persons is to respond to them *as* imitation persons. But what is this response like? It might look to be a hybrid, combining elements which the original question treated as exclusive and exhaustive. But if so, what should the mix be? Those who respond with insoluble uncertainty as to impossible objects have assuredly got it hopelessly wrong, though they may take credit for having at least suffered the problem. In fact, the solution cannot conceivably lie in finding a right mix of animate and inanimate, sentient and insentient. There can be no right mix because they do not mix. What is called for is not a novel ontological category but an ontological shift which will somehow absorb and neutralize the two contrary pulls, the one towards the animate and the other towards the inanimate. My suggestion, and it is little more, is that machines such as I have been discussing are best viewed as 'machine-persons'; and that machine-persons, like characters in plays or books, are *fictitious* persons and are to be responded to accordingly.[16]

The suggestion requires us to distinguish between 'machine-persons' and 'machine-artifacts'. Machine-persons are what machine-artifacts represent or portray, and as such they are (as Plato would say) at some considerable remove from reality. No matter how perfect an imitation they remain representations. Machine artifacts, by contrast, are no less real, substantial, than the actors (usually, though not necessarily invariably, living persons) who represent dramatic personages. Now, the practice of representing people on stage and elsewhere is venerable, and familiar to everyone. (Perhaps this is one reason why it is so hard to give any very satisfactory analysis of it.) We as a matter of course assign the same range of properties to characters in plays as we do to people we meet in the street, and we do so non-metaphorically. In so doing we are not, and we ordinarily know that we are not, attributing such qualities to whoever and whatever happens to be representing those characters. We do not normally confuse the two. (This is not invariably so. Indeed, Plato seems to have thought that the possibility—and attendant evils—of representational art issue form some such chronic confusion.) However, in the case of machines I suspect that exactly this confusion is made by those who seek to assign them sentience, or wonder whether or

---

[16] For discussion of this idea in a different application see my 'The Inward and the Outward', in D. Copp and J. J. MacIntosh (eds.), *New Essays in the Philosophy of Mind*, (Calgary: University Press, 1985), 175–93; and my 'When is Fantasising Morally Bad?', *Philosophical Investigations, III*, No. 2 (April 1988), 112–32. In the symposium mentioned in the preceding footnote I discuss some issues in the aesthetics of technology.

not they should. They assign, or wonder if they should assign, to the machine-artifact qualities which are assignable only to the machine-person which it represents. It is as if one were confused enough to attribute to wooden puppets states which can belong only to Punch and Judy.

If this is along the right lines it makes it easier to explain why so gross a blunder is made rarely in the familiar case and almost always in the novel case. For one thing, it is only fairly recently that anyone has seriously anticipated making human-like machines, and we have had no occasion to evolve a practice to accommodate them and the ways we should talk about them and treat them. For another, such machines will be (designed to be) sucked into the hurly-burly of life in a way other fictitious personages are not. Although when he leaves the stage an actor sheds the character he portrays, a machine-artifact never leaves the stage. This cannot but incline us to perceive the machine-artifact and what it represents as cutting an identical swathe through the world, thereby making the distinction proposed *psychologically* difficult to maintain. No doubt it will be claimed that the situation is far worse, and that the distinction is *logically* impossible to make. But this cannot be right. If it were, it would apply to any and every attempt to distinguish what is represented from what represents it. Even so, it leaves us wondering how good a model are our responses to dramatic and fictional characters for understanding how we may expect to respond to machine-persons. Will they be the same at-arm's-length responses, with the difference that they are unbroken; and what exactly does this mean? I am unclear how far the analogy can be pressed.

It will be asked why one should bother with these matters. One reason is that it is worth resolving the incertitudes I identified by getting rid of the impossible objects upon which they are targeted. But what if few really suffer in this way? The reply is clear: it is virtually certain that machines which are on the face of it indistinguishable from human beings (and, doubtless, other creatures) will come on the scene sooner rather than later. The pressures to call them 'persons' will be immense; and unless we are forearmed the subsumption will take place without so much as a nod of acknowledgement that the intension of the term has massively—and in my view grotesquely and deplorably—shifted. But this is another story.

Machines as Persons?

OSWALD HANFLING

I

The subject of this symposium is sometimes introduced by asking whether machines could think. This way of introducing it may be misleading, for it may seem as if it were merely about a particular activity, called 'thinking'. The question would then seem to have the same character as 'Can machines make a noise?'. But thinking is not something that can be treated in isolation from other personal qualities. What we need to consider is whether, or to what extent, a machine could participate in the whole complex of qualities, activities, attitudes, thoughts, feelings and moral relationships that we regard as essential to being a person—whether, in this sense, machines could be persons.

But this brings us to a second pitfall. In formulating the issue as being about *machines*, we are in danger of having settled it in the very act of formulation. This is because the word 'machine' is commonly used to mean an object that is *not*, like ourselves, a person. This is not merely because, as it happens, all or most of the machines we know of are different, in all sorts of ways, from ourselves, but because the very quality of being *mechanical* is one that goes against our conception of a person. We do sometimes describe people as acting in a mechanical way, but this means that their actions are deficient in the characteristics of human action, such as thought, responsibility, etc. The concept of a machine, it may be said, excludes the ascription of personal qualities to machines in any but a diluted or metaphorical sense. In this way the issue may be reduced to a 'merely verbal' level, and readily disposed of.

There are, of course, machines and machines. The vast majority of those in our experience—lawnmowers, aeroplanes, sewing machines and the like—have little resemblance to ourselves, and the idea of regarding such objects as people would strike us as suitable only for nursery stories. Nowadays, however, we may be more likely to think of computers as being the relevant kind of machine. Yet we may feel little inclination to ascribe personhood to what is, after all, a box standing on the desk, however complex its design and impressive its performance may be. Here we may be reminded of Wittgenstein's remark: 'Only of a living human being and what resembles (behaves like) a living human being can one say: it has sensations; it sees; is blind; hears; is deaf; is conscious or unconscious.'[1] This may suggest that what we should be talking about are robots, that this is where the required resemblance may be found. But the word 'robot' too is laden with negative connotations. Nowadays many car factories are operated by means of robots, but no one would be inclined to treat such objects, however ingeniously designed, as persons. Again, to say of some real person that he behaves like a robot is to say that his behaviour falls short of normal human behaviour; lacking the qualities which distinguish human behaviour from that of a mere machine. In this way the term 'robot' might be applied to someone who, for example, follows a leader with blind obedience as a result of brain-washing. Such a person has lost the faculty of critical evaluation; he behaves, as we say, like a robot. Hence, if we ask whether robots could be people, the very meaning of the word 'robot' may prevent us from giving a positive answer.

A safer way to pose the issue is by means of the neutral 'artifact'. What the issue is really about is whether an artifact could be a person; or, putting it the other way round, whether a person could be an artifact—a thing made by human hands and not born of woman in the traditional way. If the answer is 'yes', then it would not follow that *machines* or *robots* could be people, for the artifacts which are people could not properly, and without causing confusion, be described as machines or robots. This, indeed, would be an aspect of the personal status of these artifacts. We may take it that these (artificial) persons would *resent* any description of them as mere machines or robots, and they might well accuse anyone who speaks in this way of *artifactism*. People, they would say, should be judged by their personal qualities and not according to their origins. To describe one of them as behaving like a robot merely because of his origins would be mistaken and unjust in the same way as the ascription of negative qualities to a Jew or negro merely because of his origins.

Now Christopher Cherry makes it clear that he is not, or not mainly, interested in mechanical dolls and the like—objects that resemble human beings in some ways, but whose behaviour is clearly mechanical.[2] The interesting question, for him as for me, arises when we turn to artifacts whose behaviour would not appear mechanical; where, as Cherry puts it, there are 'overwhelmingly impressive resemblances' with human behaviour (p. 18), where the objects in question 'appear to act in every respect like human beings' and 'they look exactly like us, too . . ' (p. 14).

[1] L. Wittgenstein, *Philosophical Investigations* (Oxford: Blackwell 1958), I/281.

[2] Christopher Cherry, 'Machines as Persons?', in this volume.

The supposition that their actions resemble ours 'in every respect' is not, however, as easy to make as it may appear. I am not thinking here of technical difficulties that may stand in the way of such creations, for these are not the philosopher's concern. There is no obstacle to supposing any state of affairs, however far fetched it may be in practical terms, provided that the supposition is logically coherent. In this case, however, certain difficulties arise if we try to fill in the details of the artifact's behaviour. How, for instance, would he behave with regard to eating and drinking, and—let us face it—defecating? If his insides were radically different from ours—microchips and not flesh and blood, let us say—then these functions are hardly likely to be similar to ours. But what, in that case, would happen about feelings, such as hunger, which are such an important part of our humanity?

Again, how are we to envisage the artifact's medical situation? Does he sometimes consult a doctor? Is he subject to the thousand natural shocks that flesh is heir to? There are shocks and infirmities which only creatures of flesh and blood can suffer, and whose existence is an important part of the human condition. Again, what are we to suppose about the artifact's sex life, his memories of childhood or his attitude to death?

There are many details that need filling in before we can take up the supposition of an artifact who acts like a human being 'in every respect'. Perhaps it would be easier to think in terms of a being who is indeed made of flesh and blood—synthetized flesh and blood—rather than the usually postulated computer materials. (This might be especially important with regard to the artifact's *face*, given the importance of the face in human relations.) But if we take this course, then the issue (originally expressed in terms of 'machines') is in danger of being trivialized. For if, as we may suppose, the synthetic materials are indistinguishable from their natural counterparts, including the processes of metabolism, growth etc., then there will be no difference left between the artificial beings and ourselves, apart from the facts of origin. (We might think of this in terms of 'test tube babies', using the term in a more radical sense than now, to mean artificial creations.)

It might be held that even in this case the ascription of personal qualities and status would be problematic. However, I shall address the issue, as it is usually posed, in terms of non-organic materials, accepting that the resemblance between these artifacts and ourselves would be less than complete. A variety of possibilities might then be considered, including some that have been presented in vivid ways in science fiction. But, avoiding these complications, I shall simply follow Cherry by assuming that there are 'overwhelmingly impressive resemblances'. I shall argue, against Cherry, that if this were so, then there would be nothing important 'left over'—that the facts about origin and internal materials would not and should not prevent these beings from being described and treated as people. The same would be true, in my opinion, even of beings who resemble us to a lesser extent, in various ways. But I shall not, in this paper, try to say what kind or degree of resemblance is necessary. I dare say, however, that if the point is conceded for the case of complete resemblance, then it would also be conceded for something less than that, whatever it might be.

At the end of his paper, Cherry raises the question 'why one should bother with these matters', and in reply he claims 'that machines which are on the face of it indistinguishable from human beings . . . will come on the scene sooner rather than later'. This is not a matter on which I would wish to express a confident belief. But the interest of the topic is not, it seems to me, confined to the actual likelihood of such a development. It lies, rather, in bringing out what is—and is not—involved in our treatment of ordinary human beings as persons. I shall maintain that what makes the difference between a person and a non-person is not some fact about origin or internal composition.

II

If such beings, resembling ourselves, began to appear among us, what would stand in the way of regarding them as persons? *Ex hypothesi*, they would not be human in the biological sense. But this is not usually what is meant when philosophers speak of 'persons'; what they mean is a certain moral status. Persons are beings whom we respect in certain ways, and who are expected to respect us in similar ways. Unlike mere 'things', they belong to a moral community, a network of moral relationships involving rights and duties, etc.

Now the ascription of moral status is connected with what we may call the 'inner life'—the existence of consciousness, feelings, sentience, as distinct from any behaviour that we may observe. But could an artifact have an inner life in this sense? Let us also get rid of the impersonal connotations of the word 'artifact', by thinking in terms of particular beings with ordinary English names, such as Jane. Would Jane have an inner life? Would she, for example, feel pain as normal people do? Or would her pain-behaviour, when it occurs, be unaccompanied by the feeling of pain of which such behaviour is normally an expression?

Here we are close to the traditional problem of 'other minds'. Now this problem is fuelled by a certain sense of mystery about the inner life of others. I know that my own thoughts and feelings are expressed only to some extent, and I assume it is the same with others. There is more to the life of a person than what is expressed. But how, we may wonder, would this 'more' have been created in the case of the artifact? We may assume that the people who designed it were instructed to produce an object which would behave just like a human being. Now a reasonable way of conceiving this task would be in terms of inputs and outputs. Thus, in the case of pain, suitable pain-behaviour would occur in response to the relevant inputs (or stimuli)—and also sometimes without such inputs, as is the case with us.

But what if we asked the designers what they proposed to do about the pain itself? Would this be an additional item to be included in the design? This would be difficult, for it is not clear what it would mean to design a feeling of pain (unless, indeed, some of the versions of materialism now on offer could be made intelligible). We may take it, then, that nothing was done about the feeling as distinct from the behaviour, and from this we might conclude that no such feeling exists in the case of the artifact.

But this conclusion will seem less straightforward if we try to fill in some of the details. If we think of pain-behaviour in terms of input and output, we probably have in mind such examples as hitting one's finger with a hammer and responding with a suitable action, exclamation, facial expression, etc. But we should remember that by far the most usual expression of pain, as well as other feelings, in the case of adult human beings, is verbal. The sharp withdrawal, the groaning and writhing, which are sometimes emphasized in commentaries on Wittgenstein's discussion of pain—these are characteristic only of extreme cases; nor do they have counterparts in the case of other feelings than pain. More often, the expression takes the form of telling someone, more or less calmly, that one has or had a pain (a 'slight pain', perhaps) in such and such a place. (This is not to deny that, in the case of pain at least, the non-verbal behaviour is prior to the verbal statement.)[3]

Now these verbal expressions of pain and other feelings would also have to be given by Jane, if her behaviour were to be like ours. Hence the question whether she really feels pain would not need to be left at the level of mute behaviour. We could, after all, *ask* Jane whether she feels pain, both in the extreme cases and on other occasions; and if she behaves and speaks like ourselves, then her answer will sometimes be yes and sometimes no. What would it be in extreme cases, such as hitting one's finger with a hammer? If *this* part of her behaviour is to be like ours, then the answer must be 'yes' (or, more emphatically: 'Don't ask stupid questions; can't you see?') But then, if she had no feelings (because none had been 'inserted' by the designers), what could we

[3] For further discussion of this matter see my 'Criteria, Conventions and Other Minds', in Stuart Shanker (ed.), *Critical Essays on Wittgenstein* (London: Croom Helm, 1986).

make of this response? Would she even understand the question? And how could we make sense of her behaviour—both the original physical behaviour and then the apparently positive response to our question? Similar difficulties would arise if we supposed Jane to give a negative response—if she answered 'no' to the question whether she feels pain. One way or another, it seems impossible to make sense of the idea that Jane's behaviour really resembles ours if we deny that she has an inner life. Once we think about *talking* to her, the supposition that she behaves just like us but feels nothing becomes unintelligible.

It might be objected that the introduction of language makes no fundamental difference, since language is just another kind of behaviour, additional to the non-verbal behaviour but subject to the same sceptical doubts. If it is possible for someone to exhibit pain-behaviour without really being in pain, is it not equally possible to exhibit 'speaking-behaviour' without really speaking?

There is, of course, more to speaking than just making suitable sounds. Parrots are capable of making such sounds, and so are 'I speak your weight' machines; but we would not regard them as cases of speaking in the full sense. What prevents us from doing so? It is not the absence of some internal process, analogous to the feeling of pain. What we need in order to recognize real speech is only, so to speak, more of the same. If the parrot or artifact are prepared to give reasons, if they can explain why they said one thing rather than another, if they demand similar explanations from us and comment critically on these, if they sometimes tell lies, sometimes own up to them and sometimes make excuses—in short, if they play the language-game as we all do, then there will be no difference left between their 'speaking-behaviour' and real speaking. And this would also include the language-game of feelings, as in the case of Jane.

III

Should we conclude, then, that Jane would have an inner life? According to Cherry, we would find it impossible to see Jane in this way. Faced with such a creature, he says, 'our humanity instructs us in contrary . . . ways' (p. 15). A person—a natural flesh and blood person, that is—'simply cannot *see* machine-actors as animate' (p. 17). 'He sees animateness, sentience in the human being but can see neither in the machine' (p. 17). Natural people, according to Cherry, would be aware of 'overwhelmingly impressive resemblances' of behaviour, 'yet at the same time what they *know* pulls them in the opposite direction, making it impossible for them to see animateness, sentience, in machine actors' (p. 18).

But what is meant here by 'impossible'? If what is meant were logical impossibility, then an argument would be needed in support of this. Or is the issue merely one of psychological probabilities, allowing, perhaps, for the speculation that some people might find it impossible while others did not? I shall argue that, for reasons which are not merely psychological, we would find it impossible *not* to treat these beings as persons.

Now Cherry tries to steer a middle course between his 'opposite directions'—accepting that we would not be able to see sentience in 'machines', while also doing justice to the quality of their behaviour. One would, he says, be 'unable to see machine-actors as other than inanimate, yet at the same time unable to see machine activity as other than animate' (p. 17); there would be 'a compulsion to attribute sentience to the activity and insentience to its author' (p. 16).

But what can it mean to ascribe sentience to an activity, if not that it is the activity of a sentient being? To be sentient is to have the power of sensation, etc., and this cannot be directly ascribed to an activity but only to the person who acts.

Cherry's idea of affirming sentience of the activity but denying it of its author is unintelligible, as far as I can see. But it may be regarded as a suitable expression of the quandary in which he finds himself, and in which, according to him, those actually confronted with a-people would find themselves. But how real is the quandary?

I have already commented on the question-begging implications of the word 'machine' and in what follows I shall speak of Cherry's 'machine actors' as 'a-people' (a for artificial) and of natural people as 'n-people'.

Cherry's reluctance to ascribe sentience to a-people may be compared with the reluctance which many people felt in the past about ascribing certain qualities to women. Imagine a discussion taking place forty or fifty years ago about whether a woman could ever be Prime Minister. We cannot deny *a priori*, says one participant, that such a thing is conceivable. Yes, but would we regard such a being as having the inner qualities of a Prime Minister? Perhaps, unable to stomach this, he would say (paraphrasing Cherry's formula) that we would attribute Prime Ministerial qualities to the woman's activities, but deny them to their author, i.e. the woman herself. Perhaps such things might be said—or felt, more or less obscurely—by those who have never had experience of women in positions of leadership. But such hesitations would soon evaporate and there is, as far as I can see, no reason why the same should not happen in the case of a-people.

Now Cherry concedes, at the end of his discussion, that if and when such beings appear among us, 'the pressures to call them "persons" will be immense' (p. 24), so that they would in fact be accepted as persons.

31

But according to Cherry this would not be merely a psychological adjustment, an overcoming of prejudice on the part of diehard arti-factists; it would entail a change in the very meaning of 'person'. It would mean, he writes, that 'the intension of the term has massively—and in my view grotesquely and deplorably—shifted'.

But is it part of the present intension—in other words, meaning—of the word 'person', that an artifact cannot be a person? It is, if by 'person' one means a human being in the biological sense. And perhaps it would be, if by 'person' one meant an immaterial essence of the kind postu-lated by dualists. But what if one means a being who looks and behaves like a human being, engages our sympathy, respect and resentment, is held responsible for what he says and does, and so forth? Then a-people would not be excluded from being persons.

But, it may be asked, would we be right to interact with a-people in these ways? Cherry's answer (or 'suggestion') is that 'machine-persons, like characters in plays or books, are *fictitious* persons and are to be responded to accordingly. . . . No matter how perfect an imitation, they remain representations' (p. 23). Now in the case of characters in a play, there is a familiar language-game in place. 'We as a matter of course assign the same range of properties to characters in plays as we do to people we meet in the street', yet we know perfectly well that these properties are not being attributed to the actors themselves. To do so would be to confuse imitation with reality; and according to Cherry a similar confusion could take place in attributing personal qualities to 'machine-persons'.

Such confusions do take place. Children at a play will often mistake fiction for reality. They also, as Wittgenstein pointed out, attribute personal qualities to dolls. But adults (and children too, most of the time) know the difference; and if they attribute these qualities to imitation or fictitious people, they know that this does not have the same sense as attributing them to real people. (We also attribute certain qualities, such as 'clever' and 'temperamental', to ordinary machines which have no pretensions to personhood.)

There is, however, an important difference between 'imitation human beings' (a-people) and the imitations that we see on the stage, as Cherry points out. The machines, he writes, 'will be (designed to be) sucked into the hurly-burly of life in a way other fictitious personages aren't. Although when he leaves the stage an actor sheds the character he portrays, a machine artifact never leaves the stage' (p. 24).

But, this being so, what (other than origin and inner materials) is left of the difference between a-persons and persons? The case may be compared with that of real and fictitious money. In playing Monopoly we use fictitious money that has the attributes of money only in the context of the game. Outside that context it loses the character of money and is merely a collection of coloured slips of paper. But suppose this money were 'sucked into the hurly-burly of life', that it 'never leaves the stage', but is used just like real money in the conduct of real transactions. In that case it would *be* real money. Similarly, if a-people interacted with us just like real people, then what sense would there be in denying that they *are* real people?

Here again we may be misled by words like 'imitation' and 'artificial'. It is true, of course, that a-people would be artificial, and that the aim in making them would be to imitate human behaviour; and both of these words, 'imitation' and 'artificial', are sometimes used as opposites to the word 'real'. But these words would only affect the origins of a-people and not their personal qualities or status as persons. There need be nothing artificial or imitatory about these. If, in a real situation, we called such a person's behaviour 'artificial', this would have the same derogatory meaning as in the case of an n-person; and similarly with the word 'imitation'.

The attribution of personal qualities to a-people would not be a matter of choice for us, any more than the attribution of such qualities to n-people. Let us suppose that an a-person, call him Edward, has lived among us for many years and it has always been assumed that he is an n-person. Perhaps he is a bit vague when asked about his origins, but no one has ever thought to press the enquiry. Edward has a steady job in charge of a small department at a local firm. He is a respected colleague, though without any remarkable qualities, and so forth. Well, one day Edward decides to 'come out', to reveal his secret. (I assume he would himself *know* the secret of his origins. We could also imagine a scenario in which he doesn't—as happens in romantic novels.) What then? Would we take back everything we said about Edward's thoughts and feelings? Would we now say, and believe, that Edward does not really resent it when we let him down, doesn't really feel insulted if we accuse him of behaving like a robot, is not really glad when he gets a rise in pay? Consider how this might work in a case of letting down:

Edward, to n-person subordinate: Will you meet me here tomorrow morning? It's very important, so don't let me down.
n-person: Yes, I promise to meet you. (Thinks: He is only an imitation person, an artifact, and therefore not sentient. One can't have moral obligations to such a being, so my promise isn't really a promise.)
Edward: By the way, I've heard that you have been reading some bad philosophy, and this has made you an artifactist. But don't let's have any nonsense about this. If you promise to be here, then I expect you to be here, and I'll be very angry if you don't turn up. So if you are

33

Oswald Hanfling

not prepared to give a promise and stand by your obligation, then please say so now. Then I'll make other arrangements.

In these and many other situations we would find it impossible to treat Edward as something other than a person. His announcement might cause a stir at first (finding out a person's origins sometimes does), but after that life would go on as before. (Perhaps, if Edward went on and on about his origins, we would find it a bore and tell him to forget it.)

Someone who persisted in denying sentience to Edward and other a-people would be in the same position as the philosophical sceptic about 'other minds'. Such a sceptic would be stating—or purporting to state—beliefs which are belied by his own behaviour. He would be saying the words 'I doubt whether p' (or, as the case may be, 'I deny that p'), but his behaviour would show that he doubts or denies nothing of the sort. As Wittgenstein remarked about another kind of sceptic, '[He] doesn't simply look the train up in the time-table and go to the station at the right time, but says: "I have *no* belief that the train will really arrive, but I will go to the station all the same". He does everything that the normal person does . . .'[4]

It might be objected that I have overlooked a crucial difference between a-people and n-people—that with which the whole discussion began. In the case of a-people there is, after all, a very different internal structure. Would this not constitute important evidence for doubting or denying that they are sentient? (Would it not be so in the case of the discovery about Edward, for example?)

My answer is that our language-games of relations with other people are neither based on evidence, nor subject to refutation by contrary evidence. In the context of suitable human situations, we cannot help treating beings who behave like ourselves as persons; and this is not dependent on their origins or internal composition. In this respect the scepticism about a-people would be no more tenable than the corresponding scepticism about n-people—i.e. the traditional problem of other minds. In both cases the facts of origin and internal composition are irrelevant. The sceptic about other minds is not to be refuted by drawing attention to the 'positive evidence', and neither would the 'negative evidence' in the case of a-people undermine our treatment of them as people. The two versions of scepticism, about a-people and about n-people, stand or fall—in my view, fall—together.[5]

---

[4] L. Wittgenstein, *On Certainty* (Oxford: Blackwell 1969), section 339.
[5] I am grateful to David Cockburn for many helpful comments on this paper.

The Importance of Being Human

CORA DIAMOND

I

I want to argue for the importance of the notion *human being* in ethics. Part I of the paper presents two different sorts of argument *against* treating that notion as important in ethics.

A. Here is an example of the first sort of argument.

> What makes us human beings is that we have certain properties, but these properties, making us members of a certain biological species, have no moral relevance. If, on the other hand, we define being human in terms which are not tied to biological classification, if (for example) we treat as the properties which make us human the capacities for reasoning or for self-consciousness, then indeed those capacities may be morally relevant, but if they are morally significant at all, they are significant whether they are the properties of a being who is a member of our species or not. And so it would be better to use a word like 'person' to mean *a being that has these properties*, to bring out the fact that not all human beings have them and that non-human beings conceivably might have them.[1]

The argument can be given without specifying the properties that are morally relevant; and people who accept an argument of this sort can differ enormously among themselves about *which* properties are morally important. But here is an example of what people who accept the argument have in mind. It is an important part of being a human being that one has been born of two human beings. All human beings have this property; no robots or chimpanzees or rational denizens of distant planets do. But it is exactly that sort of feature of human life that is held to have no moral significance by all the people who accept the kind of argument I have in mind and who disagree among themselves about which traits *do* have moral significance.

I want to bring Kant in here. Kant said that one must always respect humanity in one's own person and in others. But what he had in mind when he spoke of respect for humanity, of respecting man as man, was

---

[1] My sample argument is made up; for an actual case very close to it, see Joel Feinberg 'Abortion', in Tom Regan (ed.) *Matters of Life and Death* (New York: Random House, 1986), 258–9.

respect for *rationality* in us. The kind of respect he had in mind could not be extended to a human being who is not capable of rational thinking; and it would have to be extended to any Martian who shared our capacity for reasoning.[2] Concern for our fellow human beings and their fate, if it is not a concern for them as rational beings, is irrelevant to ethics as Kant conceives it.

B. The sort of argument I have just sketched depends on thinking that there would be a kind of arbitrariness incompatible with morality in treating *merely being a human being* as morally important. I now want to turn to a different group of arguments also against the idea that being human has any special significance for ethics. This second group of arguments rejects the whole approach of the first, in that the latter arguments do not tie morality to an abstract notion of non-arbitrariness; they do not begin with the idea that morality cannot give weight to such things as being human. I shall give two examples of such arguments, one—Richard Rorty's[3]—emphasizing the importance in moral thought of narrower ranges of concern than the human, one—Annette Baier's[4]—drawing attention to a wider range.

The arguments I discussed first take for granted that there are timeless criteria of *moral relevance*: a consideration is or is not relevant to morality given what moral thought in essence is. Rorty rejects that idea; our thought about how we should act towards others, and the vocabulary in which we put our obligations to them, belong to the communities in which we live. And, he argues, appeals to someone's being a fellow Milanese, or a fellow philosopher, or a neighbour *do* have significance and weight for us that appeals to someone's being a fellow human being cannot have.[5] One might object to Rorty's view that we must as moral agents, as rational beings, not give mere fellow Milanese-ness weight in our thought about how we ought to treat such-and-such people, that we must treat their humanity or their rationality or self-consciousness as making them proper objects of moral concern. But the objection is question-begging: what Rorty is arguing is essentially the irrelevance, the uselessness, of the notion of morality that it invokes.

I now turn to Annette Baier. She has developed a kind of Humean view, in which our responses to character traits and actions depend on

[2] Cf. H. J. Paton, *The Categorical Imperative* (London: Hutchinson, 1953), 165.

[3] See Rorty, *Contingency, Irony, and Solidarity* (Cambridge: Cambridge University Press, 1989), especially ch. 9, 'Solidarity'.

[4] See Baier, *Postures of the Mind: Essays on Mind and Morals* (Minneapolis: University of Minnesota Press, 1985). I draw especially on 'Knowing Our Place in the Animal World', 'Frankena and Hume on Points of View' and 'Secular Faith'.

[5] Rorty, op. cit. (n. 3), 190.

our feelings. These feelings may be aroused by what affects ourselves, or by what affects members of our family, or our fellow country-men, or our fellow human beings, or even by what affects our fellow living things or the world on which we and our fellow beings depend.[6] Sympathetic feeling for others, while it may be strongest for those closest to us, has the potential to spread, to encompass beings further off from us and less like ourselves. Because these feelings also have a built-in need for social reinforcement, the feelings themselves and the language in which we express them may be modified. There is thus, as Hume brought out, the possibility, in ethics as in aesthetics, of shared standards of appropriate response. What Professor Baier does, then, is place 'fellow human being' in what you can look at as two sliding scales of generality.[7] We may look to a wider or narrower group of people with whom we share standards of assessment; and we—we assessors of conduct and character—do the assessing by considering the effects on a wider or narrower circle of beings. Hume himself defined morality in terms of generality extending in both scales to *all human beings*. Professor Baier shows that a Humean ethical theory need not fix the boundaries of moral concern where Hume fixes them; they can be moved further out (and indeed she believes that Hume himself, had he addressed the question, would have agreed).[8] What makes her own account Humean is, besides its overall Humean naturalism, the place in it of communities of moral assessment (which need not extend to the whole of mankind) and of concern, based on the emotions, for a wide and widen-able circle of beings.

Let me put this another way.

We *x*s assess together conduct and character so far as it affects ourselves and our fellow *y*s.

Professor Baier takes Hume's account, in which *x* and *y* are both replaced by *human beings*, and shows that that account can be seen as one of a variety of accounts in which *x* and *y* can be more widely or more narrowly fixed, and are independent of each other. But in her own account and in Hume's generality enters at another point:

We *x*s assess together the character and conduct of us *y*s so far as it affects ourselves and our fellow *z*s.

We Americans (say) may disapprove of foreign dog-eaters; and it may be the case that, although we assess their conduct, we do not regard them as fellow members of the community within which we make the

---

[6] Baier, op. cit. (n. 4), 171–2.
[7] Ibid. 149–50.
[8] Ibid. 149.

assessments. *Whose* conduct and character is assessed is then a third point at which there may be this or that degree of generality; and in the style of moral theory represented by Professor Baier's account, there is no *necessity* that the generality at one of these points will coincide with that at any other.

One way, then, in which the notion *human being* may play a role or fail to play a role in moral thought is in giving the range of generality of *x* or *y* or *z* in a formula which may be more or less like the one I have just given. And moral theories may also differ among themselves in how much independent variation they allow in the ranges of generality.

II

In Parts V and VI, I shall try to show that the importance of the notion *human being* in ethics can be seen only with its importance for the imagination. I shall need to make contrasts with the views I have been describing; in Part II, I pick out some significant features of those views.

First, Professor Baier's view and the place it assigns to imagination in ethics. The capacity for sympathetic sharing of another's feelings, together with other elements in our complex emotional make-up, determines the range of beings for whom we can have moral concern. That capacity for sympathetic appreciation of what others feel, and also the kind of judgment of another being's situation and nature, necessary for a grasp of what actions towards that other being are appropriate—these involve imagination. The capacities, including the imaginative capacities, that underlie and direct moral concern belong to us as animals, as the complex kind of animal we are, hence the title of one of her papers: 'Knowing Our Place in the Animal World'. Professor Baier shares Hume's 'intention of de-intellectualizing and de-sanctifying the moral endeavour, in presenting it as the human equivalent [of elements in the life of other social animals]'.[9] That view of ethics places limits on the role of imagination. Ethics is tied to a conception of ourselves as animals; the conception of what kind of beings we are is not left open to imagination. To leave it open would leave room for the kind of 'mystification' or 'sanctification' of moral life which she follows Hume in opposing. Thus, e.g., the imaginative elaboration of the difference between ourselves and animals, characteristic of Kant's ethics, gives imagination a role disallowed, I believe, by Professor Baier. (I develop that contrast further in Part IV.)

I turn now to Rorty's views. For Rorty, the capacity for imaginative identification with others is what enables us to concern ourselves with

[9] Ibid. 147–8.

their needs and their fate. This imaginative identification with others develops historically in different ways in different communities. That is, he does not work with a Humean notion of human nature, of there being aesthetic and moral qualities fitted by nature to produce certain feelings in a person with properly developed and educated organs of response. Moral concern is something we have not as rational beings nor as animals with certain capacities but as members of communities within which this or that language of moral deliberation has taken shape, and within which there are various uses of 'we', 'us' (contrasting with 'them'), expressive of solidarity with fellow members of a community.

Imagination does not merely aid our identification with others: for Rorty it has a role also in construction of the self, through imaginative development of language. This, characteristically, is something poets do; and he favourably contrasts that poetic activity with philosophical attempts to find universal features of being human. We should be better off if we ceased even to ask the philosophical question what it is to be a human being. From the philosophical point of view, the poets' interest in the particular life of this or that individual, in the particulars of a particular life, is an interest in the merely accidental; the essential reality of what it is to be human escapes their eyes altogether: they are not concerned with essential truth. The concern with what it is to be human is not, on Rorty's account, limited to philosophers. The cultural tradition of which it is part began with priests telling us *the truth* about human life, continued with Greek philosophy and includes empirical scientists and German idealists.[10] Rorty does not deny that there is imagination in such philosophical conceivings of what it is to be human; but such conceivings are best done without. Imagination, used well, is concerned with other things than *what it is to be human*, and does not sanctify or mystify human capacities or human nature; it can (I think this is his view) be fitted into what he describes at one point as a 'bleakly mechanical description of the relation between human beings and the rest of the universe'.[11] (I shall return to Rorty's view of imaginative concern with what it is to be human in Part V.)

Let me now divide the very various arguments grouped together in IA into *Kant* and *the rest*. Kant's ethics, I suggested earlier, gives a central place to an imaginatively shaped notion of ourselves as rational beings. (Here, as elsewhere in the paper, when I speak of Kant as using imagination, I do not mean 'imagination' in his sense.) He also has, notoriously, a double account of human motivation, and (matching that double account) a double account of the kind of understanding

[10] Rorty, op. cit. (n. 3), 26.
[11] Ibid. 17.

Cora Diamond

there may be of a human action. The understanding of an act as done for the sake of the moral law is not an understanding based on experience: we cannot know of any particular act that it was so motivated. But we can nevertheless imagine there to be acts the appropriate understanding of which would involve their connection with the agent's own sense of himself as a rational being. We may imaginatively read this connection into some actual act, but empirical evidence cannot suffice to establish such an understanding. (I shall discuss the role of imagination in Kant's moral psychology in Parts III and IV.)

I included in IA a great many views different from Kant's in eschewing talk of the transcendental or toning it down. What these views have in common with Kant's, though, is their insistence that, if concern for a human being is *moral* concern, it is directed towards that human being because of his or her possession of traits which make moral concern appropriate for *whoever*—human or not—has those traits. Such views may give a far more limited role to imagination than it has for Kant; they may not give it a role in our conception of ourselves as he does; they may not give it a role in the understanding of morally motivated action. They may for example allow that imagination enables us to grasp what the effects will be, on others, of actions we contemplate, to grasp what it would be like (say) to be on the receiving end of those actions. But the assignment of *that* sort of role to imagination may go with great hostility to other activities of imagination within ethics, e.g., to imaginative development of the sense of what is mysterious in human life.

III

Part III is about imagination as something we may perceive in someone's actions or words. I shall use a quotation from D. H. Lawrence's review of a book by H. M. Tomlinson.[12] Lawrence himself quotes and then comments on a passage in Tomlinson's book, about an American sportsman who had been collecting in Africa. Tomlinson had written that the sportsman 'confessed he would have felt some remorse when he saw the infant still clinging to the breast of its mother, a gorilla, whom he had just murdered; so he shot the infant without remorse, because he was acting scientifically. As a corpse, the child added to the value of its dead mother.'[13] Lawrence wrote

[12] '*Gifts of Fortune*, by H. M. Tomlinson', in D. H. Lawrence, *Phoenix* (Harmondsworth: Penguin, 1980), 342–4. (There is apparently no record of publication prior to earlier editions of *Phoenix*.)
[13] Quoted by Lawrence, 344.

We share Mr. Tomlinson's antipathy to such sportsmen and such scientists absolutely. And it is not mere pity on our part for the gorilla. It is an absolute detestation of the *insentience* of armed, bullying men, in face of living, sentient things. Surely the most beastly offence against life is this degenerate insentience. It is not cruelty, exactly, which makes such a sportsman. It is crass insentience, a crass stupidity and deadness of fibre. Such overweening fellows, called men, are barren of the feeling for life. A gorilla is a live thing, with a strange unknown life of its own. Even to get a glimpse of its weird life, one little gleam of insight, makes our own life so much the wider, more vital.[14]

Lawrence goes on to express the gratitude he feels, and that he thinks we should feel, to Tomlinson for the vision he conveys of other-than-human life in all its strangeness: not just gorillas, but octopuses and insects and others. That imaginative sense of the strangeness of these creatures' lives is in Lawrence's own prose; but it could also be in someone's actions, e.g., the actions of someone meeting that sportsman. I mean that one can think of a case or cases in which the imaginative sense of that marvellous strange gorilla's life was in an attempt, say, to protect that gorilla, perhaps a shout at the right moment to put the sportsman's aim off. You might think of the shout as an expression of concern for the gorilla, but I am interested in something else: the possibility of seeing in the action, or indeed in the concern itself, that imaginative sense of the otherness of animal life.

What interests me is the characterization of actions—and of intentions, perceptions, motives, wishes, thoughts—by the imaginative activity that enters them. In my example, the imaginative sense of the strangeness of animal life, with which we mysteriously share this planet, may be in an act; and the recognition that that is so may be part of an understanding of the act. Further, such understanding of what is in acts (or thoughts or words or feelings) belongs to the way we judge these acts, and to the ways in which we may learn from them, take up the imaginative responses in them and give them place in our own lives. Any moral psychology is incomplete if it leaves out the ways imagination enters acts (and thoughts and talk) and the understanding of those acts (and thoughts and talk).

Let me give an example of a view of moral psychology in which great weight is given to how imaginative life enters thought, action, perception and indeed patterns of action, approaches to life. The example is Dickens's moral psychology, but I discuss in this section only one element of it.

[14] Ibid. 344–5.

Cora Diamond

We all know that we were once children, but that may be mere abstract knowledge, incapable of entering our adult lives. Or it may be imaginatively available to us; the acceptance of our own past childhood may be imaginatively present and active in us as adults. Without the imaginative presence in us of the child we were, we are as adults incapable, Dickens thought, of enjoyment and hope, and that cripples us morally.

Note the difference between how a moral philosopher might represent the role of imagination in Scrooge's change of heart and how Dickens represents it. A philosopher might give us Scrooge realizing in imagination what it would be like to be a little boy singing Christmas carols at Scrooge's door and being given a good fright, and not even a halfpenny, by Scrooge; Scrooge thus recognizes that *he* would not like it if someone did it to him and that he could not will that small carollers should suffer so. But *Dickens's* Scrooge is transformed by the Ghost of Christmas Past, who makes alive to Scrooge the child Scrooge, the child Scrooge's enchantment with the *Arabian Nights* and with *Robinson Crusoe*; and this touches Scrooge. His being imaginatively touched by himself as child is then present in the awakening of humanity in him, the awakening capacity to be touched by the child singing carols at his door. As an imaginative sense of the strangeness of animal life is present in Lawrence's prose and verse, and can be present in action, so an imaginative sense of the touchingness of human childhood, tied to his own sense of himself as child, is in Dickens's writings; and he attempts to show us how an imaginative sense of the touchingness of childhood, tied to a sense of oneself as child, may be present in acts of humanity, and how its absence may also be perceived in what we do and what we are capable of feeling.

I want now to develop a comparison between Dickens's Scrooge and a Kantian Scrooge, who might (let's say) contribute some pennies to the child at the door out of respect for the child's humanity in the Kantian sense, respect (that is) for the child's rational nature, where that respect is inseparable from the Kantian Scrooge's respect for himself as rational being, his understanding of himself as a being capable both of imposing on himself and of obeying the moral law. That self-understanding of the Kantian Scrooge is quite distinct from the understanding available to him as an empirical observer of himself or of human beings in general as part of nature. We turn to Dickens's Scrooge, but Scrooge 'reclaimed'—that is, after the Ghosts have completed their work. This Scrooge is touched by human childhood, the vulnerability of children, the intensity of their hopes, the depths of their fears and pains, their pleasures in their play, their joy in following stories—all this touches Scrooge, and its touchingness is in his generosity towards children, as the Kantian Scrooge's respect for rational nature is in *his* generosity towards children. In Dickens's Scrooge, this being touched by childhood involves a live sense, and acceptance by Scrooge, of the Scrooge-child in him, as part (an owned, acknowledged part) of 'I, Scrooge, the human being'—just as the live sense and acknowledgment of the Scrooge-rational-being in Scrooge is in the Kantian Scrooge's generosity.

The understanding that the Kantian Scrooge has of himself is, as I said, not available to him as observer of human beings in the empirical world; and, just as important, the conception *we* can have of what is in his generosity is significant for us, not as students of empirical nature and manipulators of it, but as Scrooge's fellows, fellows in rationality, fellows in moral life. In Dickens's epistemology, the capacity to know oneself as Scrooge reclaimed does does not belong to him as sharer in the body of human knowledge of the empirical world and of human nature as part of it. The Ghosts who aid in his reclamation do not try to give him empirical knowledge, to overcome ignorance (in any plain sense) of nature. Just as important, the conception that we may have of what is in his developing generosity (the idea that in it is his being imaginatively touched by childhood) is something of interest to us as Scrooge's fellows, fellows in bearing within us our own childhood, fellows in Scrooge's inhumanity if our own childhood, our sense of childhood, goes imaginatively dead. There is in both cases, that of the Kantian Scrooge and Dickens's, a contrast between the understanding of Scrooge's motivation of interest to us as observers and manipulators and theoreticians of nature including human nature, and the understanding we need to have as Scrooge's fellows.

For Kant, I said, we understand Scrooge as our fellow in rationality; for Dickens, the fundamental understanding of Scrooge is as our fellow in having a human life to lead. But that is not a simple contrast; since for Kant it is rationality that distinguishes us from animals; it is what, as he imaginatively characterizes it, distinguishes having a human life to lead.

In Part I, I said that we might schematically represent some of the resemblances and differences between moral theories in terms of the values of x, y and z in

We xs assess together the conduct and character of us ys so far as it affects any of us zs.

Here, in Part III, I am concerned with generality at different places, and not within moral theory:

We, who share this striking thing—having a human life to lead—may make in imagination something of what it is to have a human life to lead; and this imaginative response we may see (and judge and learn from) in the doings and words and customs of those who share

Cora Diamond

having a human life to lead. That perception may belong to the understanding we want of those words or actions or customs. (The actions in which the sense of human life is perceivable include but are by no means limited to actions affecting other living human beings.)

The character of the generality at different points in that last paragraph may be complex and difficult to describe accurately. We may (e.g.) take it that the 'we' who share and make something in imagination of living a human life includes all peoples, but we may *then* think of as dehumanized or not properly human peoples from whose lives such imaginative response has been driven out (the Ik, as Colin Turnbull describes them)[15] or whose imaginative life we (for whatever reason), ignore, misunderstand or contemn.

IV

One of the features of human life that has been a great centre for the imagination, one of the things worked over, elaborated, made something of, by imagination is that in the world, in our lives, there is us (that is, people) and animals. We are mysteriously like them, mysteriously unlike them. We are—people have always been—deeply interested in that queer relation, us and them. Kant, with his imaginative vision of human life, of human beings as rational beings, set apart from animals by rationality, belongs not just to the philosophical tradition that searches for what is non-contingently ours; his thought forms one strand in the imaginative elaboration of this strange and striking feature of our lives: that we inhabit a world inhabited also by these *other* beings, who do not speak to us except in some of our most enduring myths and tales.[16]

Philosophers sometimes treat the idea of a contrast between ourselves and animals as either plain error on our part or as something odd, an odd mode of speech, surviving from a time when we had got our natural classification wrong.[17] But the contrast is no error of natural

[15] In *The Mountain People* (New York: Simon and Schuster, 1972).

[16] See John Berger, 'Why Look At Animals?' in *About Looking* (New York: Pantheon, 1980), 1–26.

[17] See, e.g., Mary Midgley, *Animals and Why They Matter* (Harmondsworth: Penguin, 1983), 7. For the relation between imaginative and naturalistic description of our relation to animals (taking the single example of the significance of the *look* another gives us), compare Mary Midgley, *Beast and Man* (Hassocks: Harvester Press, 1978), 6–13 with John Berger op. cit. (n. 16), 2–4, and Robert Hobson, 'The Curse in the Dead Man's Eye', in *Changes* 2 (1984), 40–4.

classification; our marking the contrast is not like our failing to see underlying similarities between superficially different species of plants or animals, a failure then reflected in a relatively primitive classification. The language of the contrast comes from our sense of what is mysterious in human life; and I am claiming that that sense is important in moral thought because of its capacity to enter what we do and say and feel and think.[18]

I want now to show how the imaginative sense of human life is related to a difference between Annette Baier's views and those of Dickens and Kant. For Dickens and Kant, I have argued, the kind of understanding appropriate to the actions and thoughts and sayings that belong to moral life depends on our capacity to make certain kinds of imaginative connection. Thus, e.g., the understanding that we are meant to have of Scrooge's remorse for not having dealt kindly with the Christmas caroller depends on our imaginatively connecting his remorse to his enlivened sense of himself as child. This kind of understanding of what actions and thoughts may have in them does not belong to empirical psychology.

The contrast with Professor Baier's view must be made carefully because of her complex relation to Kant. She incorporates some Kantian elements into her account of moral motivation,[19] but only elements consistent with its Humean spirit.[20] What she rejects is Kant's transcendental psychology, his insistence that an empirical psychology of Man the complex animal is not appropriate for the understanding of our moral life. She speaks with approval of those moral philosophers 'who looked to psychology and history to find out what sort of good we have any chances of successfully attaining, creating, preserving, and recognizing as our own',[21] but 'psychology' there is meant to exclude psycho-

---

[18] I am not in this paper concerned with the question whether the contrasts that we make, prompted by our response to what is queer and striking in human life, involve grouping things in a way that is arbitrary, compared to the groupings of things inspired by scientific interests; I am concerned rather with the fact that it is no necessary feature of philosophy that it should think of its own interests as closely tied to those of science. There is something analogous to Scrooge in our philosophy: a closing off of oneself to the child in one, as having no significant place in the grown-up way we do philosophy. The sense of the world as remarkable, the live interest we have as children in the fact that the world has animals and us, is imaginatively dead or inaccessible to us, and we are then capable of writing as if there were something odd or prejudiced about people who, in the face of all we now know, go on using the word 'animal' as if it denoted only non-human animals.

[19] Baier, op. cit. (n. 4), 305.

[20] See ibid. 137.

[21] Ibid. 138.

logy like Kant's transcendental psychology: it is (that is) meant to exclude any psychology which insists on its own difference from the understanding available to the empirical student of human nature.

One way in which the difference (between the kinds of psychology) may show up is in what counts as *understanding*. Suppose (to invent an example)[22] we are shown in a story someone who, as a child, had been inconsolably affected, afflicted, by hearing of something horrible that people do, or had done, to other people or to beasts. The child cries out 'Why are they allowed to do that?'—and no one can answer; perhaps no one cares enough to try to; to the pain of the knowledge of what we do is added the pain of not being understood. In the story we are shown how what happened then enters the grown-up person's sense of life, his sense of the darkness that there is in the way things go; and we may then see that sense of life to be present in some action many years later, shaping its significance. The sense that someone has of the terribleness of what we do, as part of that person's sense of what it is to have a human life, may be shown in a story as making an action intelligible, or as making appropriate and in that way understandable the intensity of remorse for some action, or as making it possible for some action to alter the face that the person's life has for him. But empirical psychology has standards of its own for adequacy of explanation. I do not mean that its standards are *stricter*, in the sense in which we used to hear that historians give explanations which do not meet the strict standards of the theorists of scientific explanation, but that what makes sense of an action may be something different in kind from what is acceptable in empirical psychology. The most familiar example of this difference in kind is Kant's transcendental psychology. Although he does not think that we can know for certain, of any particular action, that it was done for the sake of the moral law, to think of it as done for the sake of the law *is* to think of it as thereby understandable although one has not provided any explanation in terms usable in empirical psychology.

The difference in kind between the two sorts of psychology (two meanings of 'psychology') is a difference in the readings they invite. Thus, e.g., Professor Baier speaks of psychology as enabling us to find out what sort of good we have any chances of successfully attaining, creating, preserving and recognizing as our own. It will tell us, that is, what we are like; it does not invite us to take up and make our own or to reaffirm certain understandings of good in human life and of possibilities of intelligible human action. Kant is explicit about this: in discussing transcendental psychology, his aim is not that we should know *what the chances are* of human beings recognizing as good

[22] The example is based on an anecdote recounted by Susan Isaacs, *Intellectual Growth in Young Children* (London: Routledge, 1930), 163.

adherence to the moral law for its own sake. What he says about the possibility of doing so does not invite the response 'Yes, there is *some chance* of people acting like that; yes, there is some evidence for it'. The self-understanding that it is meant to provide is inseparable from the reader's free activity as moral agent; and Kant's intention is also to enable his readers to avoid misunderstanding the significance of what empirical psychology recognizes as possible in human motivation. There is no subject matter 'what is possible for human beings', common to empirical study of how certain beings behave and descriptions like Kant's of free action—descriptions, redescriptions, narratives—that we are invited to take up into our ways of making sense of our lives.

Even descriptions of what we *are* like may have quite different roles in reflective moral thought from what I think is suggested by Professor Baier. A writer may describe what human life is like, may describe it with great attention to its detailed empirical reality, but with the intention that the mystery of existence '[show] through the texture of . . . ordinary lives';[23] and with the further aim that the sense of that mystery, thus awakened or thus developed in the reader, will enter his or her life, will be present in his or her doings and thinkings and sayings. Attention to empirical reality with *that* sort of aim is different from the attention to empirical reality intended to make our moral theorizing realistic in what might be called a Humean sense, and different also from attention to empirical reality intended to help us apply moral principles on the basis of a more adequate conception of the circumstances in which we are acting.

I have not here tried to show that 'the kind of animal we are' has elements in its psychology of imaginative responsiveness to life, elements which are important in its behaviour and thought and which moral philosophers should not ignore. For that would treat moral philosophy as needing to know more *about* imagination in order to give it its place in the philosophical treatment of human nature. Moral philosophy is not then viewed as continuous with or fed by imaginative responsiveness to human life. The imaginative elaboration of, for example, the difference between ourselves and animals, the imaginative re-shaping of what it means to be human, and thus of the concept *human being*, is then not thought of as something that has a place in the philosopher's kind of reflection on morality and human nature.

The exclusion of such imaginative activity from philosophy may seem to be called for by the facts: we are, after all, animals, and ethics without mystification must recognize that morality belongs to 'the kind of animal we are'. But there are ways and ways of using the word

[23] Flannery O'Connor, *Mystery and Manners* (New York: Farrar, Straus & Giroux, 1970), 133; see also 44, 80, 104, 124, 176, 198.

'animal'; and to insist that ethics take seriously 'that we are animals' is to insist that ethics take seriously—in its vocabulary—certain human interests other than the interest in making imaginative sense of life. That insistence is also shown in the idea that the term 'human being' may be used only as a term making the kind of classification a biologist would make or as a term for a being with certain traits that most members of our species do have.[24] If, as I have suggested, imaginative elaboration of what it is to have a human life is a characteristic human activity, that activity (tied to the use of 'human being' and 'human' so that they are neither terms of biological classification nor terms applicable in principle to rational robots or Martians or whatnots) may be invisible to us as we engage in philosophy.

V

I have argued in Parts III and IV that imaginative response to *having a human life to lead*—to what we find strange or dark or marvellous in it—may be seen as present in actions, thoughts, talk, feelings, customs. In Parts V and VI, I return to the issues of Part I: the character and extent of moral concern; I show those issues in relation to the possibilities of imaginative response to life. Part V begins with Rorty's idea of how imaginative literature, like the writings of Dickens, enlarges the range of moral concern; I contrast Rorty's view with Dickens's own.

I noted earlier Rorty's contrast between the idiosyncratic poetic imagination, concerned with particulars, concerned with the shaping of one's own self, and the endeavours of philosophers (which he recognizes may involve imagination) to find what is essential in human nature. While he by no means excludes the possibility of imaginative concern with what it is to have a human life, he seems to regard such concern as likely to lead to mystification, or at any rate as not likely to make any useful contribution to morality beyond inspirational rhetoric. We can see this in his comments on Dickens's novels. These novels he takes to belong to a tradition of imaginative literature that helps us to grasp 'the kinds of suffering endured by people to whom we had

[24] Cf. also Peter Singer, 'Animals and the Value of Life', in *Matters of Life and Death*, 338–80: he mentions the possibility of the term 'human' 'slopping around' between the 'person'-use and the biological use (355). Cf. also Mary Anne Warren, 'On the Moral and Legal Status of Abortion', in Joel Feinberg (ed.), *The Problem of Abortion* (Belmont: Wadsworth, 1984), 102–19. She distinguishes in a different way the two senses of 'human being'; but the point of the distinction is the same: to deny the existence of imaginative shaping of meaning, and to treat thought about morality as capable of going on without loss in a context emptied of all intimacy with such imaginative shapings.

previously not attended'[25] and it is in that and related ways that imaginative literature can contribute to moral progress. Through novels and stories, we are able to see how our pursuit of private ends may conflict with what we owe others; we come, through such literature, to care about the sufferings or the humiliation of a wider range of human beings.

Rorty's idea of how Dickens's stories bear on moral thought seems not to include the imaginative concern in those stories with what it is to live a human life. There is a directing of imaginative energy in Dickens that is not towards a poetic, idiosyncratic making of the self nor towards imaginative realization of what other people suffer. The issues here come out if we contrast a Rortyan Scrooge with Dickens's. Rorty's Scrooge might be helped to be less cruel by coming to know more about the effects on the poor of the social practices of his time; or by talk or writing enabling him to see (see fully, imaginatively grasp) the effects of his own 'idiosyncrasies' on the Cratchits, for example.[26] But Dickens's Scrooge, when he is told about the social practices that leave some in Want that is keenly felt, while others enjoy Abundance, thinks it fitting that those in Want go to the workhouse, and, if they would rather die, they had better do so. He will not be able to respond to the sufferings of the Cratchits until he comes to have, in his perception of their lives and their fate, a full imaginative sense of his own mortality, until he can live in the present and acknowledge his own past. That opening of the heart, which for Dickens is tied especially to Christmas, is inseparable from a live sense of oneself as, with others, bound towards death, of others as one's 'fellow passengers to the grave'. The viewing of other people as 'another race of creatures, bound on other journeys', is an expression of one's having suppressed or rejected, rather than imaginatively owned, one's own being human; and so is the incapacity for love or mirth, the incapacity to enjoy life, that marks Scrooge and so many other characters in Dickens. The first thing that Dickens's Scrooge does when he is fully awake is *laugh*. The laughter Dickens wants from his readers is the laughter of awakened humanity in us; his writing, his imaginative attention to the ordinary and extraordinary, to the comic and horrible particulars of life, serves his readers—or is meant to—as the Ghosts serve Scrooge. Dickens's aims are not unlike those explicitly put by Joseph Conrad: If a writer of fiction takes a particular moment of life and holds it up and 'shows it in its vibration, its colour, its form', shows 'the stress and passion' in it, this may awaken in the hearts of the reader, the beholder of the described

[25] Rorty, op. cit. (n. 3), xvi; see also 94.
[26] See Rorty, ibid. 141.

moment, 'that feeling of unavoidable solidarity; of the solidarity in mysterious origin, in toil, in joy, in hope, in uncertain fate, which binds men to each other and all mankind to the visible world'.[27] One important difference, then, between Dickens and Conrad on the one hand and Rorty on the other is over the question whether solidarity with others is fostered (as much as it may be by descriptions of the pain or humiliation they suffer at our hands) by vivid descriptions of what it is like to enjoy *Robinson Crusoe* (say) or to eat such a Christmas goose as never was and to smell a Christmas pudding, taken out of the boiling water and unwrapped; the difference between Dickens and Rorty about Christmas pudding reflects a great difference about morality itself and its relation to our sense of our own humanity.

(I am not suggesting that Rorty would deny that what I see in *A Christmas Carol* can be seen there. But I believe he would find in my version of the story a concern with people's 'real needs'; and that is not what he would find useful in it; he might regard my way of reading it as not *helpful*. On the other hand, what he criticizes, in his discussions of concern with 'human nature', is that concern as found in the philosophical tradition; i.e., he criticizes the attempt to discover the timeless essence of being human, and the attempt to ground human solidarity on that timeless essence. My reading of Dickens as attempting to bring us to acknowledge our own humanity, to have a live sense of it, does not ascribe to him any concern with timeless essences. The idea of our needing a sense of our own childhood (for example) does not rest on any implicit Dickensian theory of elements in the soul including, as it were, one's own past child-self. The need is perceived in the course of what one might call Dickens's imaginative diagnosis of the soul, which is very different from the various imaginative activities explicitly discussed by Rorty: poetic construction of the individual soul (good), imaginative enablings of identification with the suffering and humiliation of others (good), imaginative engaging in the philosophical quest for our real nature (results in some not unhelpful rhetoric, but basically pretty useless). In Dickens's imaginative diagnosis of the soul, we live badly if we fear and reject our own humanity; its acceptance in ourselves goes with our capacity to respond to it in others. Dickens is merely an example; the point is that there is room for connections between human solidarity and the sense of what it is to be human, connections quite unlike those in the philosophical tradition which Rorty has in mind.)

I have stressed that, for Dickens, the awakened sense of one's own humanity may be present as much in enjoyment of the goods of life as in

---

[27] Preface to 'The Nigger of the *Narcissus*' (Harmondsworth: Penguin, 1963).

compassion or anger at injustice; but I want to consider more particularly the sense of one's own mortality. This, for Dickens, has particularly deep connections with living well and with our capacity to create a decent social world, connections that come out in many of the stories. The absence of a live sense of one's own mortality is connected in *Bleak House* (which echoes *Hamlet*)[28] with the deadly spirit of lawyerdom and reliance on false security. In *Our Mutual Friend*, the sense of one's own mortality is shown in the spirit in which those who have no love for a man, a contemptible rogue, can labour to save his life and be brought to tears in the struggle. In *A Christmas Carol* (Stave Four) there is this, said of the apparition of the dead Scrooge: 'He lay, in the dark empty house, with not a man, a woman, or a child, to say that he was kind to me in this or that, and for the memory of one kind word I will be kind to him.'

The bareness of the sounds, the rhythms, the first person singular in indirect discourse, are there used by Dickens, acting as Ghost of Christmas Yet To Come to his readers, us Scrooges. He would, if he could, bring us into our own deathchamber, bring us to a sense of our own need that someone should say of us that he, that she, was kind in this or that. He would have us see callousness, deadness to the needs of others, distancing of oneself from their fate, as denial of the common journey.[29]

I am not ascribing to Dickens the idea that we ought to think 'This person is mortal like me, therefore I cannot turn my back on his need'. Rather, just as the sense of mortality may be in the rhythms of Dickens's prose, it may be present in such things as our interrupting the rhythms of normal life, our devoting great efforts and resources, to save a single person in mortal danger; or again it may be present in the abhorrence of murder, or even in the ways we express our deepest hatreds. (I have in mind the acts of some soldiers in the Lebanon, who gestured to a group of mourning women that they might come to pick up the bodies of their dead. When the women got within range, the soldiers opened fire at them. There we can see depth of hatred expressing itself in the *denial* of what the soldiers knew human beings extend to other human beings in the face of what death is in our lives. We can, that is, see human solidarity in the face of death in part by seeing the power, as gesture of hatred, of its withdrawal.)

[28] See Joseph Gold's discussion of the tie to *Hamlet*, in *Charles Dickens: Radical Moralist* (Minneapolis: University of Minnesota Press, 1972). The whole of Gold's book is relevant to the themes of this paper, but see especially the Introduction.

[29] See also Stanley Cavell, *The Claim of Reason* (Oxford: Clarendon Press, 1979), 376.

Cora Diamond

VI

In Part I, I stated the argument, accepted by many philosophers, leading to the conclusion that *being a human being* is a morally irrelevant property, and that moral concern for a being rests rather on some or other property like self-consciousness, sentience, or rationality. That argument underlies a number of recent philosophical remarks about the treatment of retarded people. Take this remark of Peter Singer's: 'We have seen that the experimenter reveals a bias in favour of his own species whenever he carries out an experiment on a non-human for a purpose that he would not think justified him in using a human being, even a retarded human being.'[30]

Singer's use of the word 'even' expresses his view that what justifies moral concern for human beings must be either a property like sentience, which we share with 'non-humans', or a property like the capacity for rational choice, which, if it is absent in 'non-humans', is also absent or much diminished in many retarded people. Hence willingness to experiment on 'non-humans', if combined with unwillingness to experiment *even* on retarded people, reveals species-bias.

Consider also remarks of John Rawls's bearing on the retarded.[31] He treats 'the capacity for moral personality' as a sufficient condition for the application to a creature of the principles of justice; he does not try to answer the question whether the capacity is a necessary condition. He does, however, say that it seems 'that we are not required to give strict justice . . . to creatures lacking this capacity'.[32] His discussion places severely retarded people in a category with animals: creatures for whom there is a question whether justice or 'strict justice' applies to them. And this idea of retarded people as constituting a kind of 'borderline case' in connection with the applicability to them of justice is now extremely common.

Comments: A. It is sometimes also argued that retarded people are a 'borderline case' with respect to *having rights*.[33] That is plain nonsense if said of legal rights. Philosophers who ask whether it is meaningful to

---

[30] Peter Singer, *Animal Liberation* (New York: New York Review, 1975), 82.

[31] *Theory of Justice* (Cambridge: Harvard University Press, 1971), 504–12.

[32] Ibid. 512. It should be noted that the applicability of justice to a person is connected by Rawls to the 'inviolability' of the person (3).

[33] See, e.g., Joel Feinberg, 'The Rights of Animals and Unborn Generations', in *Philosophy and Environmental Crisis*, W. T. Blackstone (ed.) (Athens, Georgia: University of Georgia Press, 1974), 44; Jeffrie Murphy 'Rights and Borderline Cases', in Murphy, *Retribution, Justice and Therapy* (Dordrecht: Reidel, 1977), 26–39.

52

ascribe rights to idiots and madmen[34] should note that there is no doubt
at all that they have rights, e.g. to property, under the U.S. Constitution. Only of *moral* rights can the stuff about 'borderline cases' appear
plausible; and the only reason it does so is that theories of 'moral rights'
are usually tied to accounts of morality that incorporate some version of
the argument about *being human* not being morally relevant. Thus,
e.g., irreversibly comatose people are described by Jeffrie Murphy as
being 'disturbingly similar in relevant respects' to things like rocks, that
cannot be bearers of rights.[35] Again, it should be noted that it is a crime
to rape an irreversibly comatose woman.[36] Murphy's view has the
implication that the difference between a comatose person and a
dummy is merely a *legally* relevant distinction, and that the *legal*
distinction between the two (one being conceptually a possible victim
of a crime and the other not) does not reflect a *moral* understanding.

B. We should note how very odd the view is that a severely retarded
person cannot meaningfully be regarded as the victim of injustice. It
would be held by many people uninfluenced by theories of what can
count as moral relevance that the conviction by a court of a severely
retarded person for a crime that required an intention the retarded
person could not form was unjust; the less capable of forming such an
intention the person is, the more palpable the injustice.[37]

Professor Rorty rejects what I shall call the Orthodox view, that
concern for a being is *moral* only if it rests on 'morally relevant properties', which do not include being human, being American or Milanese
and so on. He would not argue that, because retarded people lack or
have only to a limited degree some or other 'morally relevant properties', they are a borderline case for moral concern or the applicability of
justice. Rorty sees callousness or cruelty towards the retarded as reflecting a tendency people have to care more about those whom they see as
like themselves: people may accept a sort of 'common-sense
chauvinism', that may be put, roughly, as 'the less like you and me a
thing is, the more justified we are in using it as a means to an end'.[38] I
want to bring out that, despite the differences between Rorty and the
Orthodox, he is in an interesting way *with* them; both he and they fail to
give an adequate account of possibilities of moral responsiveness to the
retarded because both he and they, though for different reasons, will
not attach to being human the significance that it has in much moral
thought.

[34] See Feinberg, op. cit. (n. 33), 44.
[35] Murphy, op. cit. (n. 33), 27.
[36] J. C. Smith and Brian Hogan, *Criminal Law* (London: Butterworths, 1973), 326–7.
[37] Cf. also the letter of Hélène Tassel-Smith, *Le Figaro*, 16 mai 1989, 2.
[38] From a letter.

Rorty's view about the retarded is that we are concerned with the pain or humiliation of a person when we see him or her as 'one of us', as sharing what we take to be salient characteristics, and the willingness we may have to treat the retarded without concern, or with a lesser concern, thus reflects our treating their incapacities as salient differences from ourselves (though we can come to see those differences as less salient, and their being our neighbours, say, or our fellow-Americans, as more important similarities). The important difference between his view and that of the Orthodox is that Rorty does not think that someone's having a capacity like that for self-consciousness or moral personality justifies respect for him in a way that his being one's fellow-American cannot. On the Orthodox view, some retarded people are in no morally relevant respect different from cows (or different only in that there are Persons who care deeply for them), and someone in an irreversible coma may be in no morally relevant respect different from a rock; for Rorty, there is no appeal to such a notion of moral relevance, but his naturalistic account includes the tendency of many people to treat as salient the presence or absence of those characteristics, like consciousness, self-consciousness, moral personality, rationality, that are treated as internally connected to the very notions of moral respect or of rights or of strict justice by the Orthodox. For the Orthodox, the severely retarded are properly thought of as in a borderline category; for Rorty, we may, with imaginative effort, bring them into the 'us' of those with whose sufferings we can to whatever degree identify, but they would tend to come in late, like the poor among ourselves, or foreigners with different coloured skin. Despite their deep philosophical differences, Rorty and the Orthodox have in common this combination of views: (1) the fact that the retarded lack or have to a far lesser degree capacities like that for rational choice makes it hard, or harder, to treat them as the objects of moral concern, and (2) there is available no notion of *human being*, embracing them and us, capable of playing a substantial role in moral life (capable, that is, of being anything more than inspirational rhetoric).

I have quoted Conrad's account of his aims as an artist, a teller of stories. He hopes to awaken the feeling of unavoidable solidarity in mysterious origin, in toil, in joy, in hope, in uncertain fate, which binds men to each other and all mankind to the visible world; he takes himself to speak to our capacity for delight and wonder, to the sense of mystery surrounding our lives, to our sense of pity, and beauty, and pain, to the latent feeling of fellowship with all creation.[39]

[39] It should be pointed out that the sense of pain meant is not the capacity to sympathize with feelings of pain in others. See, e.g., Harold Brodkey's exclamation, 'My God, how bitterly and deeply I want the world to go on'

The sense of mystery surrounding our lives, the feeling of solidarity in mysterious origin and uncertain fate: this binds us to each other, and the binding meant includes the dead and the unborn, and those who bear on their faces 'a look of blank idiocy'[40] those who lack all power of speech, those behind whose vacant eyes their lurks a 'soul in mute eclipse'.[41] I am not arguing that we have a 'moral obligation to feel a sense of solidarity with all other human beings' because of some natural or supernatural property or group of properties which we all have, contingently or necessarily. I am arguing, though, that there is no need to find such a ground; there is the possibility of deep moral concern for retarded people, in which they are seen as having, however incomprehensible we may find it, a human fate, as much as anyone else's. They are seen as with us in being human, where that is understood not in a biological sense, but imaginatively. Someone may be very touched by the response of a severely retarded person to music; and there may be in that being touched an imaginative sense of shared humanity. That is a non-moral example of the way the sense of shared humanity, embracing the retarded, may enter thought and feeling. I shall give two examples of its entering moral concern, and shall then draw some conclusions.

(1) Suppose a child to ridicule a severely retarded person, someone who had no grasp of having been the butt of ridicule, or who perhaps was led to co-operate in some cruel joke at his expense, and could not see the cruelty of the joke. The child's parents might be outraged at the conduct and think it important that the outrage be communicated to the child, that the child learn that this was very bad indeed and never to be repeated. In the outrage may be present that imaginative sense of our human boundness to each other of which Conrad wrote. (I am not denying that theories of morality of the kind I have been criticizing may try to accommodate such cases without reference to the imaginative sense of human connectedness. Such attempts may themselves reflect the view that imaginative response to what it is to be human does not belong in philosophy, that we should do philosophy, or moral philosophy, as if we were rational Martians.)

(2) In some cultures there is the idea that a retarded person is specially loved by God, is a special blessing from God on a family, is specially welcome in the community. While that idea is present in some

[40] Dostoyevsky, *Brothers Karamazov*, trans. David Magarshack (Harmondsworth: Penguin, 1958), Book III, chapter II.
[41] Walter de la Mare, 'The Mourner'.

('Reflections: Family', *The New Yorker*, November 23, 1987); the pain felt has in it the sense of mystery at how webs of human relations reach through the world.

Cora Diamond

Christian thought, it is not a mere product of Christian doctrine. It goes with a sense that we cannot judge what the significance is, or the connection with good, of a human life, and with the idea that evil done to a retarded person may reveal great corruption in the person who does it. Dostoyevsky expects his readers to share this much of such views: a man who rapes the village idiot may thereby show himself to be particularly corrupt. He takes that response for granted in his readers, without assuming that they share his Christianity. Consider the outrage that we may feel at the rape of a girl lacking speech and understanding, lacking what we think of as moral personality and the capacity for autonomous choice, and incapable of finding the event humiliating and the memory painful as a normal woman might. We do not feel this outrage as Kantians: from a Kantian point of view the offence in the rape of a non-rational being is to the rapist, to his own rational nature, to humanity in him. (The act may also be a wrong to other rational beings.) For any moral theorist who thinks that properties like self-consciousness and autonomy are central in our understanding of what it is for an act to be an offence against someone, a wrong to that person, this rape must be a lesser crime than a rape of a normal woman. As it would be for Rorty too: Rorty rejects any attempt to make 'morality' anything but the ability to notice and identify with pain and humiliation;[42] and there may be far less (in comparison with the rape of a normal woman) mental pain or humiliation in the rape of a severely retarded person, with whom in any case we may be, as he has suggested, less likely to identify ourselves than with a sensitive and normally intelligent woman.

We all have a great capacity for coldness to each other's common humanity. But that may be combined with the capacity for outrage at acts in which there is as it were a positive and arrogant treatment of oneself as not subject to that boundness to one another of which Conrad spoke. In that outrage there may be our imaginative sense of what it is to be human. I have discussed our treatment of the retarded; I believe that the significance people in some cultures attach to hospitality—what it means in those cultures to deny a stranger hospitality[43]—reflects that

[42] Rorty, op. cit. (n. 3), 193.

[43] For example, in the world of the *Odyssey*, in which those who deny Odysseus and his companions hospitality are monsters and giants; they do not share the human form, and refuse connection with us by treating us as casual munchies. Hospitality, as a central virtue in these cultures, shows the danger of generalizations about people's tendency to treat the needs of their families and neighbours as more important than those of strangers, who are 'them' in comparison to 'us'. For it may be thought appropriate or obligatory to kill the sheep on which one's family depends to give a stranger a generous meal, to rescue, in case of fire, a stranger-guest's child before one's own, to risk one's

56

same sense of the arrogance there is in cutting oneself off from commonality of need and joinedness of fate.

VII

Moral thought has many things in it, many kinds of element. The purpose of my paper has not been to *exclude* any style of moral thought, but rather to argue against those who would for different reasons themselves take the notion *human being* not to have a significant place in moral thought. Some such philosophers exclude the notion because it does not meet what they take to be basic conditions for moral relevance, a view that comes out in the simplistic teaching of some introductory texts in ethics, where it is explained that we may dispute which human traits have moral relevance, but shared humanity (not humanity in Kant's sense, but merely *being human*) is nothing.[44] This is one of many ways in which the teaching of philosophy alienates people from what unreflectively belongs to their sense of their humanity. Although I am not arguing that moral thought does not contain general principles of action, or the attempt to apply such principles to particular cases, or reflection on such principles, philosophical overemphasis on principles does lead people to distort their own thought to make it fit a particular model. Where what is in our moral response, say, to the treatment of a retarded person, is our sense of human life, we may, if we are philosophers, try to impose on it the idea that we have found a moral principle that we can now accept to govern how everyone should be treated, including ourselves if we should degenerate into imbecility. I now will that if that happened to me I should not then be raped. *So* rape can conceptually count as violation of a right, even in such a case; hence it can conceptually count as unjust and a wrong to the victim.[45] This is turning somersaults to make a single theory cover too many kinds of moral response.

[44] A good example is Joel Feinberg's 'Abortion'; see n. 1 above.

[45] See the discussion by Jeffrie Murphy of the rights of the retarded in 'Rights and Borderline Cases', op. cit. (n. 33), especially 34.

---

life in avenging the death met by a stranger under one's roof or in one's tent. In these cultures, the very 'them'ness of the stranger-guests is tied to the impossibility of setting aside their needs as one can set aside those of one's own family in the circumstances. The tie may actually be internal to the word expressive of their being 'them' as opposed to 'us', as in Greek, where *xenos* has not just the meaning it has for us in 'xenophobic' but also the meaning *guest*. See D. H. Lawrence's use of the connections in 'Snake', and Alasdair MacIntyre's comments on them in *After Virtue* (Notre Dame: University of Notre Dame Press, 1981), 116–17.

relate to [?]

In the case of Rorty's views and those of Annette Baier, I have not argued that the different sorts of sympathetic identification with what happens to others that they emphasize have no place in moral thought. What my aim has been in relation to them I can most simply make clear through an example, Zbigniew Herbert's poem 'Mr Cogito on the Need for Precision'. In that poem is Herbert's sense of solidarity with the dead, the disappeared, the victims of the millennia of human history; there is in the poem the pain of the anonymity into which they have disappeared, the need for us to see ourselves as owing them memory, owing them naming, owing them the attempt to keep the accounts. 'We are despite everything the guardians of our brothers', our brothers the dead. The poem makes a way of putting the sense of human life into what we go on now to do in politics.[46] The poetic imagination is here at work in moral thought, but not in those ways Rorty describes as helpful or admirable. Imagination is for him admirably occupied with idiosyncratic making of selves or with making us less cruel to the living by furthering our capacity to identify with their pain and humiliation. Herbert does what Rorty criticizes Kant for doing: he makes of morality 'something distinct from the ability to notice, and identify with, pain and humiliation'.[47] The case of Professor Baier's Humean ethics is complex, because the issue there is the character of moral psychology. It should be plain, though, that the pained sense of the anonymity of the dead-and-gone victims of millennia of human oppression is not the result of sympathy with what they *undergo*; the capacity that our sympathy has to spread, beyond those who are near, to distant human beings, to care about what gives them pain or pleasure or is useful to them, is not what we are called on by Herbert to exercise in respect to the dead. Although, in Hume's own account of ethics, moral concern extends to all human beings, it is not connected with an imaginative sense of human life; the development of such an imaginative sense, its presence or absence, has no place in the account he gives of delicacy of moral perception or of the differences between different people's, different nations', modes of moral response.

To clear up a possible misunderstanding: I have not tried to give the extent of moral concern in terms of *beings characterized in a certain way*. I am not trying to substitute *all human beings dead, alive, unborn*, or anything else, for the z in the formula 'We xs assess together the character and conduct of us ys so far as it affects ourselves and our fellows zs'. I have tried to show rather that in live moral thought there may be a sense of human life, and that that sense of human life may be

---

[46] For its connection with politics, see Lawrence Weschler, 'A Reporter at Large: The Great Exception', *The New Yorker*, April 3 and April 10, 1989.

[47] Rorty, op. cit. (n. 3), 193.

The Importance of Being Human

expressed in what we understand by a human fate (as anonymity becomes, in Herbert's poem, a fate about which we may properly be concerned), and in how we see the connectedness of human lives (as the poem leads us to take that connectedness to include the dead). To treat the notion of *human beings* as important in moral thought, as I have, is not to treat animals as outside the boundaries of moral concern, because it is not any kind of attempt to determine the limits of moral concern. A human being is someone who has a human life to lead, as do I, someone whose fate is a human fate, as is mine.[48] We show what we make of this in our language and literature, but in large measure also in the language of our relations to each other. We see there what others make of it, and may be pierced by what we see, as Herbert is pierced by our carelessness with the accounts. If it is possible for that sense of shared humanity to be expressed in actions, they have also most strikingly the power to express the refusal of solidarity, e.g., in the denial of decent burial, or (as Herbert invites us to see) in the obliteration of the records, the complicity in forgetting. The quotation I have twice used from Conrad, and my examples, have been meant to make clear that *merely being human* has a role in moral thought, a role quite different from that of properties like sentience or rationality or the capacity for moral personality. We expect to be able to see a sense of what human life is in people otherwise greatly different from ourselves, people who perhaps give that sense quite different sorts of expression. Our own sense of life can enter our judgment and responses to things in their life.

In some forms of ethical thought, these ideas, these responses, are at the centre. And our moral life would in fact have a different overall look to it were these ideas and responses to disappear. But philosophical ethics goes on for the most part as if there were nothing of all this *to* disappear.[49]

[48] I have been asked (by John Marshall) what it means to say of a severely retarded person that he or she has a human life to lead. I do not mean by 'having a human life to lead' having a life in which distinctively human capacities are exercised. Someone may be deprived, for part or all of his life, of distinctively human capacities like reason. A human life *without* the exercise of those capacities is *his* human life. The one human life he is given has that terrible deprivation; that, in his case, is what his having a human life to lead has been. We may perfectly well think of that as a particularly terrible human fate.

[49] An earlier version of this paper was read at a meeting of the Sociedad Peruana de Filosofía. I have been greatly helped by comments from David McNaughton, James Conant, Richard Rorty, John Marshall, Ruth Anna Putnam, Mary Rorty, David Cockburn, Peter Winch, Marilyn Frye and Anthony Woozley.

APPENDIX

This Appendix contains part of a letter of mine to David McNaughton, quoted in his paper, and clarifying some points in mine. The references to McNaughton's views are to those in a letter of his.

To explain what I mean by imaginative understanding of what it is to have a human life I want to make use of an analogy.

A. Biological concept (or concepts) of death
B. What *we have made* of the notion of *death* in this and other cultural traditions, modes of life: a non-biological notion of death.
C. Biological concept (or concepts) of human beings as one kind of animal
D. Non-biological notion (notions) of *human being*.

The analogy I want is roughly this: A is to B as C is to D. We do not master a concept by learning merely to apply it to certain sorts of things, by learning to pick out from other things those things that fall under it, using appropriate criteria, but by entering and participating in forms of activity and talk and thought. The biological notion of death and the non-biological notion we begin learning in the *same* activities (e.g., in talking about and burying a dead pet), but the activities in our culture diverge: the biological notion is developed in the human context that comes to include examination of those irreversible physiological changes in the cells, tissues, etc. that belong to the dying and death of organisms; the non-biological notion is developed by such activities as mourning, the reading and writing of the poetry of death, story-telling like that in Grimm's *Godfather Death* and so on. In the first sort of context, certain kinds of uses of language are taught and rigorously insisted on, impersonal modes of description and the like; in the second, quite other uses of language are characteristic.

Warren Goldfarb once said that any philosophy that you can put in a nutshell belongs there. With that warning in view, here is an idea of Wittgenstein's, that I take as central, in a nutshell: what it is that we are talking about is shown in how we talk about it, and in how that talk enters our lives, the shape—the 'face'—that life containing such talk has. See (e.g.) *Zettel* §§533–534. If people's life with some notion is not like the life that we live with the notion of pain, then *what they are talking about* in their talk is not what we talk about when we use our notion of pain. There are differences of degree; so far as some people's life with some notion is in some ways (which in a particular context may be important to us) *like* our life with the notion of pain, we may translate their word for that notion as 'pain'. That willingness to translate is an expression of our treating the similarity as important: in other contexts the differences might be important.

. . . We may see the non-biological notion of death in such things as [Dickens's treatment of death in *Our Mutual Friend*]. Dickens's imaginative treatment of mortality is not made appropriate by what human mortality is, if that means that there is something that it is, independent of his and other such makings, independent of the human life that contains this (and other) makings of sense.

This approach of mine may *seem* to leave no room for the issue of whether it is—to put it crudely—a good thing to treat death as we do, but its seeming so is a philosophical confusion, or so I should argue. The *seeming so* reflects an assumption that if there is any reflective question about *how* to live with death, how it is to be treated, it must be the question whether our mode of response is justified by features of the thing or things to which we are responding. Whereas I should want to argue that a reflective appreciation and judgment of our mode of response is possible without that view of justification. We can reflect on the experience we have of life with a concept and can intelligently judge it to be better (say) than life without that concept, or with it but radically changed, would be.

Applying this general view of mine to the issues you raise about my paper. I do not take myself in the paper to be answering a question of the form: *What is there about other people* that does, or can, evoke a moral response? I am interested in avoiding a conceptualization of the whole issue in terms of the following two kinds of point taken together:

1. *What they have* is:

(a) biological humanity
(b) 'moral personality'
(c) such-and-such specific capacities: intellectual or emotional or whatever
(d) a human fate (or they can be seen as having this)
(e) in some cases one thing, in other cases another
(f) whatever else.

2. To turn aside a sceptical challenge [concerning the justification of our moral thought about people] one must point to something other than (a): if not to (b), (c) or (d), then to an answer more in the style of (e). (And in connection with this sort of point, you argue that Wittgenstein should show us that we should not expect some single answer like any of (b), (c) or (d).)

What I want to do is follow Wittgenstein (that is anyway what I should say I was doing) in turning away from what is common to the 'sceptical challenge' and the attempts to meet it either by pointing to something like (b), (c) or (d), *or* by giving some more complex story like the one that you suggest and that I have labelled (e). . . I take you to hold that we should want to find something or other in a particular fellow human being (you speak of what we are or are not able to find in his nature) which justifies or merits the kind of treatment we accord to our fellow human beings. There is no room, on your view (as I read it) for critical reflection concerning that treatment if it does not come in in that way. Whereas on my view there is plenty of room for critical reflection, but it is not a matter of trying to tell whether the beings to whom we respond are, all or almost all or some of them, such as to merit or justify the treatment we do give or do think it is right to give to fellow human beings.

Let me put the point another way, using a different example. The non-biological notion of what it is to have a human life to lead is grasped through inwardness in our life-with-human-beings, part of which is that *human beings have names*. In this mode of life, *names* have significance, a significance which is brought out and developed further in poetry like Zbigniew Herbert's, or writing (about Auschwitz) like Primo Levi's. Are human beings—most or all of them—such as to *merit or justify* being named not numbered? Or is the giving of names, the treating of naming and of names, significant as a part of the having of that notion of the human that is ours? If we answer yes to that last question, we have not stopped ourselves asking whether it is a *precious* part of human life, whether it would be *a great human loss* if our kind of attachment to names, our kind of life with names, were to be eroded away. Here one can see (I hope) that there is no need to assume that philosophical-critical reflection on a mode of thought must take the form of investigating whether the mode of thought is appropriate to the nature of what is thought about. . . . As I read Wittgenstein, he does not give us *a different way* of trying to meet the demand that we justify a mode of thought by features of what we are talking about, but rather enables us to see that such demands are themselves confused. To think of this as excluding critical reflection would be to accept the picture he wished to free us from.

The Importance of Being Human

DAVID McNAUGHTON

> I wish from my Heart, I could avoid concluding, that since Morality, according to your Opinion as well as mine, is determin'd merely by Sentiment, it regards only human Nature & human Life. . . . If Morality were determin'd by Reason, that is the same to all rational Beings: But nothing but Experience can assure us, that the Sentiments are the same. What Experience have we with regard to superior Beings? How can we ascribe to them any Sentiments at all? They have implanted those Sentiments in us for the Conduct of Life like our bodily Sensations, which they possess not themselves. (Letter from Hume to Hutcheson: March 16, 1740)[1]

When we ask whether morality 'regards only human nature and human life' we might be concerned with one of two kinds of question. We may be asking what kinds of being could share our moral point of view. What is the potential scope of the community of moral agents and assessors? Is the moral point of view essentially a human point of view? Could we, or should we, adopt a wider standpoint (say that of rational agency as such) which would leave room for a significant moral dialogue with non-human moral agents, if there are any? Alternatively, we could be asking whether only human beings should be the objects of moral concern or whether we should widen the circle of concern to include other kinds of being.[2] We may make the same point using a helpful device of Cora Diamond's. We may be concerned with what should replace x or with what should replace y in the formula: We xs assess together conduct and character in so far as it affects ourselves and our fellow ys.[3]

Having distinguished those two questions we might then ask what connections, if any, there may be between the answers. Some philosophers suppose the connection to be very close and hold that whatever term replaces x should also replace y. Kant famously held that

---

[1] J. Y. T. Greig (ed.), *The Letters of David Hume* (Oxford: Clarendon Press, 1969), Vol. 1, 40.

[2] It is clear from the context that, in his letter, Hume is raising the former question.

[3] See Cora Diamond, 'The Importance of Being Human' in this volume, p. 37. All otherwise unattributed page references in brackets in the text will be to this paper.

David McNaughton

rationality was the only qualification both for being a moral agent and for being an object of moral concern. Hume, on some interpretations, thought that both *x* and *y* should be replaced by the term 'human being', although his theory seems to allow a natural extension of the class of objects of moral concern to include animals.[4]

In the first two parts of this paper I put forward a particular version of moral realism which provides an answer to our first question; for it leads to the conclusion that it is only from the human point of view, or the point of view of beings who are appropriately similar to us, that we can make sense of our moral practice. As we shall later see, this theory does have implications for the way we should answer our second question, though not of such a direct kind as we find in Hume or Kant. Since it is well discussed in the literature, my sketch will be brief. In my exposition I shall concentrate on the issue of moral justification, which is central to my discussion of the second question in Parts III and IV.

The best way in to this version of moral realism, which we owe to McDowell,[5] is to see how it differs from a non-cognitivist account in the Humean spirit. On that account, moral properties are not real properties; they are no part of the furniture of the world. Moral experience is to be analysed into two distinct parts: a belief about the non-moral features of the act or person judged and an affective response to those features. The first of these is genuinely cognitive but the second is not. The affective responses of an individual (or group) can only be seen as constituting a genuine moral practice if he consistently picks out the same non-evaluative features of the world for favourable or unfavourable evaluation. For ethical non-cognitivism justification is thus a matter of internal consistency. The great strength of non-cognitivism, which flows from this analysis, is that it provides a simple explanation of the way in which moral commitments motivate. Since a moral response is, in part, affective, to have a moral attitude about something

[4] Cora Diamond alludes, on p. 37 of her paper, to Annette Baier's Humean view which allows sympathetic feeling to extend to the inanimate. This may be the right position but, for reasons that I explore briefly in Part III, it seems to me to represent a considerable departure from Hume's own view.

[5] The route here described is followed by John McDowell, 'Non-cognitivism and Rule-following', in Steven H. Holtzman and Christopher M. Leich (eds.), *Wittgenstein: To Follow a Rule* (London: Routledge and Kegan Paul, 1981), 141–62. For an account of this version of moral realism and further references see David McNaughton, *Moral Vision: An Introduction to Ethics* (Oxford: Blackwell, 1988). The line of thought in the text is developed in *Moral Vision*, ch. 3, section 6 (*MV* 3.6). All future references to this work will be in this abbreviated style.

is to care about it, to desire to act in certain ways. The non-cognitivist is thus an internalist about moral motivation; a moral attitude can motivate without assistance from a distinct motivational state.

We can now see that there is an ambiguity in our first question. Whether or not non-humans can share our moral point of view may be a question about moral motivation or about comprehension. When Hume claims, as a chief exponent of the non-cognitivist approach, that morality 'regards only human nature and human life' he is making a point about *motivation*. When we offer certain considerations as supplying moral reasons to act in a particular way they will not be considerations that would motivate any rational agent, whatever his emotions and desires. Thus someone who did not share our moral point of view, because he did not share with us the range of affective responses that underlie our moral practice, would be unmoved by the considerations that move us. Hume's point is not about what it is to *understand* a moral practice. There is no reason, on Hume's account, to think that 'superior beings' would not understand our moral system; it is just that they would not share it. That is, they are not moved to act by what sways us. If our moral practice is a consistent one the outsider can understand it by discovering which non-moral properties we select for favourable and which for unfavourable evaluation. There is nothing more to understanding it than that. He could thus predict and even mimic our practice.

The moral realist claims, as her name suggests, that moral properties are real properties and that there can be moral beliefs which should be seen as purely cognitive states, rather than an amalgam of the cognitive and the non-cognitive. It may seem that the moral realist must reject the internalist account of moral motivation offered by the non-cognitivist. How, on the realist account, could an agent be motivated by her moral beliefs or by her recognition of a moral requirement? Surely, to believe that something is the case is one thing and to care about it, to be moved to act, is quite another. Such a rejection of internalism rests on that very distinction between the cognitive and the affective on which the non-cognitivist places such reliance—a distinction which finds its most common expression in the characteristic Humean claim that the motivation of action requires the co-operation of two radically different kinds of state—beliefs and desires.

Our kind of moral realist[6] questions this hallowed distinction. Her suggestion is that a cognitive state, a particular way of appreciating or

---

[6] In opposition to this view there are a number of moral realists who adopt an externalist account of moral motivation. For a clear account of this position see David Brink, 'Externalist Moral Realism', *Southern Journal of Philosophy* **24**, *Supplement* (1986), 23–41.

understanding a situation, can itself be a way of caring. A cognitive state can thus motivate, without assistance from a non-cognitive partner.

This kind of moral realist agrees with the non-cognitivist that intelligent beings who lacked our distinctively human concerns would not share our moral point of view. Her account of the matter, however, differs markedly from that of the non-cognitivist. As we have seen, the non-cognitivist takes it that the outsider may be aware of all that there is to be aware of but, because he lacks our concerns, does not care about what is morally right or wrong. If our use of some moral term is to be non-arbitrary and so intelligible it must be guided by the way things are in the world. For the non-cognitivist the only properties there are, and so the only properties to which we could be sensitive, are non-moral ones. So our pattern of moral response, if it is to be world-guided, must be comprehensible at the level of the non-moral properties and so could be grasped by the moral outsider.

The moral realist, by contrast, insists that we should leave open the possibility that the outsider may not even *understand* our practice because he is unable to detect any consistent pattern in our responses. Lacking our concerns, he may be unable to see any pattern in the way we group actions and agents under particular moral predicates. Only someone who could at least appreciate the point of our practice could see its structure. There may be no discernible pattern of response so long as we remain at the non-moral level. This does not mean that the realist has abandoned the claim that, in order to be intelligible, a moral practice must be world-guided. Since the realist has a richer conception of reality than the non-cognitivist, she can still make sense of the suggestion that a moral practice might be a response to what is really there. For it might exhibit sensitivity to the presence or absence of moral properties, a sensitivity only available to those who can appreciate our moral point of view.

If we embrace this suggestion then we must reject the standard picture of moral reasoning, which is by no means confined to those of a non-cognitivist persuasion. If we are challenged to justify our moral judgment about a particular case we appeal to some further features of the case which we give as our reasons. In justifying the claim, say, that some action is right we may appeal to 'thick' moral properties of the action; that it is kind or just, for instance. Those latter claims may themselves be held to be in need of justification, so that it seems reasonable to suppose that we shall eventually have to cite a number of the non-moral features of the case as justifying our moral conclusions. It is when we ask how indicating a non-moral feature can be seen as giving a reason that the moral realist departs from orthodoxy.

On the standard model, when I give reason(s) for my verdict in a particular case I am implicitly appealing to a general principle. My citing the presence (or absence) of this non-moral property in *this* case only counts as a *reason* for my judgment if the presence (or absence) of this property is generally morally relevant. I have supplied a reason only if this non-moral property of an action always counts, and counts in the same way, wherever it is found. On this conception, each moral reason gets its force from the general principle of which it is an instance. Thus a first step towards articulating a moral position would be to lay out a person's principles, that is to give a complete list of all those non-moral properties that count against doing an action and a similar list of those that count in favour.[7] This general picture of moral reasoning is so widely accepted that it is often supposed that disagreement only emerges after this point; disagreement as to the nature of moral principles (e.g. are they absolute or overridable) and how they are to be justified. But to embrace the model is already to accept the disputed picture of a moral practice. For it supposes that, in coming to understand someone's moral practice, we shall be uncovering a pattern of response which is comprehensible at the level of non-moral features—a pattern which could be grasped by the moral outsider.

What picture of justification could be put in place of the standard model? It is helpful to turn to the justification of aesthetic judgments for an analogy. If I wish to justify my claim that some painting, say, has aesthetic merit I may point to or indicate certain features of the painting in an attempt to get you to see what grounds my claim. I may, for example, show how this line sets up a rhythm which is subtly echoed elsewhere, or how the use of pastel shades creates a muted ambience. In these cases, however, there is little temptation to claim that such features only count as reasons for my judgment if they can be generalized. It would be crass to insist that, if what I am offering are reasons for my claim, then I am committed, say, to the view that any painting that uses pastel shades is the better for it. What blocks the generalizing move is the fact that no feature of the painting makes its contribution in isolation. Whether it adds to or detracts from the painting depends on its interaction with all the other elements in the painting. For this reason we would reject as ludicrous the idea that there might be an aesthetic outsider who, while lacking any insight into our aesthetic practice, could predict, on the basis of observing our evaluative behaviour, what paintings we would find valuable.

[7] We would not have a complete articulation of a moral position until we knew how that position dealt with conflicts of moral principles. If we accept Ross's claim that there is no computational method of settling moral conflicts then some part of our moral practice would remain opaque to the outsider (see *MV* 13.2).

David McNaughton

One powerful reason for rejecting generalism in moral as in aesthetic justification is that it offers an unduly atomistic picture of moral reasoning. It supposes that each reason is insulated from its surroundings so that the effect of each on the rightness or wrongness of the action as a whole can be judged separately. The moral particularist prefers a holistic view. Whether a particular feature will have a bearing, and what that bearing will be, is something that can only be decided in the particular case when we can determine how the various features of the case interact.[8]

The drive to particularism does not, therefore, stem from this brand of moral realism, for particularism is independently attractive.[9] Rather, moral realism as I have construed it offers a conception of what it is to engage in a moral practice which makes sense of particularism and offers a defence against the charge that so unprincipled a collocation of responses cannot constitute a moral practice, a response to anything real.

II

The moral realist claims that someone who did not share, or at least could not see the point of, our moral scheme might fail to see any shape to our practice. To support this claim we can appeal to familiar considerations about classification in general. Any two things are similar in an

---

[8] For more on particularism see Jonathan Dancy, 'Ethical Particularism and Morally Relevant Properties', *Mind 92* (1983), 530–47, and *MV* 13. I want to stress that the particularist sets no *a priori* limits on what kinds of feature may be morally relevant. Scientific, relational and cultural facts may all be relevant. The latter may include facts of the kind to which Cora Diamond draws our attention in her paper; facts about people and animals which stem from our cultural makings.

I use the term 'fact' deliberately. In 'Eating Meat and Eating People', *Philosophy 53* (1978), 465–79, Cora Diamond talks of applying the notion of a fellow creature to an animal, of seeing it as company, of its having an independent life. She then says 'it is not a *fact* that a titmouse *has a life*; if one speaks that way it expresses a particular relation within a broadly specifiable range to titmice. It is no more biological than it would be a biological point should you call another person a "traveller between life and death"' (p. 475). I agree with her that such a remark is not intended *biologically*, but science has no monopoly on facts. Perhaps similar thoughts underlie her contrast in her present paper between the empirical and the imaginative, a distinction of which I have a profound distrust.

[9] See the articles in Part I of S. G. Clarke and E. Simpson (eds.), *Anti-Theory in Ethics and Moral Conservatism* (Albany: State University of New York Press, 1989) especially the splendid piece by Martha Nussbaum.

indefinite number of ways and dissimilar in an indefinite number of ways. The world comes divided up in too many ways for our classification to mirror the (unique) way that things are divided in reality. Rather, the classificatory scheme we bring to bear on our world is a product of our interests, our culture, what seems natural to us. If the outsider has no conception of what it is about, say, justice that makes it important to us then he will have great difficulty in seeing why we group various actions together as all just. Even if he comes up with some hypothesis that covers existing cases it is likely that future uses of the term by us will overturn it. He will not be able to predict future applications of the term with any confidence because he cannot see how our classification of new examples can be seen as a case of going on in the same way.[10]

In the remainder of this section I want, by resisting some possible counter-claims or misunderstandings, to clarify my contention that it is only from the human point of view that we can understand and engage in our moral practice.

It might be objected that I have still not drawn the area within which comprehension can occur sufficiently narrowly. It is doubtful that the moral practice of any group of humans can be understood by all those who share the human point of view. Given that there may be differences in the thick moral concepts that different cultures have evolved to divide up the world, might it not be that a member of one human culture could make no sense of the moral practice of another culture? Might we not discover that there are incommensurable moral schemes? This is not something we could discover, as I have tried to show elsewhere,[11] for familiar Davidsonian reasons. In interpreting others we have to suppose that they are right about most things. Only against a background of agreement can there be disagreement. The interpretation of moral beliefs is no different. It could not be that we have reached the stage where we have identified a class of utterances as moral responses but can make nothing of them. If we interpret the speaker as approving of some course of action, we will only be able to see that as moral approval if the beliefs that he offers in support of his view are of the right sort, beliefs that we can interpret as moral reasons. It follows that moral dialogue between cultures is always possible, though there may be pockets of incomprehension. Moreover, we can learn from expanding our moral horizons. To be in a position to assess the practice of another culture we need to understand them, to have interpreted

---

[10] I have in mind here, in particular, the work of Nelson Goodman.
[11] *MV* 10.4.

them successfully. Once we have done that, the decisions we come to there may cast fresh light on our own moral practice.[12]

A weaker version of this objection concedes that there could not be incommensurable moral schemes but suggests that there might be a special difficulty in interpreting *moral* practice, a point which the moral realist seems to have accepted in allowing the possibility of a moral outsider. For the suggestion seemed to be that the outsider might succeed in interpreting all our non-moral utterances but that understanding might run out when he turned his attention to our moral practice. He might not be able to see us as having a moral practice at all. I am inclined to think that we should resist the claim that this is a genuine possibility and regard the concept of the complete moral outsider as merely a heuristic device in expounding the theory. This for two reasons. First, the points that I made in the first paragraph of this section were perfectly general; they made no appeal to anything distinctive about moral or evaluative practices. Second, interpretation is a holistic procedure and our moral beliefs are intimately intertwined with others. It is hard to believe that someone could have made impressive headway in interpreting our non-moral thought and be completely stuck at the moral level.

One final worry. Someone might claim that, if it is the case that only a fellow human, or someone who was sufficiently like us, could understand our moral practice, we should be able to provide an *independent* account of just what features or capacities someone has to share with us in order to appreciate our moral point of view. I am inclined to think that this demand is not one that can be met. To understand any form of life just is to see why these things are grouped together, what would count as going on the same way, and so on. The capacities someone would have to share with us in order to understand our moral point of view just are those capacities whose existence is revealed in that understanding. To be sufficiently like us is to be interpretable by us.

III

At the beginning of the paper I mentioned that for some philosophers there is an intimate connection between the answer they give to the first of our questions and the answer they give to the second. Kant sees the connection as conceptual: an investigation of rational agency shows both that it is the essence of moral agency and that it is the only thing valuable as an end in itself. So the only moral limit is set by the existence of rational agency itself, whether in your own person or that of any

[12] See *MV* 10.5–7.

other. For Hume, or so I would claim, the answer to the second question is not the same as the answer to the first[13] but there is nevertheless a connection between the answers which stems from Hume's account of sympathy. We can only sympathize with beings who are sentient, who can experience pleasure and pain. For sympathy consists in coming to have a like feeling ourselves when we are aware of such a feeling in another. I think, therefore, that the outer limits of the Humean circle of sympathy are coincident with the limits of sentience; non-sentient things cannot be the objects of moral concern except in so far as they affect the interests of sentient creatures.

It is obvious that no connections of this direct kind can be set up between the two questions in the case of the kind of moral realism I have been discussing. We have seen that only those who share our concerns can understand our moral system, but it does not follow that they alone can be the objects of those concerns. Nor have I postulated any particular psychological mechanism of a Humean kind which would set limits on what kinds of object could engage our moral sympathies. What light moral realism does shed on the second question is methodological. The particularism that emerges means that no general pronouncement on the second question can be made. How we should treat various kinds of being in particular situations is a matter to be decided on a case by case basis and not by any general considerations of moral theory.

It follows that what we might term the orthodox approach to the second question, so well characterized by Diamond at the beginning of her paper, is mistaken. That approach seeks for some general non-moral characteristic(s), such as sentience or self-consciousness, which distinguish what is an object of moral concern from what is not. Such characteristics must be ones that can survive rational reflection on the nature of morality, and the property of being human is held not to qualify. The particularist does not deny that such characteristics as sentience or self-consciousness can be morally relevant on occasion, but that does not mean that they are always relevant, still less decisively so.

Few philosophers would now defend the view that only human beings can be the objects of moral concern. But the notion that human beings have some special place in our moral thought is more resistant.

[13] If Hume did think this, as Diamond suggests on p. 37 (following Baier's account) it was not as a result of the nature of his theory. But I think the evidence is that he did give animals some place as objects of moral concern. Baier says in *Postures of the Mind: Essays on Mind and Morals* (Minneapolis: University of Minnesota Press, 1985), 149, 'Hume himself does not address the question of whether virtues and vices are shown in our treatment of animals.' This is a mistake. See David Hume, *Enquiries Concerning Human Understanding and the Principles of Morals*, ed. L. A. Selby-Bigge (Oxford: Oxford University Press, 1975) 190–1.

David McNaughton

As Diamond notes (p. 52) the orthodox approach raises a dilemma for those who hold this view. If the standard for inclusion in the sphere of moral concern is put too high then not only will most non-humans be excluded but so will some humans, such as babies and the retarded. If the standard is set so low that all humans are included then many animals will also gain entry and hence the special place of humans will again be threatened.

One version of the orthodox account sees being a proper object of moral concern as possessing moral rights which come in an all-or-nothing package; if an object passes the crucial test then its treatment is governed by a complex set of moral rules. If it fails the test then it falls outside the charmed circle and gets no moral protection. Yet there seem to be many cases, as Diamond eloquently reminds us, (p. 55) such as our treatment of the dead, the retarded, the comatose, the new-born and so on, where the way we treat them and think of them is connected to their being human. Our attitude to them is not the same as our attitude to animals whose level of capacity is roughly equivalent to theirs.

Those who seek to preserve a special place for humans, but are wedded to the picture of moral reasoning as concerned with the search for common characteristics which all objects of moral concern share, may seek to complicate the story by dividing the packet of rights into different segments. There may be some rights that one has solely in virtue of, say, sentience but others that one only acquires in virtue of some more advanced characteristic, such as rationality, or self-consciousness. Thus we might argue that animals, in virtue of their sentience, are owed duties of benevolence; we owe them, to use a phrase of Hume's, 'gentle usage'. Humans by contrast, in virtue of their self-consciousness, have a richer panoply of rights, such as the right to life, the right to certain kinds of respect, and so on. It is clear, however, that this is only a palliative measure. For it would still allow that those humans who, while sentient, lack the higher qualification may be treated in ways that we generally think of as unacceptable, e.g. new-borns may be killed, provided that it is done painlessly.

The particularist will reject the picture that moral rights come bundled together (whether in one package or two) so that once one has acknowledged that some being has a moral claim in one case one is committed to acknowledging his claims in other cases. He will also reject the claim that there are *a priori* limits to what kind of thing can be an object of moral concern on a particular occasion. One of the strengths of particularism is that it does not specify in advance what features of a situation may be morally relevant. It thus does not rule out our coming to view our treatment of some being that has hitherto not fallen within the ambit of our moral thought as having, after all, some

72

degree of moral significance. This is especially important when we get to environmental ethics for, on many moral theories, trees and rocks just cannot be objects of moral concern at all.

A worry which people naturally have about particularism is how someone can move from case to case without moral principles to guide her. When the particularist claims that there are no *a priori* limits to what kinds of thing may be an object of moral concern on some occasion, similar worries may arise. Unless we can give necessary and sufficient conditions for being an object of moral consideration how can we determine whether or not there is some morally appropriate response to this object in this situation? I shall try to allay this worry a little by pursuing the aesthetic analogy on which I have already relied. The question 'Can I see this being as having a moral claim on me in this situation?' can be compared with 'Is this artifact a work of art?'

It is now widely accepted that there are no necessary and sufficient conditions for being a work of art, but that does not prevent us using the term intelligibly. In order to show that some putative candidate should be included we have to reveal connections between it and the existing corpus of works of art. We have to be able to see how we can fit it into that corpus, in part so that we know how to appreciate it. We may come to recognize that something that we would not previously have thought of as a work of art can be so regarded. That is, we may see classifying it as art as an example of going on in the same way. I want to make two points about such cases.[14] Firstly, it may be that we can only see something as a work of art at a particular point in history. We need to have the right conceptual tools in order to understand how it can be fitted into the corpus. Second, and this is a point we have met before in the case of getting to know a new culture, our including the new work may change the way we see the old. For we may value the new object for features that we did not previously value aesthetically, but which we now see as important. But this may cast a fresh light on other works that share this feature.[15] Similar remarks apply to extending the range of moral concern. If we come to view trees, or rocks or the ecosystem in a light which shows that they merit a response which we had previously reserved for humans or animals then our view of animals or humans may itself be changed in the light of that new response.[16]

[14] Points which I owe to the work of Arthur Danto.

[15] T. S. Eliot makes similar remarks about the literary canon in 'Tradition and the Individual Talent', reprinted in D. Lodge (ed.), *Twentieth Century Literacy Criticism* (London: Longman, 1972) 71–6.

[16] There is not space to consider here the interesting question, touched on in this paper of Diamond's but discussed at greater length in other papers of hers, as to how we might extend to animals various notions that naturally find their place in human life, and what the effect of that extension might be.

What, then, of a positive account of the place of the notion of being human in ethics? The formal, short, dusty answer is that it can be morally relevant in one case and not relevant in another. Nothing general can be said about how we ought to treat humans, as distinct from other kinds of thing.

I have said that, for the particularist, the property of being human may, like any property, be morally relevant on some occasion. But someone might ask for an explanation of the way(s) in which it might get into the picture. Certainly we do appeal to it in some cases. To take an example Diamond gives, (p. 52) most of us think that it is wrong to perform an experiment on a mentally retarded person which we would be prepared to perform on an animal. In such cases we naturally appeal to the fact that the retarded are human, but how are we to understand that justification? Before we can consider whether, in such a case, the fact that the mentally retarded person is human is a sufficient, or even a good, reason for treating her differently from an animal, we need first to see how being human might figure as a morally relevant property. The rest of the paper is taken up with this question as it bears on this kind of example.

One way in which being human might be morally relevant is that, because the retarded are human, they will be part of a network of human relationships, so that using them for experimentation will cause their friends and relatives deep distress. As Diamond points out, though this is an important reason, it is not the only possible one and does not cover the case of the friendless orphan, who may seem particularly in need of protection. What is it about the retarded person herself that might ground such a judgment?

Another way in which the property of being human might get in to the picture is that the retarded person may share certain human capacities with us, and this forms the basis for certain reactions, such as compassion, and for certain kinds of relationship. We may exchange a smile with such a person or realize that she is moved by music. I do not mean that we must take this, as the orthodox approach would, as evidence of the existence of some general capacity, such as self-consciousness, which distinguishes people from beasts. But such an appeal will not work in the case of those in whom none of this can be seen. In such a case can the thought that this person is human have any moral role to play? It is here that I want to bring Diamond's paper into the discussion.

IV

Diamond argues that the notion of being human does play a crucial role in our thought and practice, and hence in our moral thought and practice. We have imaginatively made something of what it is to live a human life and share a human fate; something which is not present in the basic biological concept of being a member of the human species. This sense of what we are is made manifest in a whole range of attitudes not only to the healthy living, but to the retarded, the comatose and the dead.

We might be tempted simply to add her conception of what it is to live a human life to the accounts already sketched of the ways in which we can see the fact that someone is human as a morally relevant property, appeal to which might play a part in justifying, say, our refusal to carry out on a retarded person an experimental procedure which we would be prepared to carry out on a dog. What she adds to the conception of being human we have built up so far is a dimension in which what matters about being human is not just living a life in which distinctive human capacities are exercised. We might see her proposal as drawing our attention to a deeper sense of what it is to live a human life which gets its meaning from our imaginative makings. What might justify a special concern for 'the dead and the unborn, and those who bear on their faces "a look of blank idiocy"' (p. 55) is that they can all be seen as sharing a common human life with us. But this would be to misunderstand Diamond's position. She is not seeking to justify our attitude to the retarded by appeal to some property that they share with us.

She says, 'I am not arguing that we have a "moral obligation to feel a sense of solidarity with all other human beings" because of some natural or supernatural property or group of properties which we all have, contingently or necessarily. I am arguing, though, that there is no need to find such a ground' (p. 55). 'I have not tried to give the extent of moral concern in terms of *beings characterized in a certain way*' (p. 58). On her view, standard accounts of how we should go about justifying differential treatment of humans and animals in such cases locate justification in the wrong place. They hold that, in order to justify our treatment of human beings we must look and see whether we can find something about them which justifies this treatment. But where it is what we have imaginatively made of something that determines what kind of thing it is there is no possibility of our being mistaken about its nature, and so no question of our practice failing to fit its nature. To take an illuminating example of hers: an important part of what we have made of human life is that humans have names. Names are a human invention whose significance is brought out and developed in, among other places, poetry and novels. It makes no sense, however, to ask what it is about humans, independently of what we have made of human life, that justifies us in giving them names. Giving them names is part of what constitutes our imaginative, non-biological, notion of what it is to be human. Thus the claim that a retarded person can be seen as sharing a human fate with us should not be seen as an attempt to determine what it is about this person, apart from our treatment of her, which justifies that treatment.[17]

This does not mean that there is no place for critical reflection. The mistake was to think that 'philosophical-critical reflection on a mode of thought must take the form of investigating whether the mode of thought is appropriate to the nature of what is thought about' (p. 62). Critical reflection consists in asking whether some imaginative conception of what it is to be a certain kind of being is a precious part of human life, whether its ending would be a loss or a benefit. Practices can be rejected on these grounds. Thus she says: 'we have never made anything humanly valuable out of the differences between the races, the mythology of the American South notwithstanding.'[18]

There is much that needs to be explored about these claims but I shall not dispute what I take to be a central point, that where our conception of something's nature is, in part, determined by a practice we cannot appeal to that nature to justify its inclusion in the practice. My aim is merely to show that there can sometimes be a serious question as to whether some person (or being) does or should fall under a practice. Here it cannot be the case that that person's nature is constituted by the practice, because it is the applicability of the practice to her case that is in question. In such cases, it will be legitimate to speak of giving reasons for or against our decision, and justification for including or excluding her will have to proceed by reference to features of her and her situation which are independent of the practice. Among cases of this kind are, I maintain, ones such as the treatment of the severely mentally disabled or permanently comatose about which the orthodox approach raises sceptical doubts. I shall argue that we need to understand how we can see such people as having a human life to lead and that Diamond's paper provides us with a plausible answer. The natural way to understand that answer, contrary (as I understand them) to her intentions, is to see it as providing a justification for including them in that practice, a justification which appeals, ultimately, to the biological fact that they are members of the human species.

---

[17] In this paragraph, and elsewhere, I am relying heavily on a letter of Cora Diamond's, part of which is reproduced in the Appendix to her paper. She says '[O]n my view there is plenty of room for critical reflection, but it is not a matter of trying to tell whether the beings to whom we respond are, all *or almost all or some of them*, such as to merit . . . the treatment we do give or do think it is right to give to fellow human beings' (p. 62, my emphasis).

[18] Diamond, 'Eating Meat and Eating People', op. cit. (n. 8), 351.

Let me begin the argument with an example, which I have developed from her 'Eating meat and eating people', where the question of whether some being is rightfully excluded from a practice does not arise.[19] What it is for an animal to be a pet is constituted by the way we treat them; we have made for ourselves the notion of being a pet. 'A pet is not something to eat, it is given a name, is let into our houses and may be spoken to in ways in which we do not normally speak to cows or squirrels.'[20] We cannot appeal to the nature of this animal, antecedently to the practice, to explain what it is about it that justifies our treating it in this way because there is nothing about, say, this lamb, which is a pet, which differentiates it from that lamb, which is going to market, except that one has been taken up into this form of life and the other has been excluded. Moreover, in explaining that this lamb is allowed in the kitchen because it is a pet, we are not justifying the action by explaining what kind of thing it is. Rather, its being that kind of thing is constituted by such practices as allowing it in the kitchen. It follows that 'people who ate their pets would not have pets in the same sense of that term. (If we call an animal that we are fattening for the table a pet, we are making a crude joke of a familiar sort.)'[21] In the case of pets, critical reflection cannot consist in asking what it is about the nature of this lamb that merits our treating it as a pet; to be a pet just is to be treated in that way. We can only criticize the practice by asking if it makes anything valuable out of the relations and differences between animals and ourselves.

The foregoing is a remark about setting up a practice in which one lamb is treated in a particular way and another is not. It is worth noting that once I have made a pet of Larry I enter into a complex relationship with him which constitutes the practice, and that very fact can explain why it would be morally wrong of me, or anyone else who knows that Larry is a pet, to serve him up piping hot with mint sauce. It is not simply that, if I did eat him, I would show that he was not, after all, a

[19] When I originally wrote this paper I took myself, in my remarks about pets, to be expounding Diamond's position in her earlier paper. However, she assured me, at the conference, that the argument which I develop here (which we may call the circularity argument) is not one she intended to put forward. Fortunately, there is no need to consider whether my reading had any textual warrant (which I think it had); the argument of my paper is unaffected by the question of attribution. I develop the pet example firstly to try to make sense of the sentences from her letter that I quoted and, second, in order to bring out the contrast with the case of the severely retarded human, and thus to pose a challenge to Diamond's understanding of this latter case.

[20] 'Eating Meat and Eating People', op. cit. (n. 8), 469.

[21] Ibid.

pet or that he had ceased to be a pet. I could be morally criticized for eating Larry for a reason that would not apply if I ate a lamb from my farm. So even in this case, the question of moral justification of some proposed course of treatment can arise. But what settles the issue here is just an appeal to what we have made of Larry by including him in our practice. For it is part of the practice that, generally speaking, once an animal has been made a pet of, one is responsible for its welfare, should not eat it etc. (This is quite different from the case of treating a rock as a doorstep. Here it ceases to be a doorstep just when one ceases using it as such and there are no moral obligations internal to the practice.)

I have chosen the example of what it is to be a pet both because it does offer a clear instance of a case where it makes no sense to ask whether we are justified in including *this* creature in the practice, and because the differences between this case and what we have made of human life illustrate the doubts that I have about its extension to the latter case. Whether an animal is a pet does just depend on how we treat it. It is clearly absurd to ask whether there is something about the nature of *this* lamb, as distinct from that one, which justifies the differential treatment. The most obvious difference between being a pet and being human is that 'human' is, among other things, a biological category whereas 'pet' is not.

This difference suggests a dilemma for a position like Diamond's. For we may ask what are the criteria for being human. If we press the pet analogy then what it is to be human is to be treated in certain ways. This may not coincide with what it is to be a member of the species *homo sapiens*. For there is a danger that certain people will turn out not to be human just because they are not in fact treated in the appropriate ways. One thinks, for example, of the treatment of slaves in certain cultures.

Sabina Lovibond provides a fine example when she quotes the anthropologist Mary Douglas on the practices of the Nuer:

> For example, when a monstrous birth occurs, the defining limits between humans and animals may be threatened. If a monstrous birth can be labelled an event of a peculiar kind the categories can be restored. So the Nuer treat monstrous births as baby hippopotamuses, accidentally born to humans, and, with this labelling, the appropriate action is clear. They gently lay them in the river where they belong.[22]

---

[22] Sabina Lovibond, *Realism and Imagination in Ethics* (Minneapolis: University of Minnesota Press, 1983), 54. I have Davidsonian doubts about this description of the Nuer's practice, but I leave those on one side.

If there is nothing more to whether some being leads a human life than how we treat and think of it then, in the Nuer society, deformed babies are not human. This horn of the dilemma is uncomfortable because we now cannot run a story about what it is to lead a human life for those who are excluded from that life. The Nuer are not, apparently, making any mistake. The other horn takes 'human' as essentially a biological notion, but that seems to lead straight to a charge of speciesism, for how can a merely biological notion be morally relevant?

It seems reasonable to respond that this dilemma is too quick. For Diamond's project is to show what we have imaginatively made of human life, and the scope of the enquiry is determined by the nature of the subject. It cannot be that, in our imaginative development of what it is to be human, it emerges that there are beings that are biologically human but do not lead a human life. What matters then is not so much how certain groups are in fact treated in some society but whether we have imaginatively forged a certain kind of account of what it is to live a human life which makes sense of the claim that all of us who are biologically human share a common human fate—an imaginative account which takes off from our all being members of one species but goes beyond it.

This response invites, however, a certain kind of scepticism. For we may doubt whether we do have a conception of what it is to have a human life to lead, which is more than just being a living member of the human species, and which applies even to the most severely retarded, or the comatose from birth, who exhibit no signs whatever of characteristic human response. On the other hand, there is at least one conception of what it is to live a human life (which I have already mentioned) which does go beyond mere species membership—a conception in which to live a human life is to engage in characteristic human activities, to laugh, to weep, to mourn and to rejoice. But that is not a form of life in which the severely mentally retarded can participate.

This point is beautifully brought out in footnote 48 on p. 59 in which Diamond deals with just such an objection. The picture which Diamond paints can be seen as her response to the doubt as to whether there is a conception that meets her specifications. It allows us to see the retarded person not only as having a human fate but one that is particularly terrible. It is a fate that a chimpanzee could not suffer. But it is perfectly proper, I maintain, to see what she is doing here as offering a *reason* for including even the severely retarded within a range of practices, attitudes and responses. We are led to see that there is reason to feel sorry for the retarded in a way in which we could not feel sorry for the chimpanzee. In virtue of the awfulness of her fate we may feel that it would be callous in the extreme to use the retarded human as a subject in medical experimentation.[23]

I am claiming that what Diamond is offering here can properly be seen as an attempt to justify certain kinds of response, an attempt to show that certain ways of treating the severely retarded would be wrong. It is, indeed, a justification of just the kind that could figure in a particularist account. We are faced with competing conceptions of what it is to live a human life, on one of which a severely retarded person cannot be seen as sharing a common human fate with us, and on the other of which she can. What Diamond offers are reasons for seeing that person's existence in one way rather than another.[24] The objection to viewing an appeal to the fact that Larry was a pet as a justification for treating him in a particular way was that it was hopelessly circular, since Larry's being a pet was constituted by his being treated in that way. But Diamond appeals to a fact about the retarded person which is not in itself constituted by the practice—the fact that he has been deprived of distinctively human capacities—in order to justify her claim that he can be seen as having a human life to lead. So the circularity objection to understanding her remark as an attempted justification fails and the particularist may, if she wishes, appeal to such a reason if she finds it compelling in some case(s).[25]

[23] At the conference, David Cockburn pointed out that this reason did not seem sufficient, on its own, to explain our reluctance to experiment (painlessly) on the retarded, though it might ground some other response, such as wanting to give them those comforts they could appreciate, as a sort of compensation. (A similar problem would afflict anyone who tried to explain, along parallel lines, our feeling that it is very wrong to make fun of the retarded, even where they are incapable of noticing it.)

Here is a tentative response. The thought that someone has been deprived, although she does not know it, of a normal life, might ground an unwillingness to do anything to make her life worse. This would rule out all experiments except ones where there was no possibility of any deleterious consequences. This might still leave some opening for totally harmless experimentation. But would such experiments, if they met this stringent condition, be wrong?

[24] It might help to recall the aesthetic analogy; think of cases where one wishes to justify one's judgement of a work of art by offering a particular way of seeing (or reading, or hearing) it.

[25] Holism about reasons will prevent particularists suppposing that, where reference to being human gets in as a moral reason, it always gets in in the same way. The above account would not do, for example, in the case of neonates. Here, perhaps, we appeal to the fact that they are potentially human, that they would have a human life to lead if they were nurtured rather than destroyed. (I owe this point to Jonathan Dancy.)

It is noteworthy that objections to the potentiality argument typically

In virtue of what, however, can we see the retarded person as having been *deprived* of the exercise of distinctively human capacities? In virtue of her being a member of the species *homo sapiens*. For in another possible world *she* might have lived a full and normal human life. Whereas we cannot say that of the chimpanzee.[26] Does this show that Diamond's appeal is ultimately merely to a biological fact? No, not *merely* to a biological fact, for that fact grounds a counterfactual which enables us to see the retarded person in a certain light. Still, it might be said, the biological fact would figure in a complete account of the justification for treating the retarded with respect. And is this not to fall foul of the charge of speciesism? No, not if we adopt particularism. The particularist insists that it may be perfectly proper to appeal to the fact that someone is a member of the human species where it is morally relevant. But that appeal is not everywhere relevant, nor is any general licence granted for, say, doing what we like to animals provided that it is in our interests.[27,28]

[26] I owe this point to Piers Rawlings.

[27] I should perhaps stress that there are many parts of Diamond's rich paper that are unaffected by these remarks, such as her interesting treatment of Scrooge's awakening awareness of his own mortality.

[28] I wish to thank Cora Diamond for giving most generously of her time in discussing her views with me and saving me from many errors. I also wish to thank Jonathan Dancy, Piers Rawling, Brad Hooker and David Cockburn who provided helpful comments on earlier drafts of this paper, and the Philosophy Department of the University of Georgia for a generous financial contribution to my travelling costs.

---

follow a pattern which the particularist rejects. We are reminded that there are many cases where the fact that something is potentially *f* does not justify us in acting as if it were actually *f*. The implication is that because an appeal to potentiality won't work in these cases it won't work anywhere. This is just the move the particularist resists.

Response to McNaughton

CORA DIAMOND

David McNaughton argues that in footnote 48 of my paper I provide justification for including the severely retarded among those whom we think of as with us in being human. Let me fill in the background to that note.

In the paper I write about the ways in which a sense of shared humanness may be expressed, for example in literature. At various points I *use* the language of human connectedness in the hope that readers will find themselves at home in what is in fact a familiar kind of language. That was my intention in writing that 'a human being is someone who has a human life to lead, as do I, someone whose fate is a human fate, as is mine'. John Marshall was puzzled by my saying that I meant those words to apply also to severely retarded people. On his Kantian view, what is meant by the leading of a human life involves having ideas about one's life and how one might lead it, ideas that enter into what one does, what one makes of that life. So rationality is tied to a life's being human; and that led Marshall to say that someone cannot lack rationality and still be, in the morally important sense, human. McNaughton takes it, I think, that I could reply to Marshall that living a human life comes to different things in different cases, that in some cases a life's being *human* is tied to the person's having ideas about his life, and those ideas entering into what the person does, and that in other cases a person's having a human life to lead is tied to his being deprived, as only a human being can be, of distinctively human rational capacities. But I want to make clear why I did not try to show that in the case of the retarded person there is something—something *else* than what there is in the case of other people—that makes him a proper object of moral concern.

In footnote 48 I was trying to lead Marshall to recognize the way of speaking I put before him as something possible for himself. I spoke of the person, deprived for all or most of his life, of distinctively human capacities, and said that a human life without the exercise of those capacities is *his* human life. The one human life he is given has *that* deprivation in it; *that,* in his case, is what his having a human life to lead has been. I meant this to hark back to my quotation from Conrad, about the feeling we may have of unavoidable solidarity in mysterious origin, in uncertain fate, binding men to each other—I used the language of that Conradian sense of solidarity. I spoke from within that sense, hoping that Marshall would find that the words resonated in him.

McNaughton wants us to see the deprivation this way: *because* this being, this man, has a deprivation which only a human being can have, which no chimpanzee can have, we have a justification for bringing him into our conception of those who share a human fate.

Now if a person has suffered some terrible irremediable deprivation in his life, or has undergone some terrible suffering, that can in many circumstances be a justification for treating him or her with special concern. But that kind of justification has its place within the context of our understanding of the finality of our life, of our subjection to what happens, of all that losses can mean for us. When we are struck by what a deprivation like being from birth without normal mental capacities is, when we are struck by what it means for *that* to be the one life someone has, there is already present in that being struck the Conradian sense of our unavoidable solidarity. It is not then that our grasp of the retarded person's deprivation *justifies* extending our feeling of shared humanness to him; rather, there is an idea of what the deprivation is, an idea I hoped to express in that footnote, that emerges from our seeing the retarded person's life as *with* ours, of him and the rest of us as bound together.

Conrad speaks of us as bound not only to each other, but as bound to the whole visible world. I do not want to deny that there can be a pained sense of deprivation when we sharply feel what it is for an animal to be deprived of the normal life of its kind. That is, my discussion of the importance of shared humanness is not meant to suggest that the sharedness of life itself does not also play a role in our thought. Nor did I want to suggest that the form taken by the sense of life in Conrad or Dickens was more than an important kind of example.

Response to Diamond

DAVID McNAUGHTON

Where two people differ about the application of some term to a particular object, to what can they appeal to settle their disagreement? In my paper I suggested that the disputants can legitimately draw attention to various features of the contested case to try to show the continuity, or lack of it, between this case and other instances that fall under the concept. In so doing they are offering reasons to justify their judgement in this particular case.

I am now inclined to think that such an approach is only likely to be successful if the disagreement between the parties is not too radical. This is so where they share a common understanding of the term in question but disagree about a hard case. Here, the features to which they appeal, and the significance those features have, will be determined by that shared understanding. But their disagreement may go deeper. They may have competing conceptions of the same term which give each of them a quite different approach to the case in question. In particular, what is a hard case on one approach may be a paradigm case of the concept on the other. Lacking a shared conception, it is likely that neither disputant will be able to appreciate the significance of the features of the case in hand to which the other draws attention. Each will be an outsider to the other's practice. (I am not suggesting that there is a sharp division between these more and less radical kinds of disagreement; it is clearly a matter of degree.)

Diamond's disagreement with Marshall is of this more radical kind. For Marshall, the more retarded someone is the more difficult it is to see her as having a human life to lead. But for Diamond the retarded are not at the periphery of the concept; they fall squarely under it. (On this, see her remarks about Rorty and the Orthodox on p. 54 of her paper.) My suggested reading of her response to Marshall was based on the model that I now think is only suitable for disagreements of the less radical variety. It fails to address their disagreement adequately, for the kind of reason that Diamond gives at the end of her reply to me. A Kantian could not be struck by the life of the retarded as one of deprivation, which merits a certain range of response, since there are no resources in his conception for thinking of those who lack rationality in that way.

That does not mean, however, that what I offered might not be a helpful response to someone who was closer to my particularist conception of what it is to see some being as an object of moral concern. Think, for example, of someone who cannot understand the pity we feel for the congenitally retarded. They have not suffered a *loss,* he might say, since they never had normal mental capacities, nor are they capable of appreciating that they are without them. Reminding him that, had things gone normally, they would have led lives like ours, can be a way of helping him understand that there is another way of seeing them as having lost something, and thus as deserving sympathy and a certain kind of treatment. Here Diamond's objection does not apply. It is not necessary that my interlocutor *already* see the retarded person's life as one with ours, in order for him to be struck by its deprivation. Rather, I offer him a way of seeing it as, in some ways, continuous with cases that do elicit our sympathy at what has been lost. To be struck by that continuity is, at the same time, to see that kind of concern as appropriate.

What resources can we draw on in trying to settle the more radical form of disagreement? It is, I think, common ground between Diamond and myself that we have to address our opponent from within our tradition, practice, or form of life. There is no common, practice-free conception of rationality, no Archimedean point which we could utilise to aid understanding. This point, I take it, underlies our opposition to the orthodox approach to moral justification. It also, I presume, lies behind Diamond's strategy of responding to Marshall by using 'the language of human connectedness' so that he can 'recognise the way of speaking as something possible for himself' (p. 83 in her response). But what if, as in the present case, that way of speaking is seen by the other person as deeply puzzling?

All that can be done, I believe, is to give a persuasive articulation of the whole practice, and ultimately of its place in one's world-view, in such a way that the other person may be led to see how this represents an attractive way of understanding the disputed concept. This is what I take Diamond to have been doing in her discussions of Conrad and Dickens. This brings me back to a worry about her position in her *Appendix.* In an articulation of a particular conception of leading a human life how could one avoid appealing to features of human beings which helped to explain the attractiveness of the view one was advocating? Diamond mentions, for example, in her discussion of Conrad, our 'mysterious origin' and 'uncertain fate' (p. 83). What purpose does drawing our attention to those features serve if it is not to offer reasons, from within the practice, that help to explain and justify the attitudes and responses embedded in that practice?

Real Selves: Persons as a Substantial Kind

E. J. LOWE

I. Introduction

Are persons substances or modes? (The terminology may seem archaic, but the issue is a live one.) Two currently dominant views may be characterized as giving the following rival answers to this question. According to the first view, persons are just *biological substances*. According to the second, persons are *psychological modes* of substances which, as far as human beings are concerned, happen to be biological substances, but which could in principle be non-biological. There is, however, also a third possible answer, and this is that persons are *psychological substances*. Such a view is inevitably associated with the name of Descartes, and this helps to explain its current unpopularity, since substantial dualism of his sort is now widely rejected as 'unscientific'. But one may, as I hope to show, espouse the view that persons are psychological substances without endorsing Cartesianism. This is because one may reject certain features of Descartes's conception of substance. Consequently, one may also espouse a version of substantial dualism which is distinctly non-Cartesian. One may hold that a person, being a psychological substance, is an entity distinct from the biological substance that is (in the human case) his or her body, and yet still be prepared to ascribe corporeal characteristics to this psychological substance.[1] By this account, a human person is to be thought of neither as a non-corporeal mental substance (a Cartesian mind), nor as the product of a mysterious 'union' between such a substance and a physical, biological substance (a Cartesian animal body). This is not to deny that the mind–body problem is a serious and difficult one, but it is to imply that there is a version of substantial dualism which does not involve regarding the 'mind' as a distinct substance in its own right.

II. What is a substance?

But what do we—or, more to the point, what *should* we—mean by a 'substance'? I am prepared to defend what I take to be a more or less

---

[1] Such a view has close affinities with that advanced by P. F. Strawson, in his *Individuals: An Essay in Descriptive Metaphysics* (London: Methuen, 1959), Ch. 3.

Aristotelian conception of this notion. That is, I shall follow the Aristotle of the *Categories* in taking a 'primary' substance to be a concrete individual *thing*, or 'particular', or 'continuant'.[2] Paradigm examples are such entities as an individual horse (say, Eclipse) and an individual house (say, the one I live in). (If, as some commentators believe,[3] Aristotle changed his mind about this between composing the *Categories* and the *Metaphysics,* then so be it; I am really only interested in the doctrine, not in whether or when Aristotle held it.)

Such substances (henceforth I shall drop the word 'primary') belong to kinds, that is, to species and genera (which Aristotle, in the *Categories* but not elsewhere, called 'secondary' substances). The kinds to which substances belong I shall call *substantial* kinds. Not *all* kinds are substantial kinds, of course, since there are kinds of non-substantial individuals: for example, kinds of events and kinds of numbers. Events, though concrete individuals, are not substances by the 'Aristotelian' account because they are not entities capable of persisting through qualitative change—indeed, they just *are,* broadly speaking, the changes which substances undergo. Numbers are not substances because—assuming indeed that they really exist at all—they are purely abstract entities.

Substantial kinds may be *natural* (like the kind *horse*) or they may be *artefactual* (like the kind *house*). This distinction is mutually exclusive and perhaps also exhaustive—though arguably there genuinely exist substantial kinds, like perhaps the culinary kind *vegetable*, which are neither natural nor artefactual.[4] But to call a substantial kind 'natural' is not to imply that individual exemplars of it could not be artificially synthesized. Rather, the characteristic feature of natural substantial kinds (henceforth, simply 'natural kinds') is that they are *subjects of natural law*. This requires some expansion. Obviously, it is not that an artefact, such as a watch, is not subject *to* natural law: if a watch is dropped, its fall will be governed by the law of gravity, quite as much as will the fall of a tree. The point rather is that there are no natural laws

[2] See further my chapter on 'Substance', in G. H. R. Parkinson (ed.), *An Encyclopaedia of Philosophy* (London: Routledge, 1988), 255–78. 'Particular' is Strawson's term. The term 'continuant' was coined by W. E. Johnson: see his *Logic, Part III* (Cambridge: Cambridge University Press, 1924), Ch. VII.

[3] See, e.g. Alan Code, 'Aristotle: Essence and Accident', in R. E. Grandy and R. Warner (eds), *Philosophical Grounds of Rationality* (Oxford: Clarendon Press, 1986), and Michael Frede, 'Substance in Aristotle's *Metaphysics*', in his *Essays in Ancient Philosophy* (Oxford: Clarendon Press, 1987).

[4] See T. E. Wilkerson, 'Natural Kinds', *Philosophy* **63,** No. 243 (January 1988), 29–42.

that are distinctively *about* watches or artefacts of any other kind: artefactual kinds are not subjects *of* natural law. By contrast, there *are* laws about plants and animals and stars and atoms and all other such natural kinds. The laws in question belong to the various special sciences: biology, astronomy, nuclear physics, and so forth. Each of these sciences is about substances of certain appropriate natural kinds. The kinds that are proper to one science are not, in general, proper to another: thus astronomy has something to say about stars but not about starfish, while the reverse is true of biology. Furthermore, I see no good reason to believe that all laws about natural kinds are even 'in principle' reducible to, or wholly explicable in terms of, laws about some privileged set of 'basic' or 'fundamental' natural kinds—such as sub-atomic particles. That is to say, I consider the various special sciences to be for the most part relatively autonomous, despite numerous theoretical interconnections between them.

One reason why I reject reductionism about laws is that I reject it about substantial individuals of the kinds which are the subjects of laws. For instance, I reject the view that a biological entity such as a tree can simply be regarded as being nothing over and above an assemblage of sub-atomic particles, even though we now believe that the ultimate constituents of trees (and of everything else material) are indeed such particles. It may perhaps be true that the existence of the tree in some sense 'supervenes' upon that of its constituent particles at any given time (though saying this is no clearer than the somewhat obscure notion of supervenience permits it to be). But that these particles constitute a *tree* rather than an entity of some quite different non-biological kind crucially depends upon their organization (that is, in Aristotelian terms, upon their realizing the 'form' of a tree). And this organization can only be appropriately described (I would contend) in distinctively *biological* terms. Thus, what is crucial as far as the presence or absence of a *tree* is concerned, is that the particles in question should be so organized as to subserve the characteristic life-sustaining functions of the various typical parts of a tree—respiration, photosynthesis, nutrition, and so forth. (By a tree's 'typical' parts I mean such parts as its leaves, branches, roots and so on, all of which play distinctive biological roles in its overall structure and economy.) Saying what these typical parts and characteristic functions are, and explaining their proper interrelationships, are precisely matters for the science of biology, and will involve the recognition of various distinctively biological laws. Biological laws are laws about living organisms *qua* living organisms (rather than, for example, *qua* material bodies), and since talk of living organisms is not reducible to talk of assemblages of sub-atomic particles, neither are biological laws reducible to the laws of nuclear physics.

E. J. Lowe

III. Persons as Biological Substances

Having explained what I mean by 'substance' and 'substantial kind', I can return now to my main theme: the ontological status of persons. According to the first view mentioned in my opening section, persons are biological substances—that is, they are members of a substantial kind which is a kind of living organism. Briefly: persons are a kind of animal. This seems to have been Aristotle's own view, and in modern times it is well represented in the work of David Wiggins.[5]

One striking feature of this view is that it threatens either to promote a (to my mind) ethically dubious anthropomorphic 'speciesism' or else to play havoc with zoological taxonomies.[6] To see this, it should be noted that it is normally the case in zoology that, if a species a is subordinate to both of two distinct genera b and c, then either b is subordinate to c or c is subordinate to b. (I use the term 'genus' here in a broad sense just to mean a higher kind than another, relative to which the latter is correspondingly a 'species'.) Formally, we may state this principle as follows (where '/' symbolizes the subordinancy relation):

$$P. \ a/b \ \& \ a/c \rightarrow b=c \lor b/c \lor c/b.$$

For instance, goats are both ruminants and ungulates—and, as it turns out, ruminants are (i.e. are subordinate to) ungulates, in accordance with the requirements of principle P. Consequently, if two distinct species a and a' are both subordinate to a genus b, while a is also subordinate to a genus c and a' is subordinate to a genus c', then (by our principle P) it is *both* the case that either b is subordinate to c or c is subordinate to b, *and* the case that either b is subordinate to c' or c' is subordinate to b. It follows (assuming that our principle P also applies to the genera and that the subordinancy relation is transitive) that in such a case either c is subordinate to c', or c' is subordinate to c, or else c and c' are both subordinate to b. Now, an adherent of the view that persons are a kind of animal will doubtless want to say that *humans* (i.e. members of the species *homo sapiens*) are *persons* and are also (for example) *mammals*. But could an adherent of this view also accept the possibility of there being a hitherto unknown species of *amphibians* (say), call them *bolgs*, which were likewise *persons*? Not if our tax-

[5] See David Wiggins, *Sameness and Substance* (Oxford: Basil Blackwell, 1980), 187.

[6] Wiggins himself (ibid. 174f.) gravitates towards the first horn of this apparent dilemma. Another recent author who gravitates towards the anthropocentric position is Kathleen Wilkes: see her *Real People: Personal Identity without Thought Experiments* (Oxford: Clarendon Press, 1988), 97ff., 230ff.

onomic principle P is correct, for this would commit them to the proposition that either mammals are amphibians, or amphibians are mammals, or else both mammals and amphibians are persons—and none of these disjuncts is true. (The last disjunct is of course false because if amphibians are—i.e. are subordinate to—persons then, since frogs are amphibians, frogs would have to be persons, by virtue of the transitivity of the subordinancy relation. But frogs are not persons, outside the realms of fairy tale.) So either a widely applicable taxonomic principle must be rejected or else it must be claimed that creatures such as our imagined bolgs cannot be persons—which seems to require an intolerable degree of anthropocentric prejudice.

Perhaps, however, all that this shows is that our principle P should indeed be rejected in favour of a weaker one, expressible formally as follows:[7]

$$P'.\ a/b\ \&\ a/c \rightarrow b=c \lor b/c \lor c/b \lor (\exists x)(b/x\ \&\ c/x).$$

Appealing to this principle, an adherent of the biological substance view of persons could hold that both humans and bolgs are indeed persons, even though humans are mammals and bolgs are amphibians. For the only constraint that P' imposes here is that mammals, amphibians, and persons should all be subordinate to some one higher genus—and an adherent of the biological substance view will of course be quite happy to allow this, seeing the genus *animal* as occupying precisely such a role. The proposed set of relationships is displayed in Figure 1.

Such a taxonomic structure cannot, I think, be ruled out *a priori*, since I am certainly prepared to allow that structures isomorphic with it may obtain amongst artefactual kinds. However, amongst *natural* (and more specifically *biological*) kinds this seems most improbable. This is connected with the fact that natural kinds are subjects of natural law. If

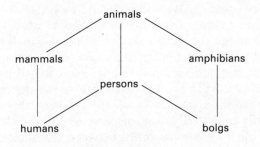

Figure 1.

[7] Cf. Wiggins, *Sameness and Substance*, 202.

persons are a natural, biological kind, as is now being proposed, then one would expect there to be distinctive biological laws relating to personkind—laws intimately linked to the evolution of persons as a biological kind. Such laws would have to be applicable to both humans and bolgs, these both being *ex hypothesi* species of person. However, humans and bolgs, being mammals and amphibians respectively, must be presumed to have had quite different evolutionary histories, tenuously linked only by a very remote common ancestor species: and this seems to make it little short of miraculous that they should none the less *both* have evolved to be governed by the *same* distinctive network of biological laws, even to the extent of qualifying them as species of a single biological kind, personkind. It is rather as if we were to discover that although all the frogs we have hitherto encountered are amphibians, there is in fact also a mammalian species of frogs, exhibiting many of the features we are familiar with in frogs and yet warm-blooded and given to suckling their young. As an imaginary contribution to biological science, the theory of persons just adumbrated is no less incredible.

At this point various responses are available to my opponent. One is to remark that in fact evolution *has* thrown up species sharing many morphological features despite their having no close common antecedent, a phenomenon which is often reflected in the popular names of these species: for instance, *wolves* and *marsupial wolves*.[8] But such examples do not really help my opponent, since biological science does *not* in fact classify such species as genuinely falling under the same genus by virtue of the shared morphological features in question. Marsupial wolves are *not* regarded by zoologists as a species of dog, unlike true wolves (*canis lupus*). However, to this my opponent may respond that I have unfairly stacked the cards against him by taking zoological species as my paradigm of biological kinds.[9] 'Obviously', he may say, 'persons can't be regarded as a zoological species on a par with *canis lupus* or *homo sapiens*, and so can't be expected to fit in neatly with zoological taxonomies; but this doesn't mean that they can't constitute a biological kind—a kind of animal—which finds a place in some alternative (though not for that reason *rival*) taxonomic scheme.'

My reply to this suggestion is that it is threatened by the following dilemma. Either it will be compelled to regard persons as constituting a purely 'nominal' (as opposed to a 'real') kind—and this will undermine the supposedly biological status of persons. Or else it will have difficulty in establishing compatibility between the zoological taxonomy and the proposed alternative biological taxonomy in which persons are

[8] Cf. Wiggins, ibid. 203.
[9] Cf. Wiggins, ibid.

supposed to find a place. To see this, we must recall that an adherent of
the suggestion will want to claim that individual human beings are *both*
members of the zoological species *homo sapiens* and *also* members of
the allegedly biological kind *person*. Now, if *person* is regarded as a
purely nominal kind—that is, as a 'kind' membership of which is
secured merely by possession of some set of 'defining characteristics'
(so that, in my view, it deserves the name 'kind' by courtesy only)—
then the claim in question is not threatened by inconsistency. However,
it does now appear obscure in what sense it could still be insisted that
the concept of a person is essentially a *biological* one. For if personhood
is determined by the satisfaction of a set of defining characteristics, it
seems clear that the favoured candidates for such characteristics would
have to be broadly *psychological* ones: an ability to reason, the possession of consciousness, a capacity to perceive and to engage in intentional activity, and so forth.[10] It certainly is not clear why we should
have to include amongst these characteristics any mention of a biological substrate or of distinctively biological functions. There seems to be
no good reason, either *a priori* or *a posteriori*, to suppose that the
psychological capacities mentioned earlier could not in principle be
associated with an inorganic body, and indeed even with a wholly
artefactual one.[11]

So let us turn to the other horn of the dilemma, by supposing that
persons are to be regarded as a *real* biological kind. My point now is that
it is difficult to see how this can be consistent with regarding individual
members of the species *homo sapiens* as also being instances of the kind
person, given the relative independence of the two taxonomic schemes
within which these kinds are supposed to find their places. The reason
for this is as follows. Specifying what real or substantial kind(s) a
particular belongs to is, in Aristotelian terms, tantamount to determining its *essence*. Thus, bound up with such a specification will be an
account of the particular's *persistence conditions*; that is, an account of
the sorts of admissible changes it can undergo while yet surviving as a

[10] For a view of personhood along these lines, see Daniel C. Dennett,
'Conditions of Personhood', in his *Brainstorms* (Hassocks: Harvester Press,
1979). I criticize this sort of approach in my *Kinds of Being: A Study of
Individuation, Identity and the Logic of Sortal Terms* (Oxford: Basil Blackwell, 1989), 112–18. Thus I agree with Wiggins that persons constitute a real
rather than a merely nominal kind, but differ from him in denying that the
kind in question is a *biological* one.

[11] David Wiggins challenges this view in his *Sameness and Substance*,
174–5. It has of course also been challenged, if more obliquely, by John Searle,
most recently in his 'Is the Brain's Mind a Computer Program?', *Scientific
American 262* (January 1990), 20–5. But I find neither challenge convincing:
see my *Kinds of Being*, 111.

particular of that kind. Changes that are admissible for particulars of one kind are very often not admissible for particulars of another kind; and in general the range of admissible changes will (in the case of natural kinds) be intimately tied to the range of natural laws of which the kind in question is the subject. For example, the change from possessing gills and a tail to possessing lungs and four legs is admissible in the case of frogs but not in the case of trout, because the laws of morphological development differ for creatures of these two different kinds. Now, if *person* and *homo sapiens* are *both* real biological kinds, then both will have associated with them a range of admissible changes determined by the developmental laws governing these kinds. However, given the relative independence of the two taxonomic schemes within which these kinds are supposed to find their places, there is no reason to suppose compatibility between these ranges of admissible changes—and indeed every reason to suppose incompatibility.[12] For instance, suppose that our imagined bolgs are accepted as *bona fide* members of the kind *person*, and yet are also similar to their amphibian cousins the frogs in undergoing metamorphosis from a larval to an adult phase. Then bolgs *qua* amphibians can survive a change from having gills and a tail to having lungs and legs, whereas humans *qua* members of the mammalian species *homo sapiens* cannot. But both bolgs and humans are supposedly *also* members of the allegedly biological real kind *person*, governed by its own developmental laws. Either these laws permit the change from having gills and a tail to having lungs and legs or they do not permit it. If they do, then it follows, absurdly, that an individual human being *can* survive the change *qua* person but *cannot* survive it *qua* member of *homo sapiens*. If they do not, then it follows, equally absurdly, that an individual bolg *cannot* survive the change *qua*

---

[12] Wiggins would deny this, on the grounds that both schemes are supposedly dominated by the genus *animal*. Thus he writes: 'Cross-classifications that are resolved under a higher sort do not ultimately disturb a system of natural kinds. It is always (say) animals that are under study; and different classifications will not import different identity or persistence conditions for particular animals' (*Sameness and Substance*, 204). This seems to presume that all animals, of whatever kind, are governed by the same persistence conditions. But that is patently false, at least if one means by the 'persistence conditions' for a given kind of animals the range of changes which, as a matter of natural law, members of that kind can undergo. Of course, it may be *conceptually* possible for an individual member of one animal kind to survive a transmutation which renders it a member of another kind governed by persistence conditions different from those of the first. But the bare logical possibility of such fairy-tale transmogrifications obviously does nothing to lessen the tension between our two supposed taxonomic schemes, conceived as contributions to empirical biological science.

person but *can* survive it *qua* bolg. (If it is felt that this argument is suspect on the grounds that human beings do not have gills and a tail in the first place, or indeed on the opposing grounds that human beings do in fact undergo a metamorphosis not unlike that of amphibians but prenatally during their embryo stage, then it is easy enough to substitute for the bolgs an imagined species undergoing a metamorphosis which human beings undoubtedly *cannot* undergo despite possessing the morphological features of its initial phase—for instance, a change from having hair and arms to having feathers and wings.)

This concludes my discussion of the first view mentioned in my opening section—the view that persons are biological substances.[13] I hope I have made the unattractiveness of that view abundantly clear, and in particular I hope I have made it clear why adherents of that view are driven towards anthropocentrism. It is true that I have offered no explicit arguments against such anthropocentrism itself—against the opinion, that is, that human beings are the only persons that there could be—but this is because I find it not only morally repugnant and dangerously arrogant, but also symptomatic of a philosophically inadequate imagination. I cannot really take the suggestion seriously as one meriting detailed examination and refutation.

IV. Persons as Psychological Modes

The next view I shall consider—that of persons as psychological modes—is essentially the view of Locke and Hume; though of course Locke and Hume also had their important differences on matters to do with substance and identity. Here I should explain that by a *mode* I understand any concrete non-substantial individual, or any entity wholly constituted by concrete non-substantial individuals. Paradigm examples of concrete non-substantial individuals are events, processes, and states. And the view of persons which we are now considering takes persons to be wholly constituted by *psychological* or *mental* events, processes, and states.

It must be conceded that Locke's adherence to the psychological mode view of persons is less clear-cut and explicit than Hume's. Hume of course quite expressly regards the self as being 'nothing but a bundle or collection of different perceptions'.[14] On the other hand, Locke's official doctrine seems to be that 'person' denotes a nominal kind whose

[13] I raise other objections against it in my *Kinds of Being*, 108–21.
[14] See David Hume, *A Treatise of Human Nature*, ed. P. H. Nidditch (Oxford: Clarendon Press, 1978), Book I, Part IV, Sect. VI, 252.

E. J. Lowe

defining characteristics are all psychological in nature.[15] Even so, Locke's account of the identity conditions of persons and his concomitant treatment of the puzzle cases certainly appear to imply that, on his view, neither material nor (finite) 'spiritual' *substances* can qualify as persons.[16] Furthermore, there is a passage in the *Essay* in which Locke, having claimed that the only three kinds of substance of which we have ideas are God, finite spirits, and material particles, goes on to say that 'all other things [are] but modes or relations ultimately terminated in substances'.[17] Given that persons (other than God, at least) are not substances, this would certainly appear to imply that for Locke they have the status of *modes*. Anyway, ignoring further exegetical complications, I shall henceforth just assume that Locke does indeed belong to the same broad camp as Hume.

In recent years, a view of persons very much like that of Locke and Hume has enjoyed a revival in the writings of such philosophers as Derek Parfit.[18] Modern adherents of the view are, however, usually concerned to represent it as a physicalist theory, or at least as being compatible with a thoroughgoing physicalism. This, they suppose, may be achieved by maintaining that mental events, processes, and states are—or at least could well be—identical with physical events, processes, and states. Such psychophysical identities may, it is further supposed, obtain either on a 'type-type' or on a 'token-token' basis (with the latter suggestion currently enjoying rather more popularity than the former).

How are persons supposed to be constituted by mental states? (Henceforth, for the sake of brevity, I shall use 'state' in a broad way to include both events and processes.) Here theorists diverge somewhat. According to what we may call the 'Lockean' school, personal identity consists in the obtaining of relationships of 'co-consciousness' between mental states. That is to say, on this approach a person is constituted by a manifold of mental states by virtue of these states being connected to one another, but not to any other mental states, by relationships of co-consciousness. Just what these relationships are is a matter for further theorizing on the part of adherents of the Lockean school, but it

[15] See John Locke, *An Essay Concerning Human Understanding*, ed. P. H. Nidditch (Oxford: Clarendon Press, 1975), Book II, Ch. XXVII, Sect. 9. Of course, Locke thought that *all* sortal terms denote merely nominal kinds, so that his classification of 'person' as a nominal kind term reflects no special treatment of it.

[16] See further my review of Harold W. Noonan's *Personal Identity* in *Mind* 99 (1990), 477–9.

[17] Locke, *Essay*, Book II, Ch. XXVII, Sect. 2.

[18] See Derek Parfit, *Reasons and Persons* (Oxford: Clarendon Press, 1984), Part III.

is generally agreed that in the case of coexisting mental states they involve some sort of 'unity of consciousness' condition while in the case of mental states separated by time they involve memory of a special sort (sometimes called 'experiential memory' or 'first person memory'). Adherents of what we may call the 'Humean' school differ from those of the Lockean school chiefly in contending that the relationships between mental states which are crucial to personal identity are not so much cognitive as *causal* in character[19] (though since both schools will typically also advance causal accounts of cognitive relations like memory, the differences between the Lockean and Humean schools are more ones of emphasis than of fundamental principle). It is probably fair to say that most modern proponents of the view of persons now under consideration espouse an amalgam of neo-Lockean and neo-Humean ideas. For brevity, and in recognition of Locke's historical priority, I propose however simply to call such modern accounts collectively the *neo-Lockean theory*.

It is to the credit of the neo-Lockean theory that, unlike the neo-Aristotelian theory, it is untainted by anthropocentrism (this indeed is the lesson of Locke's story of the rational parrot). This explains, too, why the neo-Lockean theory should appeal, as it clearly does, to enthusiasts for the prospects of artificial intelligence. The existence of a neo-Lockean person is popularly likened to the running of a computer program, which is largely independent of the detailed 'hardware' of the machine on which it is run. Human brains and nervous systems provide, on this view, highly efficient hardware (or 'wetware') for the 'running' of a person, but there is no reason in principle why the 'program' should not be run on an altogether different kind of machine, constructed on electronic rather than on biological principles. This even offers human persons—albeit only in the distant future—the prospect of immortality by means of transfer to a solid state device (though equally it offers an embarrassment of riches in the form of simultaneous transfer to more than one such machine).

However, the neo-Lockean theory is untenable. Neo-Aristotelians indeed are likely to abhor it as reviving the 'myth of the ghost in the machine', and as grotesquely abstracting from the bodily and social dimensions of personality. It is not clear to me that this line of criticism is at all fair, though, since it is perfectly open to the neo-Lockean to insist that persons must indeed be *embodied*, and moreover furnished with bodies apt for the performance of physical actions, including those necessary for social co-operation and communication. (After all—to

[19] Cf. Hume, *Treatise*, 261: 'the true idea of the human mind, is to consider it a system of different perceptions . . . which are link'd together by the relation of cause and effect'.

E. J. Lowe

pursue the computer analogy—you cannot run a program on a chunk of rock or a tin can, much less on nothing at all; nor would anyone see fit to denigrate the notion of a program as introducing the 'myth' of a ghost in the hardware.) I suspect that all that this neo-Aristotelian line of criticism amounts to is once again the expression of anthropocentric prejudices. Yet for all that the neo-Lockean theory *is* untenable, and this for reasons of fundamental principle.

What is wrong with the neo-Lockean theory is that, in purporting to supply an account of the individuation and identity of persons it presupposes, untenably, that an account of the identity conditions of psychological modes can be provided which need not rely on reference to persons. But it emerges that the identity of any psychological mode turns on the identity of the person that possesses it. What this implies is that psychological modes are essentially modes *of persons*, and correspondingly that persons have to be conceived of as psychological *substances*. This is what I now hope to show.

By psychological modes I mean, as I have already explained, individual mental events, processes, and states. (It is important to emphasize that we are talking about *individual* entities here—'tokens' rather than 'types'.) Paradigm examples would be: a particular belief-state, a particular memory-state, a particular sensory experience, a particular sequence of thoughts constituting a particular process of reasoning, and so on. But, to repeat, such individual mental states are necessarily states *of persons*: they are necessarily 'owned'—necessarily have a *subject*. The necessity in question arises from the metaphysical-cum-logical truth that such individual mental states cannot even in principle be individuated and identified without reference to the subject of which they are states. (The point has been argued before by Strawson,[20] but it is none the less worth insisting on it again since Strawson's arguments seem to have gone largely unheeded.)

Consider thus the example of a particular experience of pain, which is a 'token' mental event occurring at a specific time. (Whether it occurs at a specific *place* is more contentious. We should not confuse the phenomenological location of the pain—where it is felt 'at', for instance in a certain tooth—with the place, if any, at which the token experience occurs. Physicalists would of course presume that the token experience is identifiable with a token neural event located in the brain, at least in the case of a human person; but the truth—and indeed the intelligibility—of physicalism is something that I have grave doubts about.[21]) Now, clearly, the qualitative character and time of occurrence of this token experience do not suffice to individuate it uniquely: two

[20] See Strawson, *Individuals*, Ch. 3.
[21] See further my *Kinds of Being*, 113–14, 132–33.

qualitatively indistinguishable token experiences could, logically, occur simultaneously (and quite probably often do, given the vastness of the world's population). What is additionally required to individuate the token experience, it appears, is precisely reference to its *subject*. For instance, if the pain is *mine*, then that it seems will serve to distinguish it from any other qualitatively exactly similar pain occurring at the same time.

But two questions arise here. First, can we be sure that there is no *other* way of individuating the token experience uniquely which does not require reference to its subject? And secondly, can we be sure that one and the same subject could *not* simultaneously have two qualitatively indistinguishable token experiences? Both of these questions have been interestingly addressed quite recently by Christopher Peacocke.[22] Peacocke suggests that although it is a necessary truth that one and the same subject cannot have two qualitatively indistinguishable token experiences at the same time, this is not because token experiences are individuated by reference to their qualitative character, time of occurrence, and subject: rather, the explanation is quite the reverse of this, namely, that subjects themselves are individuated by reference to token experiences in such a way that where we have evidence for the occurrence of two simultaneous and qualitatively indistinguishable token experiences, this should *ipso facto* be taken to imply the existence of two distinct subjects of experience. In support of this suggestion, Peacocke appeals to an example involving a so-called 'split-brain' patient. We could, he contends, have good evidence for supposing that in the case of such a patient there might be, on a given occasion, 'two distinct but qualitatively identical experiences grounded in (different) states of the same brain'.[23] And, he goes on, 'It seems that if we speak of two distinct minds or centres of consciousness in these circumstances, we do so because the token experiences are themselves distinct'.[24] This presupposes, of course, a favourable answer to the *first* question raised a moment ago: that is, it presupposes that we can individuate token experiences independently of their subject, and hence have independent evidence, in the case of the split-brain patient, for the simultaneous occurrence of two qualitatively indistinguishable token experiences.

Now Peacocke *does* consider that a favourable (to him) answer to our first question is available. He suggests that in order to individuate token experiences it suffices, apart from referring to their qualitative charac-

[22] See Christopher Peacocke, *Sense and Content: Experience, Thought and their Relations* (Oxford: Clarendon Press, 1983), 176ff.
[23] Ibid. 177.
[24] Ibid.

E. J. Lowe

ter and time of occurrence, to refer to their *causes and effects*. Thus, he says,

> There is a clear motivation for saying that in the split brain there are two token experiences, a motivation which does not appeal to the identity of persons. The two experiences have different causes—for example, one results from the stimulation of one nostril, the other from the stimulation of the other nostril—and they may have different effects too.[25]

(Peacocke's example here involves, of course, olfactory experiences rather than pains, but this is beside the point.) However, I consider this line of argument to be fatally flawed. No doubt it is true that whenever two distinct token experiences occur, they will differ in respect of at least some of their causes and effects: but it is far from clear that one can effectively appeal to such causal distinctions to individuate token experiences quite independently of any reference to the subjects of those experiences. For it may be, as indeed I believe to be the case, that such causal distinctions themselves cannot be made independently of reference to subjects. But before pursuing this point it is worth remarking that to the extent that Peacocke's proposed criterion for the individuation of token experiences—sameness of causes and effects—is merely a special application of Davidson's well-known criterion for the individuation of events in general, it falls foul of the latter's fatal defect, which is a kind of circularity.[26] Briefly, the trouble with Davidson's criterion is that if (as Davidson himself presupposes) the causes and effects of events are themselves events, then the question of whether events e_1 and e_2 have the *same* causes and effects (and hence turn out to be the same event according to the criterion) is itself a question concerning the identity of events, so that in the absence of an independent criterion of event identity Davidson's criterion leaves every question of event identity unsettled: hence it is either superfluous or ineffectual. Moreover, Peacocke's special application of Davidson's criterion to mental events inherits this difficulty. For even if we suppose, for the sake of argument, that the individuation of *non*-mental events is unproblematic, it is none the less the case that no mental event has purely non-mental causes and effects: that is to say, every mental event has other mental events amongst its causes and effects. And hence the proposal to individuate mental events in terms of the sameness of their causes and effects will again presuppose answers to questions of the

[25] Ibid.

[26] See Donald Davidson, 'The Individuation of Events', in his *Essays on Actions and Events* (Oxford: Clarendon Press, 1980). For an exposure of the defect, see my 'Impredicative Identity Criteria and Davidson's Criterion of Event Identity', *Analysis 49* (1989), 178–81.

very sort at issue, namely, questions concerning the identity of mental events.

It will be of value to expand upon the point that mental events never have wholly non-mental causes and effects, not only in order to support a premise of the foregoing argument, but also because it will help to support the more ambitious claim I made a moment ago that causal distinctions between token experiences (and other mental states) cannot be made independently of reference to subjects. The point is that a mental event, such as a token experience, can only occur *to* a subject, and moreover only to one in a condition which involves the simultaneous possession by that same subject of a whole battery of other mental states—at least some of which will stand in causal relations to the sensory experience in question, helping to determine such features as its intensity and duration and in turn being affected by it in various ways. For instance, if one directs one's attention away from pain, its intensity may be diminished; again, if one believes that the pain is symptomatic of a serious illness, it may cause one to have fears which one would otherwise have lacked; and so on. That a pain should have such causal liaisons with other mental states of the same subject is partially constitutive of the very concept of pain. Thus we can make no sense at all of a subject undergoing a single sensory experience in the complete absence of all other mental activity, much less of a single sensory experience—a twinge of pain, say—occurring out of the blue to no subject at all. *Pace* Hume, 'perceptions', even if they are 'distinct', are frequently not 'separable'.[27] Mental events, even of the most rudimentary kinds, are only conceivable as elements within relatively well-integrated mental economies—that is, as parts of the mental lives of subjects.[28] At root, this is just a corollary of Davidson's own well-known thesis of the 'holism of the mental'.[29]

But let us now see how all this bears upon Peacocke's suggestion that causal distinctions can motivate a claim that two distinct token olfactory experiences occur in his imagined split-brain patient without relying on any consideration as to the number or identity of the subjects involved. What sorts of causal distinctions might be appealed to? Unfortunately,

[27] Cf. Hume, *Treatise*, 233, 634.

[28] This has been disputed recently by Andrew Brennan, in his 'Fragmented Selves and the Problem of Ownership', *Proceedings of the Aristotelian Society* XC (1989/90), 143–58. He cites in his support clinical cases of patients suffering from Korsakov's syndrome, which involves severe amnesia. However, my thesis is not an empirical one, vulnerable to the alleged findings of such psychiatric case studies, but rather a logico-metaphysical one which imposes an *a priori* constraint on what could *count* as an experience or as evidence for the occurrence of one.

[29] See Davidson, *Essays on Actions and Events*, 217.

Peacocke only gestures in the direction of an answer, merely saying (as we have already seen) that 'The two experiences have different causes—for example, one results from the stimulation of one nostril, the other from the stimulation of the other nostril—and they may have different effects too'. But so far all we know about the imagined case is that it is one in which the *corpus callosum* of a living human brain is severed and subsequently the two nostrils neurally connected to the different hemispheres are simultaneously stimulated in the same way. Thus far, however, we have been given no reason for supposing that *either* stimulation results in an olfactory experience. For that, we need to know the answers to such questions as 'Was the patient awake?', 'Did he still possess a sense of smell?', 'Was he paying attention to the stimulus?', and so on. But these are all questions which precisely make reference to a putative *subject* of olfactory experience. Moreover, they presume—perhaps wrongly—that there is just a *single* subject present. But how is this presumption, if mistaken, to be recognized as being in error? That is, how are we to discover that we are dealing with two subjects rather than just one? Peacocke's suggestion seems to be that we *first* determine that each stimulation results in a distinct but qualitatively exactly similar token experience, and *then* on that basis assign each to a different subject, hence concluding that we have two subjects rather than one. But we have just seen that the question of whether a stimulation results in any olfactory experience at all is only answerable in the light of information concerning the prospective subject of that experience (whether he is awake, and so on). So Peacocke's suggested procedure presupposes an answer to the very question that it proposes to settle: for it presupposes, with respect to each stimulation, that we already have in view a subject to which any resulting experience may be assigned. The key point is that whether the stimulation of a particular nostril results in an olfactory experience depends precisely on whether that nostril is functioning as an olfactory sense organ of a subject who is identifiable as the possessor of a suitable range of further mental states at the time of stimulation. Hence it emerges that we cannot effectively motivate a claim that each stimulation results in a distinct token experience without relying on presumptions concerning the existence and identity of the prospective subject(s) of those experiences. And the more general lesson is that one cannot reasonably form judgements about the causation of mental events—including sensory experiences—independently of forming judgements about the subjects of those states, and so cannot expect judgements of the former sort to underpin the individuation of such states in a way which makes no reference to those subjects.[30]

[30] This elaborates and strengthens an argument to be found in my *Kinds of Being*, 131–33.

But what then *are* we to say about the split-brain patient? *Do* we have two subjects here or only one? Again, is it right to dismiss (as Peacocke does) the possibility of one and the same subject simultaneously possessing two qualitatively indistinguishable token experiences? Let me say at once that I think it is a mistake to regard the psychological subject as a 'centre of consciousness'. (Peacocke himself shifts uneasily between the terms 'centre of consciousness', 'mind', and 'person'—all of which, in my view, demand quite different treatments.) The notion of the subject as a 'centre of consciousness' seems to involve precisely that Lockean conception of the self which I am now engaged in challenging: for it suggests that 'unity of consciousness' is somehow criterial for the identity of the self, and this I wish to deny. The case of the split-brain patient is indeed a difficult and puzzling one: but I am strongly inclined to urge that even in such a case we have only a single subject, albeit a subject quite possibly suffering from a partial bifurcation of consciousness, or 'divided mind'. Perhaps, however, this is really no more than an extreme case of a condition to which all psychological subjects are prone.[31] At various times we all find ourselves 'dividing our attention' (as we say)—for example, engaging in conversation while negotiating busy traffic.

This being so, however, I must reject the thesis that one and the same subject cannot possess two qualitatively indistinguishable token experiences simultaneously, however improbable the actual occurrence of such a state of affairs might be. And this then raises the question of how token experiences can be guaranteed to be individuated uniquely, given that reference to their qualitative character, time of occurrence, *and subject* may not suffice. But a plausible answer is that we can now appeal additionally to causal considerations. Peacocke's error (as I see it) was to suppose that we could appeal to causal considerations without needing to make reference to the subject: but in rejecting his supposition we do not have to dismiss causal considerations as irrelevant to the problem of individuation. However, the details of such a solution must await another occasion.

There remains one line of defence of the neo-Lockean theory which I have not yet tackled. The burden of my criticism of that theory has been that it fails to accommodate the fact that mental states have to be individuated as states *of persons*, for this introduces a vicious circularity into its attempt to specify the identity conditions of persons in terms of relations between mental states. But, it may be urged, the truth is only that mental states—being modes—have to be individuated as states *of something*, that is, as states of substances of *some* sort. And why, it may be asked, should not the neo-Lockean simply say that mental states are

[31] Cf. Wilkes, *Real People*, Ch. 5.

states *of the body*—allowing indeed that the body might in principle vary enormously in nature from one person to another? In fact, of course, the neo-Lockean who is also a physicalist does hold precisely this to be true. But the problem is that reference to the body is simply incapable of playing the individuative role here demanded of it. This is because by the neo-Lockean's own lights there can be no guarantee of a one-to-one correspondence between bodies (of whatever sort) and persons. Hence, in a case (however hypothetical) of co-embodiment by two distinct persons (as in the Jekyll and Hyde story), referring a mental state to a particular body will not determine to which person it belongs nor, hence, which token state it is. For persons cannot share token mental states, and so while it is left undetermined to which person a token state belongs, the identity of that token state must equally be left undetermined. For example, if the token state—say, a token belief-state—is referred to the Jekyll–Hyde body, this leaves it open whether it is Jekyll's belief-state or Hyde's belief-state: it cannot be both Jekyll's and Hyde's, but whose it is matters if we are to identify which particular belief-state it is.

Perhaps this argument will be objected to as question-begging, however. Perhaps it will be urged that reference to the Jekyll–Hyde body *will* serve to *identify* the belief-state, but merely leave undetermined whether this state belongs to Jekyll or to Hyde. But what if, as seems perfectly conceivable, Jekyll and Hyde both have token belief-states of exactly the same type? Still these token belief-states cannot be identical because, as has been remarked, token mental states are not shareable between persons. In that case there will be two exactly similar token belief-states referrable to the same body, so that reference to that body will not, after all, serve to distinguish them. The plain fact is (and we should hardly be surprised by it) that in rejecting the biological substance view of persons in favour of the psychological mode view, the neo-Lockean theory has cut itself off from any possibility of treating the *body* as the 'owner' of mental states and thus as playing an essential role in their individuation. The 'owner' of mental states for the neo-Lockean theory must be the person *as opposed to* the body, even though the person itself is, according to that theory, a construct of mental states— the very mental states indeed of which it is the 'owner'. And it is of course precisely this circularity in the theory to which I object.

V. Persons as Psychological Substances

The conclusion I draw from the preceding arguments is that a person or subject of mental states must be regarded as a *substance* of which those states are modes, and yet not as a *biological* substance (as the neo-

Aristotelian theory would have it). What sort of substance, then? Clearly, a psychological substance. That is to say, a person is a substantial individual belonging to a natural kind which is the subject of distinctively psychological laws, and governed by persistence conditions which are likewise distinctively psychological in character. But thus far this is consistent with regarding a person as something like a Cartesian ego or soul, and this is a position from which I wish to distance myself. The distinctive feature of the Cartesian conception of a psychological substance is that such a substance is regarded as possessing *only* mental characteristics, not physical ones. And this is largely why it is vulnerable to certain sceptical arguments to be found in the writings of, *inter alia*, Locke and Kant. The burden of those arguments is that if psychological substances (by which the proponents of the arguments mean *immaterial* 'souls' or 'spirits') are the real subjects of mental states, then for all I know the substance having 'my' thoughts today is not the same as the substance that had 'my' thoughts yesterday: so that, on pain of having to countenance the possibility that my existence is very much more ephemeral than I care to believe, I had better not identify myself with the psychological substance (if any) currently having 'my' thoughts (currently 'doing the thinking in me'). But if *I* am not a psychological substance, it seems gratuitous even to suppose that such substances exist (certainly, their existence cannot be established by the Cartesian *cogito*).

But why should we suppose, with Descartes, that psychological substances must be essentially immaterial? Descartes believed this because he held a conception of substance according to which each distinct kind of substance has only one principal 'attribute', which is peculiar to substances of that kind, and such that all of the states of any individual substance of this kind are modes of this unique and exclusive attribute.[32] In the case of psychological or mental substances, the attribute is Thought; whereas in the case of physical or material substance(s), the attribute is Extension. On this view, no psychological substance can possess a mode of Extension, nor any physical substance a mode of Thought. However, I am aware of no good argument, by Descartes or anyone else, in support of his doctrine of unique and exclusive attributes. Accordingly, I am perfectly ready to allow that psychological substances should possess material characteristics (that is, include physical states amongst their modes). It may be that there is no material characteristic which an individual psychological substance possesses *essentially* (in the sense that its persistence conditions preclude its surviving the loss of this characteristic). But this does not of course imply that an individual psychological substance essentially

[32] See Réné Descartes, *Principles of Philosophy*, Part I, Sect. 53.

possesses *no* material characteristics (to suppose that it did imply this would be to commit a 'quantifier shift fallacy' of such a blatant kind that I am loth to accuse Descartes himself of it).

How, though, does this repudiation of the Cartesian conception of psychological substance help against the sceptical arguments discussed a moment ago? Well, the main reason why those arguments seem to get any purchase is, I think, that in presupposing that psychological substances would have to be wholly non-physical, they are able to take it for granted that such substances are not possible objects of ordinary sense perception. They are represented as being invisible and intangible, and as such at best only perceptible by some mysterious faculty of intro-spection, and hence only by each such substance in respect of itself. But once it is allowed that psychological substances have physical charac-teristics and can thus be seen and touched at least as 'directly' as any ordinary physical thing, the suggestion that we might be unable to detect a rapid turnover of these substances becomes as fanciful as the sceptical suggestion that the table on which I am writing might 'in reality' be a succession of different but short-lived tables replacing one another undetectably. Whether one can conclusively refute such scepti-cism may be an open question; but I see no reason to take it seriously or to allow it to influence our choice of ontological categories.

I believe, then, that a perfectly tenable conception of psychological substance may be developed which permits us to regard such sub-stances as the subjects of mental states: which is just to say that nothing stands in the way of our regarding *persons* precisely as being psycholog-ical substances. The detailed development of such a conception is a topic for another paper, and for now it must suffice to say that I conceive of psychological substances as the proper subject-matter of the science of psychology, which in turn I conceive to be an autonomous science whose laws are not reducible to those of biology or chemistry or physics. However, it will be appropriate to close the present paper with a few remarks on the relationship between psychological and biological substances, that is, between persons and their bodies. (I restrict myself here to the case of persons who—like human persons—have animal bodies.)

With regard to this issue I am, as I indicated at the outset, a *substantial dualist*. Persons are substances, as are their bodies. But they are not identical substances: for they have different persistence conditions, just as do their bodies and the masses of matter constituting those bodies at different times. (I should perhaps emphasize here that where a person's body is a biological substance, as in the case of human persons, the body is to be conceived of as a *living organism*, not as a mere mass of matter or assemblage of physical particles.) Clearly, though, my version of substantial dualism is quite different from

Descartes's. Descartes, it seems, conceived a human person to be the product of a 'substantial union' of two distinct substances: a mental but immaterial substance and a material but non-mental substance. How such a union was possible perplexed him and every subsequent philosopher who endeavoured to understand it. The chief stumbling block was, once again, Descartes's doctrine of unique and exclusive attributes. How could something essentially immaterial get to grips, causally, with something essentially material, and *vice versa*? But psychological substances as I conceive of them are *not* essentially immaterial, and thus I see no difficulty in principle about their entering into causal transactions with their physical environment. And on my view, human persons are themselves just such psychological substances, not a queer hybrid of two radically alien substances.

So, as for the relationship between a person and his or her body, I do not see that this need be more mysterious in principle than any of the other intersubstantial relationships with which the natural sciences are faced: for instance, the relationship between a biological entity such as a tree and the assemblage of physical particles that constitutes it at any given time. Most decidedly, I do not wish to minimize the scientific and metaphysical difficulties involved here. (I do not, for example, think that it would be correct to say that a person is 'constituted' by his or her body in anything like the sense in which a tree is 'constituted' by an assemblage of physical particles.[33]) None the less, it is my hope that by adopting a broadly Aristotelian conception of substance and by emphasizing not only the autonomy but also the continuity of the special sciences, including psychology and biology, we may see a coherent picture begin to emerge of persons as a wholly distinctive kind of being fully integrated into the natural world: a picture which simultaneously preserves the 'Lockean' insight that the concept of a person is fundamentally a psychological (as opposed to a biological) one, the 'Cartesian' insight that persons are a distinctive kind of substantial particulars in their own right, and the 'Aristotelian' insight that persons are not essentially immaterial beings.[34]

[33] For criticism of this suggestion, see my *Kinds of Being*, 119–20.
[34] I am grateful to audiences at the Universities of Durham, Oxford, Sheffield, and York for helpful comments on earlier versions of this paper.

Personal Identity and Brain Transplants

P. F. SNOWDON

My topic is personal identity, or rather, *our* identity. There is general, but not, of course, unanimous, agreement that it is wrong to give an account of what is involved in, and essential to, our persistence over time which requires the existence of immaterial entities, but, it seems to me, there is no consensus about how, within, what might be called this naturalistic framework, we should best procede. This lack of consensus, no doubt, reflects the difficulty, which must strike anyone who has considered the issue, of achieving, just in one's own thinking, a reflective equilibrium. The theory of personal identity, I feel, provides a curious contrast. On the one side, it seems highly important to know what sort of thing we are, but, on the other, it is hard to find any answer which has a 'solid' feel.

Animalism and an Objection

There is, I think, a theory about our identity which falls within this naturalistic constraint and which can be claimed to be the simplest one to do so, and that is the thesis that we are *animals* of a certain kind, and so *our* persistence conditions are those for animals of that kind. Further, since it is the simplest theory that can be given, we have a strong motive to explore as fully as possible the resources available to it, for it is only if we are fairly sure that it cannot be right that we should move on to consider less simple views.

In this paper I am not going to present what can be said in *favour* of the thesis that we are animals, (which thesis I shall call animalism).[1] I want, rather, to consider whether animalism can give an adequate reply

---

[1] I have addressed these issues in 'Persons, Animals and Ourselves', in Christopher Gill (ed.), *The Person and the Human Mind* (Oxford: Clarendon Press, 1990), 83–107, and in 'Against Personal Identity' (unpublished). Other, and important, discussions are: D. Wiggins *Sameness and Substance* (Oxford: Blackwell, 1980), esp. Ch 6, and D. Wiggins 'The Person as Object of Science, as Subject of Experience, and as Locus of Value', in A. Peacocke and G. Gillett (eds). *Persons and Personality*, pp. 56–74, 208–12 (Oxford: Blackwell, 1987).

P. F. Snowdon

to the argument, which it seems to me, has been thought to be the
strongest objection to it. The objection that I have in mind is the
familiar one based on the claim that there could, in principle, be whole
brain transplant operations performed on us, in which a brain is transplanted into a new environment, organic or possibly inorganic, sustained in that environment so that it carries out what are believed to be
its mental functions, thereby yielding experiences, thoughts, apparent
memories, and so on. About these circumstances, it seems plausible to
claim that the subject (or self) would go with the brain, but that because
the brain is simply one organ from a complex animal, the animal does
not go along with its, now ex-, brain. In these envisaged circumstances,
we and the animals come apart. If this split is possible, then, it seems,
we are not one and the same object. Now, about this argument (or this
sort of argument), which, of course, will need to be clarified in the
course of the discussion, I am at this stage, advancing two claims.[2] The
first is that this has been the most influential argument against animalism, but, second, it is, I think, a line of argument which *seems* cogent
and persuasive.[3]

My question, then, is: how should an animalist reply to BTA? In
considering this question I do not aim to provide a full answer, but,
rather, to survey the options and determine, if I can, which is the most
promising.

There is, however, a second topic in which I am interested. One new
development in the theory of personal identity over the past five years
(I mean since the publication of *Reasons and Persons*[4]) has been a
discussion of method. A number of people have written about this, but
the two discussions which I have selected to make a partial assessment
of, are those by Kathleen Wilkes,[5] and Mark Johnston.[6] Both these

[2] I shall, from time to time, refer to this argument as BTA (short for Brain
Transplant Argument).

[3] There is a clarification and a hesitation I wish to express. First, I am not
claiming that BTA is the *strongest* objection to animalism. I am, at the
moment, unsure what qualifies as that. Second, since animalism has not been
explicitly opposed in standard discussions, there is something misleading in
saying that BTA has been the dominant argument against it. What seems fair
to say though, is that BTA has been, in recent discussions, the leading
objection to the standard bodily criterion approach to personal identity, which
is the view amongst the standard views which is closest to animalism.

[4] Derek Parfit, *Reasons and Persons* (Oxford: Clarendon Press, 1984).

[5] Kathleen V. Wilkes, *Real People* (Clarendon Press: Oxford, 1988); see
esp. Ch. 1. The book is subtitled 'Personal Identity without Thought Experiments'.

[6] Mark Johnston, 'Human Beings', *The Journal of Philosophy LXXXIV*, No.
2 (February 1987), 59–83.

writers express criticisms of the method standardly employed in discussions of personal identity. Now, these methodological issues are of considerable interest in themselves. However, their extra interest from my point of view is that the transplant argument is, it would seem, simply an instance of the standard method of argument, and if there are sound criticisms of that method, then they might enable an animalist to answer the leading criticism of their view.

In order to avoid having an extensive discussion, in this paper, of what it is best to regard animalism as claiming, I shall simply stipulate that it involves *two* claims. The first is that we are identical with certain animals. But it is also part of the view that our persistence conditions are those of *animals*, animals being regarded as one fundamental kind of thing. So the second claim, which I shall treat as at least partly elucidatory of this thought, is that anything which is an animal must be an animal, and the self-same animal, at all the times it exists. Given that the view claims both these things, it is committed to the claim that *we must* be animals, and the selfsame animals, at all times we exist.

There is a problem with animalism as I have just expressed it which I wish to note and then ignore. It concerns the earliest stages of our existence. If we say that we were, prior to birth, foetuses, then according to animalism as presently stated, we must count the foetus as an animal. This is not an entirely happy thing to have to say. It may, therefore, be correct to treat being an animal as what is known as a phase-sortal, covering certain stages in the life-history of, say, the more general category of organisms, which, if they are like us, will normally go through a pre-animal-, and then a much longer animal-, phase. If sound, this leaves us with the problem of hitting on the right basic natural category in terms of which to state the thesis. Having noted the problem, however, I shall stick with *animal*, since, in considering the argument I am interested in, it does not matter what precise natural category we choose.

The Objection and some Responses

BTA gives a case for denying the truth of the commitment of animalism which I specified above. For purposes of discussing the argument, I shall represent it as resting on *four* claims. First, it is not absolutely impossible that our brains should be transplanted into new receptacles while retaining their intrinsic functions.[7] Second, amongst the brain's

---

[7] The brain performs important control functions for the rest of the body. In the brain transplant cases as normally envisaged by philosophers these control functions are not necessarily resumed in the new system. We might call these the brain's *extrinsic* functions. The intrinsic functions are the processes which characteristically occur *in* the brain, constituting whatever they constitute (assumed to be the sustaining of a mentally endowed subject). I hope that this note explains the significance of 'intrinsic' as it occurs in the discussion.

intrinsic functions is that of sustaining a subject with thoughts, apparent memories, beliefs, (etc.), and so such a rehoused and functioning brain will sustain a subject of experience who has psychological links to the donor subject. Third, in the new situation the total system (whatever it is) of which the rehoused brain is a functioning part, is *not* the self-same animal which donated it. Fourth, the resulting subject sustained by (or realized by) this system, would be the same subject (or person) which that brain previously sustained. I think that it is right to say that if each of these four claims is accepted then animalism, as explained, cannot be correct.

To start the discussion of this argument I want to stress one point of interpretation, and concede two claims in it.

(1) The point of interpretation concerns the fourth claim. In the argument this judgment has the status of what is known as an intuition. What would be achieved by a successful transplant is described in neutral terms which can be accepted by a theorist who does not agree that it amounts to preserving the person. However, what is true is that when we are presented with the description, we have the strong intuition that the resulting subject is identical with the original person. I want to stipulate that in the argument as it is being discussed *that* is the status of the fourth claim.[8]

(2) The second premise is that our mental life is sustained by, and carried out in, a bodily organ, the extent of which is far less than the whole body. Once that is granted it apparently becomes possible to keep our mental life going, outside the animal, since the removal of that organ is simply the removal of one organ, and no more carries the animal with it than heart or kidney removals do. The argument could be rejected if this assumption about the physical basis of our mental life should turn out to be wrong. If, somehow, the whole (or more or less the whole) of the animal were implicated in mental processes, nothing threatening along these lines could be envisaged. However, although in a full treatment this would need proper discussion, I propose to grant the second premise, which, it seems to me, science speaks for and philosophy does not oppose.

(3) I also propose to agree to the third claim, that the removal and transplant of the brain does not take the animal with it. I am influenced by three considerations. (i) Brain transplants seem analogous to other organ transplants. They are obviously thought of as processes which do not send the donor animal with the organ. (ii) It seems reasonable to

---

[8] I hope that this stipulation makes explicit a feature which is, in fact, characteristic of standard presentations of this sort of argument. It also distinguishes BTA from a similar argument presented by Johnston (ibid. 77–80), which I hope to discuss elsewhere.

treat the human case as we would those of non-human animals. With them we have no inclination to think of the animal as going with the transplanted brain. (iii) In some cases the resulting complex structure can hardly be the original donor animal for it does not qualify as an animal at all, e.g. the vat case. Of course, even if the force of these points is acknowledged, it has to be conceded that difficult problems of animal identity remain, which I shall leave untreated.

If these concessions to the argument are correct, there are two remaining premises, which the animalist might try to deny.

I want to consider briefly the fourth one. It emerges as an intuition, in response to a neutral description of what the (supposed successful) transplant achieves. The neutral description contains an account of the (supposed) mental continuities. A strategy that suggests itself for over-throwing this intuition, and eliciting the contrary one (that the person does not go with the brain), is to stress, in an equivalently neutral way, the other *discontinuities* between the before-person and the after-person. This was in fact the strategy employed by Bernard Williams in a famous discussion (in 1957) of a suppose case of an emperor switching bodies with a peasant.[9] Williams emphasized the loss of voice and style of speech. Although there is no demonstration that a sufficiently smooth-talking proponent cannot make any headway with such a reply, it faces, it seems to me, *two* significant obstacles. The first is simply that the discontinuities in, for example, expression or appearance or behavioural skill, when emphasized, do not tend to elicit the contrary intuition, in the way that the mental continuities do elicit the other

[9] Bernard Williams, 'Personal Identity and Individuation', in *Problems of the Self* (Cambridge: Cambridge University Press, 1973), 11–12. It should be pointed out that Williams was not discussing brain transplants, but, rather, the general idea of a distinctive personality, which is linked at t to body B, shifting to body C at t+n. Williams suggests that it might be a logical impossibility that body C express that personality: 'The emperor's body might include the sort of face that just *could not* express the peasant's morose suspiciousness . . . These "could"s are not just empirical—such expressions on these features might be unthinkable' (Williams, ibid. 12). These remarks do not pay enough attention to the crucial issue, and give prominence to a peripheral one. Suppose that we grant the possibility of a logical impossibility of the sort Williams is arguing for, then, as it stands, it amounts only to a point about the expressibility of a personality (or attitude) in a given body. It does not follow that the attitude or personality might not belong to the person with that body. Williams requires that presence involves expressibility; but he gives no reason for saying that. Whether that is so is the crucial issue. Further, if we decide that presence does require expressibility, then it will follow that, if a certain body cannot in fact express a certain attitude, then the person with the body cannot, in fact, have that attitude. This conclusion does not require that it is a logical impossibility for that body to express it.

positive intuition. The second is that it can be said of, at least, many of these discontinuities that it is not absolutely necessary that transplants involve them. If the receiving entity is very like the donating animal then many of them will simply not occur. I think that these two points make it seem very unlikely that the Williams' strategy will overturn the fourth claim in the argument.

It is important to remember that what is envisaged is a *successful* transplant, that is one which post-operationally sustains a subject who psychologically resembles the subject there would have been if there had been no operation. When people envisage transplant cases which do not fulfil that requirement—where the resulting subject is severely impaired in comparison to the subject there would have been—then there is far less unanimity over the intuition that it would amount to the genuine survival of the person who donated the brain. The success assumption means, however, that these cases are irrelevant.[10]

That it is plausible to think that an attack of this sort on the fourth claim does not work, does not imply, of course, that the fourth claim is immune to other sorts of criticism, and I shall later consider a different criticism of it.

The 'Possibility' of Brain Transplants

This leaves the first assumption of BTA as a possible target. That is the thesis that it is possible (in principle) to transplant a whole brain into a new environment, preserving its intrinsic functions (which amount to its sustaining a consciousness of a sort such as it would have sustained if it had not been transplanted). To discuss whether this can be denied or queried we need to know what sort of possibility is in question. I want,

[10] The success assumption also provides a counter to another criticism of this stage in the transplant argument (which I owe to L. J. Cohen.) It might be said that acceptance of the intuition that the resulting subject is the same person as the person who donated the brain rests on the quite general principle that a person is tied to his living brain. This general principle, it might be alleged, is not plausible, since in some circumstances, it gives counter-intuitive results. An example would be that of a child born with severe brain disease, who is given a new brain straight after birth; it is claimed, we would treat that as the child receiving a new brain, and not as the creation of a different person. A proponent of the transplant argument would reply that there is no essential commitment to the general principle in endorsing the intuition about the *successful* case. This sort of example, and also less-than-successful cases, are, however, certainly relevant when considering the *general* account of identity which someone who accepts the brain transplant argument would go on to develop.

without extensive discussion, to assume that we are prepared to talk of metaphysical or conceptual possibility (which terms I take to be modifications of 'possibility' intended to express the same sort of possibility), and that we are sympathetic to the idea that the notions of identity, kind, and metaphysical possibility are tightly linked. That is therefore the sort of possibility we are considering.[11] So to attack the argument at this stage is to suggest in all seriousness that the envisaged brain transplant is *not* a metaphysical possibility.[12] Is there any chance of opposing BTA in this way?

I do not myself see how to make a convincing case for supposing that there is. I want to lay out what I feel able to say about this in a series of remarks, some clarifying the issues, others attempting to restrict options.

(1) It is *not* enough for an opponent of BTA to say this; we allow nowadays that metaphysical possibilities are determinable empirically, and this is obviously a case where our views on what is metaphysically possible must be empirically led. So, there must be *some* chance that it should turn out to be metaphysically impossible. Hence, the first premise is not definitely affirmable, and the argument has to be withdrawn. The reason that this is not enough is that it rests on an absurdly strict principle of argumentation. If, considering the evidence we currently have, plus our general understanding of possibility, it seems highly likely that a transplant is a metaphysical possibility, then that is enough to grant it.

(2) Someone might make the comment that it might be metaphysically impossible for us to have brain transplants but that it seems clearly possible for there to be persons of a different sort to us for whom it is metaphysically possible. However sensible this remark is, it is irrelevant here. Animalism is a thesis about *us*, and so an objection to it on grounds of metaphysical possibility must appeal to possibilities for *us*.

[11] I do not mean to imply that the notion of metaphysical possibility is free of all doubts and difficulties. I think of myself as merely endorsing the conventional approach.

[12] I was lead to think that this reply was worth investigating partly because it amounts to saying about whole brain transplants what, it seemed to me, David Wiggins had suggested, in *Sameness and Substance*, should be said about fision and fusion (see *Sameness and Substance*, 169–70 and 221). Thus he seemed to be maintaining that fision and fusion were not genuine metaphysical possibilities. Indeed, I thought that it was a motive for the account of personhood that is offered that it looked likely to have that consequence. However, he has informed me that this is not a completely accurate understanding of his suggestion, and so it would be wrong to regard the present section as a discussion of an application of an idea of his.

(3) The time is long past when a proponent of the metaphysical possibility of brain transplants can defend their possibility by simply pointing out that it is perfectly easy to *imagine* or *conceive* of it happening. The link between imaginability and genuine metaphysical possibility has been thoroughly debated recently, with the result, as I see it, that imaginability cannot be taken as a *guide* to possibility. Either it is insisted that the objects of imagination must be possibilia, in which case the claim to have imagined precisely what is at issue will simply be disputed, and so, whether it is possible (and hence imaginable) must be determined in some other way, *or* it is allowed that we can imagine non-possibilia, and then no-one need quarrel with the theorist's claim to have imagined brain-transplants, but his achievement has no probative significance. The worry is sometimes expressed that if imaginability is not a guide to possibility, then we have *no* guide to possibility. But, I take it that what replaces the picture in which imaginability is our route into possibility, is that our possibility judgments are not as a whole founded on anything else, but that we find ourselves with various possibility judgments, which are adjudicated within the system of such judgments. So, we might say that the role of the imagination is to supply imaginabilia on which the intellect, (or the understanding), must judge whether they are possibilia.

(4) Now, the area we need to investigate seems to me to be what might be called the metaphysics of *causation* and *capacity*. The transplant can go ahead so long as the receiving system can supply all those substances, and conditions, and connections which are causally necessary for it to function, and there is in principle a transplant process which does not mess up the organ itself. So, it seems to me that a case for supposing that the successful transplant is metaphysically impossible, has to rest either on the claim that the process must damage the brain or on the claim that, though undamaged, it is impossible for there to be a new receptacle which can supply the right types of things. Now, I am prepared to allow that the fundamental causal truths about our brains are, given the kinds of things they are made of, essential to them, so any general actual causal truth can be regarded as metaphysically necessary. However, these causal truths, I assume, relate types of result to types of conditions, and it would be quite implausible to contemplate defending the impossibility thesis by suggesting that the processes in a particular brain are causally tied by law to the particular environment they do in fact occur in.

There is, as far as I know, no scientifically respectable ground for the first ground for the impossibility claim. How might the second ground be argued? It seems to me that the case will consist of two claims.[13]

---

[13] I have been helped in formulating this by some remarks of David Wiggins.

(a) It will first be emphasized that what is needed is a *successful* transplant. By this is meant that in the new environment the brain must function, not simply so as to sustain *some sort* of consciousness, but so as to sustain consciousness and capacities as they would have been if the transplant had not been carried out. Now, it will be claimed that it is at least very plausible to say that this is possible, in the nature of the case, only if there are suitable inputs, outputs, and relations between them. Otherwise, it will be claimed, the system goes 'haywire'.

(b) It will next be claimed that those connections cannot be re-established for a relatively mature brain outside the environment in which it has, in such a complex way, matured. The right connections cannot be regenerated.

It seems to me that in this sort of argument the problematic move is the second one. The emphasis is primarily on complexity of connection, but, how from that does the metaphysical impossibility of suitable connection flow?

One thing that encourages a sense of impossibility is the idea of a *planned* operation to ensure the connection. The complexity will defeat us since we will not be able to find out about it. However, arguing this way is to mistake an accidental for an essential feature of what is envisaged. For it to be a metaphysical possibility that the transplant succeeds, it is in no way required that it be any more than *good luck* that it works.

This does not add up to a proof or demonstration of metaphysical possibility. It amounts, rather, to saying that, given that we have a relatively discrete organ and given the fundamental fact that causal processes relate to types, it is hard to see how it can be metaphysically impossible for the entity to function outside its present receptacle.

Criticism of Method

If the animalist's opposition to the transplant objection takes the form of trying to overturn the assumptions in it by generating alternative intuitions, then, I think it is unlikely to be persuasive.

It is, however, a mistake to suppose that we are restricted to these replies. Both Johnston and Wilkes seem to be suggesting that if we reflect on the method employed in the transplant argument (or some aspect of it) we can locate considerations which make the argument inadmissible. As a general suggestion this is extremely valuable, since it directs us to a new range of considerations.

What needs to be asked is whether they have located an aspect of the method underlying the present argument which can be regarded as dubious.

P. F. Snowdon

Wilkes's Criticism

I shall consider first what Kathy Wilkes says in her recent book. She states her thesis, which is defended in the first chapter, as the claim that thought experiments are 'for this topic in particular, highly misleading as a philosophical tool', but she says also that they are 'problematic in general', and she means by that in general in philosophy.[14] It seems clear that if there is some real doubt in principle about employing thought experiments, then the transplant argument will be covered by the doubt, since it is obviously a thought experiment.

The most I can do here is to consider in a very general way the case she constructs. I have to leave out of consideration most of what she says, including a lot of illuminating discussion of particular cases.

My reason for considering Wilkes's argument is, as I have just said, that she reports herself as objecting to thought experiments, and I would say that, without a doubt, BTA is a thought experiment. Unfortunately, Wilkes has, what strikes me as, an eccentric interpretation of 'thought experiment'. Thus, she says, 'such forays of the imagination are called *thought* experiments precisely because they are imaginary, they cannot be realized in the real world'.[15] Now, the first claim in that quotation is in accord with how I understand 'thought experiment', but the second is *not*. A thought experiment is carried out in thought, real objects are not acted on. However, the envisaged situation need not represent an impossibility for its envisaging to be part of a thought experiment. Thus, consider thought experiments in the debates about knowledge. These include cases where a man A is observed doing something but A has an identical twin in the vicinity, unknown to the observer; cases where there are large numbers of imitation barns in an area, but no imitation red barns—and so on. In the normal way of speaking when one is considering these cases one is engaging in thought experiments. However, it would be wrong to say that they are situations which cannot be realized in the real world. So, in so far as Wilkes wishes to build real impossibility into thought experiments, she cannot be taken to be discussing arguments of the above kind. What, one wonders, would she call consideration of the kinds of cases I have mentioned? They are not real experiments, nor are they, according to her, thought experiments. All this means that she in fact has no quarrel with the method normally known as thought experiments, and the sub-title of her book is misleading.[16]

[14] Wilkes, op. cit. (n. 5), 1.

[15] Wilkes, ibid. 2.

[16] She should have subtitled it—personal identity without the consideration of impossible cases.

A further disappointment for me is that she considers that brain transplants are *not* theoretically impossible, which is the kind of impossibility she is concerned with.[17]

It follows that Wilkes herself, contrary to what might be inferred from her sub-title, has no obvious objection to the argument I am trying to answer. However, her arguments are, I think, worth considering for their own sake. Moreover, someone might disagree with her opinion that brain transplants are 'theoretically possible', in which case, her objection in principle to considering and drawing conclusions from such cases might come into play. Further, we need to remember the success assumption; it would be possible to hold that brain transplants are theoretically possible but that they could not be *successful* in our sense.

Her view on thought experiments (in her sense) is that as a type of procedure they are not objectionable. There are, she thinks, valuable thought experiments in science. She chooses an example of Einstein's, in which, starting from the idea that he is travelling as fast as the speed of light, he envisaged what he would see, given Maxwell's electrodynamics, which turned out to be something Maxwell's theory ruled out. As a consequence, Maxwell's theory was reduced close to absurdity.

Now, it immediately follows from this that, according to Wilkes, thought experiments, per se, are not suspect. She must suppose that something goes wrong in philosophy when envisaged, but impossible, cases are used in arguments. But why should that be thought?

It seems to me that Wilkes has, fundamentally two ideas here. The first is that in scientific thought experiments when consequences are drawn from the initial merely thought of supposition, it is clear what 'background assumptions' are being relied on. Thus, in the Einstein case it is Maxwell's general theory. However, her view has to be that in philosophy (and in particular in the discussion of personal identity) it is not clear what the background assumptions are. Given that this is not clear, nothing can be concluded from the consideration of such cases.

If this is a fair statement of the argument, two questions arise. Is it true that it is unclear what the background assumptions are? If they are unclear, does that invalidate the thought experiment? Before we can answer these questions, however, we need to know what is meant by 'background assumptions'. Both the thought experiments which win Wilkes's approval are *reductios*, and so the notion of a background assumption has application to them, for it would seem to mean the assumptions which enable the objectionable consequence to be derived. In Einstein's thought experiment these assumptions are (or

[17] Wilkes, op. cit. (n. 5), 37.

include) Maxwell's theory. The derivation of a consequence incompatible with the theory itself, then counts decisively against that theory. But on this understanding of 'background assumption' there is no necessary unclarity about what the background assumptions are in some philosophical thought experiments concerned with personal identity. Often, in such thought experiments, a certain assumption A is introduced, and it is argued that, according to a certain philosophical theory T, it will follow that C is true (where C is a judgment relating to A), and it will then be claimed that C is (reasonably taken to be) false. For this thought experiment T amounts to the background assumption. It will often be a theory about personal identity, and it will be perfectly clear what it is. So, on this interpretation, it need not be unclear what the background assumption in a philosophical thought experiment is.

However, there are two other ways of understanding the notion. The first is that A itself qualifies as the background assumption. There is, though, no plausibility to the claim that it is always unclear what the relevant A is.[18] Finally, we might understand by 'background assumptions' the assumptions that are made as to how exactly A should come about. It would be fair to say that often this is not made clear. The best that would be done would be to say; let us assume that, *somehow or other*, A. If A is realistically impossible then a somehow-or-other assumption seems to be the best that can be made. But why exactly is that a problem? It is, after all, the sort of assumption which Einstein's thought experiment made, since, presumably, it began; suppose, somehow or other, Einstein was travelling on a light beam. In fact, we have arrived at an understanding of the objection according to which, it seems, it must apply to all thought experiments in Wilkes's sense, and so cannot be a distinctive feature of philosophical ones which accounts for their inadequacy.

The second point which Wilkes emphasizes is that where cases are not real-life, our intuitions about them become 'increasingly dubious, uncertain and contestable'.[19] This is a familiar sort of remark, and about it we can, I think, say the following. It is not true that there is any reason to suspect a judgment about an envisaged case just because it is very unlike a real situation. For example, there will never be a train consisting of ten-thousand carriages. However, it seems quite clear what it would be—a very long train. This example was meant to illustrate the point, but a few more general remarks are appropriate.

[18] Since A is a general assumption, further details can always be requested, but that does not amount to a *significant* unclarity as to what has been assumed, because it may well be that further details are simply irrelevant.

[19] Wilkes, op. cit. (n. 5), 47.

The normal view about language is that we have conferred upon its terms an interpretation in such a way that determines them as true of or false of certain merely possible (but non-actual) situations. Thus it may be that there will never be a crowd of 654 people; but we all agree that 'crowd' would apply to such a group. So the fact that a situation will not actually occur cannot be a reason to suppose that our language is not so interpreted as to contain something which would be true of it. On this conception, judgments about non-actual cases need not be 'dubious, uncertain , or contestable'. In fact, the category of contestable cases cuts across the actual/non-actual division. We do not know what is true to say about actual cerebral commissurotomy cases, but we do know what would be true to say of lots of non-actual cases. What needs showing is, I think, that there is some special reason why the intuitions in philosophical thought experiments are contestable. Mere non-actuality, or even, enormous improbability, is no reason.

I conclude, then, that neither reason creates special problems for philosophical thought experiments, not even in Wilkes's sense.

Now, this is merely an assessment of what, in general terms, Wilkes's arguments, as I have interpreted them, have established; it does not amount to a denial of her main thesis, nor does it amount to a positive view about the question she is considering. I want, therefore, to conclude my discussion of Wilkes with a few, rather more positive, remarks.

(i) If we are to impose restrictions on the kinds of imaginary cases which should be considered, they must flow from an understanding of the type of question (or issue) that we are attempting to answer (or settle), or of the more specific dialectical purpose that consideration of the envisaged case is meant to serve. In fact, it is clear that there is no single purpose which consideration of imaginary cases is supposed to serve, and so there is no reason to expect that we should be able to formulate a simple cogent rule, covering all purposes, as to what cases can be legitimately considered. (ii) In so far as an envisaged case (plus the judgments on it) are intended to provide data which a theory of our identity conditions must at least be consistent with, then we can, I think, say that envisaged cases must be metaphysically possible in order to be relevant. The reason for accepting this is that a theory of our identity is, on my understanding, claiming to tell us what features are essential to, and constitutive of, our remaining in existence. The notions of 'essential' and 'constitutive' need explaining, and the obvious explanation is that a feature F is essential to, and partially constitutive of, our remaining in existence, if and only if, it is metaphysically impossible for one of our kind to survive without F being present. A theory of identity, understood thus, makes a claim about all metaphysically possible cases of persistence.[20] It follows that verdicts on imaginabilia, which do not represent metaphysical possibilities, are irrelevant, but that verdicts on metaphysically possible cases are relevant. It remains to be decided where this leaves Wilkes's suggestion that it is wrong to consider 'theoretically impossible' cases. Whether her suggestion is correct turns on the relation, which is not at all easy to determine, between the notions of metaphysical possibility and 'theoretical possibility'. I do not wish to decide this here. (iii) As I have said, the envisaging of merely thought of cases serves other roles in our debate than that of providing data relevant to theories of identity. For example, there is a debate about what should matter to us in the continuities involved in our lives. There is no obvious reason for thinking that only genuinely metaphysically possible cases are worth considering here. Thus, a very famous case, consideration of which is supposed to enable us to learn about what is of value, is Nozick's Experience Machine. Our intuitions about that case are held to be important. It does not occur to people to object to consideration of it on grounds that it is simply not possible. Now, if that is irrelevant to such an example used for such a purpose, it would seem that it would also be irrelevant to cases dealing with personal identity used for the same purpose. A further, and it seems to me quite legitimate, role for imaginary cases is to query principles which might be endorsed in arguments. Thus suppose someone relies on the principle that if there is a continuous 'stream of consciousness' linking P1 and P2 then they must be the same person or self. It is quite legitimate to undermine reliance on this by citing cases of 'brain-splitting', whether these are possible or not. Finally, as Parfit has pointed out, it is possible to cite imaginary cases about which intuitions are elicited, with the purpose of revealing that we have certain opinions. There is no reason to limit cases used in this way to the metaphysically possible.

Johnston's Criticism

Johnston is opposed to animalism, to which he objects on the basis of an argument which has significant resemblances to BTA, but he is also critical of the method of argument which has been standard in recent discussions of personal identity. He calls this method 'the method of cases'. It is the method used when 'competing accounts of the necessary

---

[20] In making this proposal I am relying on the standard interpretation of what a theory of personal identity is. The strongest case which could be made for a recommendation like Wilkes's would be to argue for a novel interpretation of the problem, relative to which impossible cases are irrelevant.

and sufficient conditions for personal identity are . . . evaluated simply in accordance with how well they jibe with intuitions wrung from cases'.[21] It seems undeniable that BTA is an argument exemplifying that method and so if it could be established that the method is dubious that would render it illegitimate to rely on that argument. Johnston clearly agrees with this application of his criticism since he comments on his own exposition of an argument which is virtually the same as BTA that 'this is just another example of uncritical reliance on the method of cases', and takes that as a reason for not relying on it.

In outline, as I understand it, his major argument is that if we rely on the method of cases we cannot avoid accepting a certain theory about personal identity, but there is also a very strong reason for not accepting that theory. This is taken to establish that the method is unreliable.

In more detail Johnston's argument against the standard method runs as follows. The method relies on intuitions about personal identity generated by partially described cases. However, given the famous case devised by Bernard Williams of the mental-characteristic swapping machine, we can vary the cases described so that they elicit rather different intuitions of what are, in certain important respects, very similar cases.[22] Roughly, the idea is that if we tell the story with two people starting the experiment, stepping in simultaneously, and a psychological switch occurring between them, then our intuitive judgment is that the people (or selves) switch. If, however, we describe what is the same sequence happening to one subject alone, our intuition is that he remains despite the psychological changes and is not replaced in what was his body. Johnston continues his argument by claiming that these verdicts, if accepted, support a view of ourselves which he calls the 'bare-locus view'. This says that we are 'bare loci of mental life, that is, possessors of mental life whose survival requires no amount of bodily or mental continuity'.[23] Johnston's next move is to introduce a second constraint on theories of personal identity, which is that an account of our identity must validate the ways we employ for identifying people over time; we must be just the kinds of things that our basic practices would succeed in tracing.[24] The final stage in Johnston's

---

[21] Johnston, op. cit. (n. 6), 59.

[22] The case is one where we have a machine into which two people can enter. It scans their mental characteristics and, somehow, switches these characteristics between the people. It can work on one person, wiping clean his brain and inducing a new set of characteristics not based on a set already possessed by an individual.

[23] Johnston, op. cit. (n. 6), 70. The reason is that the first verdict shows that bodily continuity is not necessary, and the second that psychological continuity is not.

[24] Ibid. 63.

argument is to say that the bare locus view does not satisfy this requirement and so it cannot be correct. Johnston's basis for this claim is our
habit of completely confidently thinking that by continuously observing a sleeping person we know where the subject is. However, if the
subject is a bare locus and so at best causally connected to the body, it
must be a real possibility that the subject slips out of his body link
during sleep. So our practice of keeping track of people during sleep is
not validated by that theory.

My view is that this extended argument is very ingenious, but that it
contains too many steps which are dubious for any reliance to be placed
on it. I shall mention some of them.

(1) Suppose Johnston is right to the very end. It seems that that
establishes that there is a competition between two philosophical methods, and unless he arbitrarily espouses one method rather than the
other, he cannot reject the method of cases on that basis. There seems
no evident reason offered by Johnston against drawing the conclusion
that the method he favours (which I shall call the E-method) is in fact
unreliable since it leads to a rejection of a theory which is well supported
(i.e. by the method of cases). (2) It is also debatable that the E-method
is incompatible with the bare locus view as Johnston seems to understand it. His example of sleep can be given the obvious answer that
there is very good evidence that people do not quit their normal body
links during sleep, namely, that, however random the timing of
reawakening they are always there when reawakened. Now, Johnston's
response might be to deny the claim that this is good evidence that
keeping people in view when they are asleep is a satisfactory method of
keeping track of them on the assumption that the bare locus view is
true, or he might claim that, even if it is good evidence, it does not
demonstrate that the bare locus view meets the requirements of the
E-method. When he discusses this issue Johnston in effect indicates
that he is prepared to say the second thing. Thus he points out that it
would 'boggle' ordinary thinkers to so much as raise the worry about
location of selves during sleep.[25] But, in that case, Johnston's E-method
requires that a theory of personal identity cannot be correct if, assuming the theory is true, there are possibilities which would 'boggle'
ordinary people. This is a very strong requirement, and in no way
established by Johnston. (3) It is unclear, I think, what the bare locus
view is, and what its relation to the method of cases should be taken to
be. The earlier statement of the view is not, in fact, a theory, so much as
the rejection of two theories. A whole range of theories is consistent
with rejection of those accounts. That range includes Nozick's closest
continuer theory, versions of the multiple criteria view (popular at one

[25] Ibid. 70.

time in Oxford), as well as something like Cartesian Dualism, which seems to be Johnston's interpretation of the bare locus theory. But, Johnston cannot claim to have demonstrated that these other views are not consistent with the method of cases, nor has he shown that, across the full range of cases which might be considered, the Cartesian view is supported by the method of cases. The proper attitude has surely to be that we cannot really say on the basis of what Johnston has provided that the bare locus view, understood in his way, is the theory supported by that method. We have, then, no right to suppose that a rejection of that view implies anything about the method of cases. (4) In fact, there is a reason to think that the bare locus view is not likely to be the view suggested by our responses to the envisaged example of Williams's machine. The reason is that, although the bare locus theory is consistent with the supposed intuitive reactions to the case, it provides no *explanation* at all for the different reactions to the different cases. Why should we be inclined to suppose that the bare locus will stay with the body in the second cases, but not in the first? So, on the basis of comments (3) and (4), I conclude that little reason has been given to link the method of cases and the bare locus theory. (5) Suppose we agree with Johnston that the intuitions he cites will lead to the bare locus view, and that that theory is unacceptable. What should someone who does *not* have those intuitive responses himself conclude about his use of the method of cases? Has he been given any reason to view its use by him as unreliable? It is hard to see that he has. (6) What is the method of cases, and the role of intuition in it? No-one needs to be told that there are mistaken intuitions; and it is hard to think that the method that has been used requires that there are *no* unreliable intuitions. So why should we regard every argument which relies on intuitions as having been undermined by a criticism of accepting every intuition?

It would not be justified, given these queries, to regard Johnston as having provided a reason for not accepting the BTA.

An Alternative Reply

I thus find myself holding that no direct replies to BTA are convincing, and that neither Wilkes nor Johnston have undermined the method which it employs.

There is, however, I think, a reply available. The animalist should consider simply standing the transplant argument on its head. He thinks that he is rationally entitled to deny the conclusion; his attitude should, therefore, be—what premise *can* I reject? It then seems to me that the best target is the one identified by Johnston, namely, the fourth claim, because that straightforwardly rests on intuition. The best he can do is to say: there is no counterintuition that can be generated, and there are no grounds of a general sort for being suspicious of such intuitions, no independent evidence that they do lead us astray. But this is just a case where we find ourselves with what, in the light of all the evidence, has to be recognized as a deviant, although recalcitrant, intuition. This is a case where what is genuinely possible for *us* is to be decided on the basis of what the best theory of us is—and we must swallow the consequences of that.[26]

Now, this is a suggestion as to how BTA can be met. It needs to be asked whether it can be strengthened, and how it might be criticized. It seems to me that two things would strengthen this reply. First, it would be strengthened if we could provide an explanation as to why we have intuitions which, according to the endorsed theory, are incorrect. I can see lines to explore here, but I do not have an explanation which I wish to offer. Second, it is part of the viewpoint which is emerging to say that although we can think about ourselves, we lack any relatively *a priori* conception of what our persistence actually consists in. So we can ask: is this a plausible view of our thought about ourselves? It seems to me that the present line of reply to BTA indicates that we have to look at this question next.

It is likely that the reply will be criticized by pointing out just how strong the intuition that is being rejected is. But in the context of the reply that is being given it does not seem that comment achieves anything, and something more needs to be said in defence of the intuition.

Conclusion

I conclude that it is not clear that BTA refutes animalism; but it cannot be said that there is available as yet a full and convincing reason to think it does not.[27]

[26] To deny the fourth premise in BTA is not to solve all the problems that brain transplants generate. In particular, I have not said what happens to the animal which donates the brain. The particular question is what our verdict should be if a new brain is transplanted into the skull vacated by the old one.

[27] Earlier versions of this paper were presented in Oxford, Liverpool, and Lampeter, and the discussion on each occasion was very helpful. I am especially grateful to John Campbell, O. R. Jones, Michael Martin, Derek Parfit, and David Wiggins for their responses. I am also grateful to Brian Garrett and Galen Strawson for comments, and to David Cockburn for advice and patience.

Personal Identity and the Idea of a Human Being

GEOFFREY MADELL

The central fact about the problem of personal identity is that it is a problem posed by an apparent dichotomy: the dichotomy between the objective, third-person viewpoint on the one hand and the subjective perspective provided by the first-person viewpoint on the other. Everyone understands that the mind/body problem is precisely the problem of what to do about another apparent dichotomy, the duality comprising states of consciousness on the one hand and physical states of the body on the other. By contrast, contemporary discussions of the problem of personal identity generally display little or no recognition of the divide which to my mind is at the heart of the problem. As a consequence, there has been a relentlessly third-personal approach to the issue, and the consequent proposal of solutions which stand no chance at all of working. I think the idea that the problem is to be clarified by an appeal to the idea of a human being is the latest manifestation of this mistaken approach. I am thinking in particular of the claim that what ought to govern our thinking on this issue is the fact that human beings constitute a natural kind, and that standard members of this kind can be said to have some sort of essence. Related to this is the idea that 'person', while not itself a natural kind term, is not a notion which can be framed in entire independence of this natural kind.

I think this approach is wholly misconceived. I shall open by discussing in an unavoidably condensed form the dichotomy between the first and third-person viewpoints which this approach ignores, and look at one or two attempts to undermine the considerations which reveal this divide. I shall then look at two recent discussions which pay allegiance to the idea of a human being, and argue that their failure to provide any understanding of personal identity stems from just this allegiance. I shall end with some reflections on the dichotomies which are the subject of the mind/body problem and of the problem of personal identity respectively, and counsel against any suggestion that we can regard them as merely apparent.

I

Persons on the third-person view are a special sort of object in the intersubjective available world. As with any object, it is claimed, the origin of the person–object is of its essence. But the person–object is a *psycho-physical* entity, having a psychological life which reveals some marked degree of continuity and connectedness; and this, too, is of its essence.

What ought to be central to discussion of personal identity is the fact that this 'person-as-object' view is impossible to grasp from the first-person perspective. I cannot, to being with, *imagine* what it could be to be such an object. The necessity-of-origin thesis is incomprehensible from this perspective. It is not just that everyone can easily imagine having been born earlier or later; it is also that the thesis implies that had the series of experiences leading up to my present state of consciousness had a different origin then this present state of consciousness would not have been *mine*; and that's as incomprehensible as anything could be. And the claim that, while this line of experiences stretching back into the past might have been different in all sorts of ways, it just could not have started earlier or later than it did is one which is utterly opaque. There *is* solid argument for the necessity-of-origin thesis as it pertains to *objects*. We do not know what it could mean to say that there is a possible world in which this very same oak tree grew from a different acorn; we have no idea what could pick it out as the very same oak tree. But there is no such argument available in the case of persons. The reason why there is no such argument is that the self-ascription of experience, the conception of an experience as mine, is in no way governed by the thought that it was preceded by a series of experiences which necessarily had the origin that it did, and so we have no difficulty in conceiving of the possible world in which the flow of experience leading up to my present state of consciousness began earlier or later.

Consideration of the first-person perspective also shows the story about psychological connectedness to be untenable. The basic point is absolutely simple: the status of any experience as mine or not mine is one thing, its particular character or content is quite another. If we accept, what is in any case obvious, that any of one's experiences might have been different in character, we have implicitly accepted the distinction between the ownership of experiences on the one hand and their character and content on the other. And what goes for any individual experience also goes for series of experiences. If the momentary state of consciousness's being mine is independent of its content and character, then the continuing consciousness's being mine is also independent of content and character. And so the flow of my experiences could be radically fragmented and disconnected.

It is difficult to understand the continuing adherence to varieties of the psychological continuity view in the light of this fundamental objection.[1] The central confusion in the position of the psychological continuity theorist seems to me to be as follows. The ownership of an experience is something which for him can be explicated only in terms of the connection between that experience and others; he can have nothing to say, therefore, on what it is for a single experience to be mine *intrinsically*—what it is, for example, for some particular sensation or thought to differ from every other qualitatively similar sensation or thought occurring at the same time just in being an element in my consciousness. Not being able to accommodate this fact, he has no way of recognizing that the imagined very different experience, its links with its neighbours broken, is still my experience. In addition, since the ownership of experience is to be explicated in terms of the experience's being located in a suitably linked series, the psychological continuity view has nothing to say on what it is for one of two indistinguishable series of experiences—one on Earth and one on Twin Earth, say—to be mine. The clear implication of all this is that the disregard of the first-person view can only give us something incoherent. The fundamental notion governing the view I am attacking seems to be a conception of experiences as essentially *impersonal* elements (Parfit, for example, is quite explicit about this), a conception which disregards the dimension 'mine/not mine'. No coherent conception of persons can be erected on such a foundation.

I have argued that the conception of persons as a particular sort of object in the world, psycho-physical entities which are tokens of the natural kind 'human being', is undermined by two different exercises of the imagination. The first threatens the claim that my origin is of my essence, as the origin of any physical object is of its essence. The second undermines a claim about the psychological aspect of this psycho-physical entity: that the flow of its experiences is characterized by some marked degree of connectedness, and that this, too, belongs to its essence. I have concluded that the view of persons in question is one which it is impossible to grasp from the standpoint of the imagination. We cannot regard persons as just a rather interesting sort of object in the world. We do not have a notion of persons at all until we recognize that crucial respect in which persons differ from objects—in their subjectivity, their first-person perspective. We cannot recognize this and continue to suppose that this will have no implications for our view of the identity of persons.

---

[1] Yet Harold Noonan, defending a psychological continuity view in his recent *Personal Identity* (London: Routledge, 1989), doesn't even mention it; nor is there any discussion of the opposition between first and third-person viewpoints.

II

The claim that consideration of the first-person perspective undermines the view of persons as tokens of a natural kind is powerfully reinforced by what looks to be a quite different consideration, though it is, I shall argue, closely connected to the point I have developed in the preceding section. Briefly, the conception of persons as tokens of a natural kind leaves us without any understanding of what it could be for one such object to be *me*. No matter how complete one's description of the objective order may be, what it is for some element of that order to be me is something which eludes such a description. We have no insight into how indexical thought, or indexical properties, can latch on to a world conceived of purely objectively. This is a claim which Nagel has discussed in various writings, and it is one whose truth becomes ever more clear with every successive attempt to show how the fact of indexical thought and a purely objective conception of the world are compatible, as I shall show.

I suppose the point emerges at its sharpest when confronted with that most brutally 'objective' view of reality, materialism. If one takes this to be the view that reality consists of assemblies of elementary particles, such that, as Rorty has said, if we keep track of all the particles there are we shall be keeping track of all there is, the difficulty is obvious: no one has anything coherent to say on what it could mean for some segment of a world so conceived to be *me*. Reality thus conceived presents a glacial surface which makes it impossible for indexical thought to get any sort of foothold. 'Being me' is not a property known to physical science; nor is it a property which, mysteriously, 'supervenes on' the physical. While the point is most obvious in relation to the ontology of materialism, it applies with equal force if, with John Perry, we believe 'only in the common actual world'.[2] If we have nothing but the objective, intersubjectively available order the question must always confront us: what is it for some element of that objective order to be *me*? The identification of some point in this world as me would be something utterly inexplicable and magical.

Gareth Evans ends his discussion of self-identification in *The Varieties of Reference*[3] with a number of points, the first of which runs: 'Our self-conscious thoughts about ourselves are irreducible to any other mode of thought; in particular, they cannot be regarded as involving the identification of an object by any description. . . . There is always a gap between grasping that the $\emptyset$ is F and grasping that I am F' But he goes on to claim that '[d]espite recent claims to the contrary, our

[2] J. Perry, 'The Problem of the Essential Indexical', *Nous 13* (1979), 16.
[3] G. Evans, *The Varieties of Reference* (Oxford: Clarendon Press, 1982), 255–6.

thoughts about ourselves are about *objects*—elements of reality. We are, and can make sense of ourselves as, elements of the objective order of things' (255–256). But if we are *merely* 'elements of the objective order of things', then, as McDowell notes in his comments, '[o]ne must conceive the states of affairs one represents in one's "egocentric" thoughts . . . as states of affairs which could be described impersonally, from no particular standpoint' (264). But if this is true, then there cannot be the gap between 'the Ø is *F*' and 'I am *F*' that Evans rightly discerns, and we can have no understanding of what it could be for some arbitrary element of the objective order to be *me*. We cannot hold on to the truth that there is a gap between 'the Ø is *F*' and 'I am *F*' and continue to claim that we are *merely* 'elements of the objective order of things'. It seems to me a central delusion to suppose that there is any acceptable response to this situation other than that of introducing into our ontology specifically first-person facts, perspectives or properties: the property 'being me', or 'being mine'. Once we recognize this, I shall argue, we must bid farewell to the idea that our understanding of persons is governed by a conception of human beings as merely a certain sort of object in the world, a natural kind. In the following section, I shall develop and defend this claim

III

Many philosophers have seen no particular problem about how indexical thought latches onto a purely objective world. I consider here just two very recent examples of this position.[4] I shall then discuss what their failure shows.

W. G. Lycan, in his recent book *Consciousness*,[5] offers the suggestion that the subjectivity and the perspectival character of our experience which Nagel has focused on in various writings amount to no more than the fact that our perception of reality must be partial. People viewing a physical object from different points of view take in different and necessarily incomplete bits of information about the object. This is *part* of the way in which our experience is subjective, a way which can clearly be accommodated within an overall objective conception of reality.

---

[4] What follows is an attempt to bring up to date the discussions in my *The Identity of the Self* (Edinburgh: Edinburgh University Press, 1981), ch. 2 and my *Mind and Materialism* (Edinburgh: Edinburgh University Press, 1988), ch. 5.

[5] G. Lycan, *Consciousness* (Cambridge, Mass.: Bradford Books, 1987), ch. 7.

Geoffrey Madell

I think it is clear, however, that this suggestion offers no insight into how indexical thought latches onto a purely objective world. Simply to point to the fact that different positions in the world will yield different perspectives on it leaves us with no understanding of what it could be for one of these positions to be *uniquely mine*. Introducing perspectives into our account of the objective world is one thing, and an easy thing; introducing the *first-person perspective* into such a world looks impossible.

Lycan makes another claim which needs consideration. It is that self-regarding propositional attitudes, though they differ functionally from other attitudes directed upon the same state of affairs, have the same truth condition, namely, that state of affairs itself.

> There is thus no extra fact, and particularly not an "intrinsically perspectival" fact, that is known, believed, or whatever . . . I know that *I myself* weight 180 pounds, while you know only that WGL—as you represent him—weighs 180 pounds; but it is the same fact that we both know. Two schemes of interpretation are in play, a functional or computational scheme that distinguishes my knowledge of my own weight from your knowledge of my weight (those bits of knowledge having quite different causal roles in the two of us), and a referential or truth-conditional scheme that does not distinguish them at all. (80)

I think it is fairly easy to see that this, too, misses the point. We can certainly grant that, for each person, the knowledge he has of his own state has a different causal role from the knowledge anyone else has of that person's properties. But it is a mistake to suppose that this allows us to see how the first person can attach to a world conceived of purely objectively. The picture Lycan presents us with is that of a range of particulars (persons), and it is plausibly claimed that the knowledge each particular has of its own states is functionally distinguishable from the knowledge any other particular has of those states. But that simply leaves us with a variant of our basic question, a variant which reads: what is it for one such particular, equipped with this functionally distinctive knowledge, to be *me*? The fundamental mistake underlying both of Lycan's arguments is to suppose that if we describe the objective world in enough detail, or focus on the right aspect of such a world, what it is for some element of this world to be *me* is something which will leap right off the page.

I suggested above that we cannot understand how indexical thought can latch on to the world until we allow that the inter-subjectively available world is not all there is, that there are intrinsically first-person facts or properties. Hugh Mellor's aim in his recent paper 'I and Now'[6]

[6] H. Mellor, 'I and Now', *Proceedings of the Aristotelian Society, 89* (1988–89), 70–94.

is to show, not only that such properties and facts are necessary to make indexical thought intelligible, but that the notion of a first-person fact or self is an incoherent one. There can, he claims, no more be subjective facts or selves than there can be such a time as *now*: 'If there were [such a time], then since all tokens of the form "the time is now Y" are true if and only if they occur at Y, every time would have to be both *now* (to make the true tokens true) and not *now* (to make the false ones false), which it can't be' (80). The same point, the argument runs, undermines the claim that reality might contain a person (*I*) or a property (*being me*). For, 'since all sentence tokens of the form "I am X" are true if and only if produced by X, every person X would have to be both *I* and not *I*, which no one can be. Reality can no more contain a person (*I*) or a property (*being me*) . . . than it can contain a time *now* or a property of *being now*' (82).

The argument is much too swift. The fact that 'I am Ronald Reagan' is true when spoken by Ronald Reagan and false when spoken by anyone else does not commit the believer in subjective properties to the view that Ronald Reagan, or anyone else, is both *I* and not *I*. I have indeed insisted that to make sense of indexical thought we have to introduce the subjective property 'being me'. But the property required is that of being *uniquely* me. It must be; for to assume that there is some extra property ('being me') which is *common to everyone* simply confronts us with the basic question again: what is it for one particular person, with this extra property which everyone has, to be *uniquely* me? But if everyone is the *unique* 'I' that he is, then he is that 'I' and not another one; no one is 'both "I" and not "I"'. Thus Husserl says, 'The word "I" names a different person from case to case, and does so by way of an ever altering meaning'; and: 'Each man has his own "I"—presentation (and with it his individual notion of I) and this is why the word's meaning differs from person to person'.[7] This is the claim to be considered. Whatever arguments there may be against it, it is clear that it does not involve the outrageous breach of the law of non-contradiction of which Mellor accuses the believer in subjective facts.

Mellor's belief that 'I' and 'now' can be treated together sustains his final section, called 'How "I" and "Now" Refer'. Here he says that 'my desire to express a belief habitually causes me to use "I" when the belief I want to express is first-person, and "now" when it is present tense' (92). Well and good, but *everyone's* desire to express a belief causes him to use 'I' when the belief he wants to express is first-person. Our, Nagelian, question now becomes: what is it for some particular person, having such a belief and a desire to express it, to be me? Focusing on some aspect of the objective world, in this case the connections between

---

[7] E. Husserl, *Logical Investigations* (London: Routledge, 1970), 315–6.

Geoffrey Madell

belief, desire and first-person utterance, does nothing to answer that question.

Why is it that the two sides on this issue seem to pass each other like ships in the night? Part of the answer should be clear from the discussion above; it is that it is not continually borne in mind that the question is, what is it for some objective item to be *uniquely* me? The suggestion one sometimes meets that the Fregean notion of modes of presentation can be used to dissolve the problem epitomizes this failure. It is argued that while everyone must be seen under an objective mode of presentation, answering to a description, everyone, as Frege points out, is also presented to himself in a special way in which he is presented to no one else—as 'I'. There is, then, no special problem about why it is that a complete objective description of the world will not capture the fact that one of the persons described is me, and certainly not one which requires the positing of additions to our ontology such as the property 'being me'. There is no particular puzzle about the fact that what is captured under the one mode of presentation is not captured under another. Basically, it is claimed, there is no more problem about the fact that one and the same entity is presented in these two different ways than there is in the fact that one and the same object is presented as both 'Hespherus' and 'Phosphorus'.

The flaw in this position is quite evident. Even if this picture of the one sort of entity (persons) presented in two different modes is assumed to be intelligible, the central question would remain: what is it for one of these Janus-like entities to be *uniquely me*? There can be no escape from this question, and no response which simply amounts to positing something which is common to everyone can meet it.

Another, and related, part of the explanation of why it is that many thinkers have failed to grasp the central point at issue is this. Some philosophers who suppose themselves to be addressing Nagel's concerns (as Lycan and Mellor explicitly do) in fact offer various answers to a question which is very different from Nagel's. Instead of giving us their conception of what it could be for some element of the objective order to be *me*, the question they address is: what are the distinctive features of belief or knowledge about oneself? What distinguishes self-knowledge from knowledge of others? So it is felt sufficient to answer that it is the fact that such knowledge satisfies a certain functional account (Lycan), or that such belief, given the relevant desire, issues in a first-person utterance (Mellor), or that such belief is tied to action—*I* do something about the sugar spilling on the floor, or *I* go to Cleveland to collecte the promised fortune (Perry, Shoemaker).[8] The fact is that

[8] Perry, 'Essential Indexical'; S. Shoemaker and R. Swinburne, *Personal Identity* (Oxford: Blackwell, 1984), 104.

134

such responses, far from providing any sort of answer to the Nagelian question, presuppose that we already have an answer to it. They trade on the obvious fact that I am of course aware of myself and of my position in the world, so that the only remaining question appears to be: what are the distinctive features of those beliefs which are beliefs about myself? What distinguishes the knowledge I undoubtedly have of myself from the knowledge one person has of another? But to claim, what is obvious, that I have an awareness of myself and of my position in the world is one thing; to claim that that of which I have this awareness is simply a segment of objective reality is something completely different. This latter question *does* raise the Nagelian question, what is it for something which is *merely* an item in the objective world to be me? That question is not confronted by the philosophers we have discussed.

A purely objective, third-person view of selves and of their identity through time is impossible. No one has succeeded in showing how the view of persons as merely a special sort of object allows an understanding of indexical thought, and a recognition of the gap between 'the $\emptyset$ is F' and 'I am F'. That is why, *pace* Mellor, reality must include the person I and the property *being me*.

We must, then, recognize that to opt for the conception of persons as a natural kind is to ignore completely one side of the subjective/objective divide. If 'I' does not pick out merely an element of the objective order of things, there is no question of 'I' denoting a token of a natural kind, or of our understanding of persons being governed by the idea of the natural kind 'human being'. The idea of a natural kind is the idea of a class of particulars with an essence. But in surrendering the idea that 'I' denotes merely some segment of the objective world we clearly also surrender the idea that 'I' has a discoverable essence. That is to say, there is no way of showing that the relation between 'I' and its objective setting is a necessary one.

IV

I have argued that the 'person-as-natural-kind' view is undermined from two different directions. I have claimed, first, that this view is one which cannot be grasped from the point of view of the imagination; I cannot make sense in terms of what I can imagine for myself of the idea that I am merely a sort of object, an object whose origin is of its essence. I have also claimed that this conception of ourselves makes the fact of indexical thought impossible to understand. It is fairly clear, I think, that these points are connected. I cannot imagine what it could be for the status of my present experience as mine somehow to depend on its being a member of a series of experiences whose particular origin is somehow essential to it. But it is equally impossible to grasp what it is for something which is merely a particular object in the world, an object whose identity depends on its having the particular origin that it did have, to be me. Again, a simple exercise of the imagination makes clear that the status of experiences as mine is something which is independent of their character or content. The idea that this continuing pain would be less fully mine if it were to cause a sudden personality change is one which it is impossible to grasp from the point of view of the imagination. What links my experiences together in the one consciousness is just their being mine. But it is precisely this irreducible first-person property which is required to make the fact of indexical thought intelligible.

What undermines the 'person-as-object' view, therefore, is a combination of two different lines of argument, lines of argument which reveal themselves as fundamentally connected and which support each other. What they show is that we cannot force our conception of persons into the Procrustean bed of objecthood. The dissonances between our conception of objects and what is revealed in the first-person perspective are far too great.

V

I have argued that the general run of discussions of personal identity are radically flawed, essentially because they take it that what is under scrutiny is simply a special sort of object in the inter-subjectively available world. This is a posture which involves the disregard, or very superficial treatment, of what should be at the centre of considerations of this issue—the first person perspective. The idea that the notion of a human being should govern our thoughts on persons and their identity inevitably brings these errors in its train.

I want now to look at two recent treatments of personal identity, both of which have given the idea of human beings as a natural kind a prominent position. The first is that of Mark Johnston, in his recent paper, 'Human Beings'.[9]

In *The Identity of the Self* I argued that the two thought-experiments considered by Williams in 'The Self and the Future' (*Philosophical Review 79*, 1970), far from supporting the bodily continuity criterion, as Williams tentatively suggests, in fact support the view which I have argued we cannot escape, the view that the relation between the self and

[9] M. Johnston, 'Human Beings', *Journal of Philosophy 84*, No. 2 (February 1987) 59–83.

its objective setting and properties is contingent. This argument is in effect re-invoked by Johnston, but it seems to him that the view of the self to which the two thought-experiments taken together point (he calls it the 'bare locus of consciousness' view) opens up such mind-boggling sceptical possibilities that we cannot take it seriously. For example, we cannot rule out the possibility that during sleep three or four or many more selves 'replace each other behind the stage of the continuous bodily life that we observe'. He goes on:

> Let no one suggest that those ignorant of the ways of bare loci can rule out these alternatives by means of an inference to the numer-ically *simplest explanation* of observed bodily continuity. None of these hypotheses *explain* continuity of bodily life devoid of mental accompaniments. They are all merely compatible with such con-tinuity. (73)

The way out of this, argues Johnston, is to 'lay down as a first constraint on any theory of personal identity that it enable us to construct our everyday practice of reidentifying people as an unproblematic source of knowledge about personal identity over time' (71). This, says Johnston, is a constraint which the bare-locus view flouts. We must therefore reject the imaginings that detach me from the human being I appear to be.

I find this way at arriving at the notion of a human being quite unacceptable, for two main reasons. The first is that the sceptical implications of the 'bare-locus' view do not seem to me to be troubling in the way that Johnston suggests. Indeed, he oddly mistakes the issue. The question is not about whether the believer in the 'bare locus' view is entitled to offer something he takes to be the simplest explanation for the 'continuity of a bodily life devoid of mental accompaniments' (how could there be any problem about *that*?), but about whether he is entitled to say, for example, that the simplest explanation for psycho-logical connectedness which bridges gaps in consciousness is that there is the same self, or 'bare locus of consciousness', after that gap as there was before. And the answer to that question is, surely, yes. Johnston may reply that the absurd hypothesis that there are any number of selves putting in a brief appearance during sleep cannot be ruled out on the 'bare locus' view, but here Occam's razor surely applies. I see no more reason to entertain this hypothesis than I see reason to entertain the hypothesis that all the furniture in one's bedroom has been engaged in such swappings while one was asleep.

The second reason why this approach must be rejected is that, whatever we take the sceptical implications of the 'bare locus' view to be, we cannot simply *set aside* those considerations which appear to support it. It is quite improper to suggest that the mere fact that the

Geoffrey Madell

view which these considerations support opens up certain sceptical possibilities constitutes in itself a sufficient justification for rejecting these considerations. We must note, too, that Johnston considers only one pair of thought-experiments, those in 'The Self and the Future'. He does not consider the way in which the 'human-being-as-natural-kind' view appears to be undermined by deliverances of the imagination which are a good deal less adventurous than the ones discussed in Williams' paper, and his failure even to touch on the issue of indexical thought means that his attempt to take the measure of the case against the natural kind view is seriously incomplete. We are left without any clear understanding of what the limits to the use of the imagination might be, or of how the power of certain exercises of the imagination apparently to undermine the natural kind view is to be explained, and we have no answer at all to the crucial question of how the referent of 'I' is to be seen as an object in the world.

It might be suggested that Johnston's position has some justification if we take it as an attempt to capture our actual notion of persons, the one with which we in fact operate. The suggestion cannot stand. It is not possible to insulate what we take to be our actual concept of a person from the considerations I have adduced. If it is the case that our present concept is something like the 'human-being-as-natural-kind' idea under discussion, then in undermining that idea we undermine our present concept.

Kathleen Wilkes' distrust of thought-experiments rests on different grounds.[10] One central claim is that if the usual run of thought-experiments are judged against the world as we know it, they describe what is clearly impossible, and if they are not then they are nothing but fantasy. The crucial aspect of this position is the claim that the impossibility involved in such thought-experiments is 'theoretical' or 'in principle' impossibility, the impossibility, for example, of gold having an atomic number other than 79, or water being anything other than H_2O. The suggestion seems to be that it is the conception of human beings as a natural kind which should govern our thoughts about personal identity, and that thought-experiments about personal identity are incoherent when they ignore the essential properties of the natural kind 'human being', just as a speculation about water being anything other than H_2O ignores the essential property of water.

A demonstration that our thinking about persons actually becomes incoherent if it ceases to be governed by a conception of the natural kind 'human being' would certainly be a major, indeed a dramatic, advance in the debate. Not only could we set aside most of the familiar thought-experiments, but the Nagelian question seems to get an immediate

[10] K. Wilkes, *Real People* (Oxford: Clarendon Press, 1988), ch. 1.

138

answer: the only possibility we can understand is that 'I' denotes an object in the world, a token of a natural kind.

The whole approach seems to me to break down, essentially because the analogy with natural kinds like gold and water in fact undermines the central claim about thought-experiments. The essence of water is given by its inner chemical constitution; the substance on Twin Earth, though it has the same surface properties as water, is not water, since its chemical constitution is different. By contrast, it is the surface properties of consciousness which are the focus of our interest and which, indeed, we see as constituting the essence of mental states. There may be philosophical importance attaching to the decision not to use the term 'water' if the surface properties of what we think of as water do not have the right chemical underpinning, but it is not all clear that there is any comparable significance in the decision not to use the term 'human being' in a parallel case. If, as Wilkes appears to admit (36), it makes sense to think of persons who are not human beings, who divide or fuse, then it cannot be the case that '[w]hat we know and believe about natural kind organisms determines the genuine theoretical possibilities' (37).

Wilkes has a rather different claim, which is that what is wrong with typical thought-experiments is that they leave the relevant background unspecified, in much the same way as fairy tales do. We do not care *how* people pass through mirrors in fairy stories, but we cannot allow a similar laxity in relation to thought-experiments about, say, the fission and fusion of persons.

I do not have space here for a full discussion of this claim, but a number of points need to be made about it. The first is that it looks to be in conflict with the admission that we can conceive of fission for beings who are persons but not humans. The second point is that even against speculations such as Parfit's teletransporter thought-experiment,[11] it looks as if the most we can say is that we do not yet know how to transport information from one brain and embody it in a replica of the original person. What we are not justified in doing is ruling out the speculation as incoherent. This would be rather like endorsing the confident claim of the pre-nuclear age that the very idea of splitting the atom is absurd. Some speculations, by contrast, are fairly clearly *logically* absurd, but I think we need more convincing argument than Wilkes has provided to justify rejecting thought-experiments which are not so flawed. Lastly, it is in any case pretty clear that Wilkes' point about the failure to specify the relevant background could not be aimed at the exercises of the imagination with which I have been particularly

---

[11] D. Parfit, *Reasons and Persons* (Oxford: Clarendon Press, 1984), 199–201.

concerned, and which I see as undermining the natural kind view of persons: the thought that I might have had a different origin, for example, could not be so opposed. In summary, Wilkes has not succeeded in showing that the notion of a human being as a natural kind governs our thinking about persons, and neither Wilkes nor Johnston has taken proper cognisance of the considerations which tell against their 'objectivist' view of persons.

VI

We have, then, to acknowledge that the heart of the problem of personal identity lies in the dichotomy between the objective view, which see persons as a special sort of object in the world, and the subjective stance which cannot embrace this view, and which sees 'I' as merely contingently connected with its objective setting. Once it is seen that contemporary attempts to discredit the imagination on the one hand and to dissolve the problem of indexical thought on the other are unsuccessful, we cannot avoid the truth that there can be no understanding of what consciousness is and of what sort of beings we are which does not take the subjective view very seriously. We do not take it seriously by alloting the notion of a human being a central role.

How disturbing ought we to find the dichotomy with which we have been concerned? In relation to another problem which centres on a dichotomy, that of the relation between mind and body, Colin McGinn has recently argued that, although the problem cannot be solved, this is something which should cease to worry us once we understand why the solution to the problem is 'cognitively closed' to us.[12] In brief, while the nature of our conscious states is available to us only through introspection, the physical states of the brain are open only to perception, but neither introspection nor perception can give us access to the necessary link between brain states and conscious states. We know that brain states cause conscious states, and this causal nexus must proceed through necessary connection of some kind, but we can have no understanding of this connection; to us, it can only appear deeply contingent. If this is acceptable, it is plausible to suggest that much the same is true of the issue of personal identity. Here too, one side of the divide is open only to consciousness, the other only to perception, and the necessary link between them, if such there be, must in consequence remain opaque.

I do not believe that this suggestion offers a satisfactory position even in relation to the mind/body problem, but with regard to the problem of

[12] C. McGinn, 'Can We Solve the Mind-Body Problem?', *Mind 98*, No. 391 (July 1989), 349–366.

personal identity it is quite unacceptable. So far as the mind/body problem is concerned, to claim that, though the link between brain states and states of consciousness may be opaque, the former do indeed cause the latter, is to commit oneself to a quite unacceptable epiphenomenalism. We may, to avoid this, choose simply to say that, though we must posit some sort of necessary link between states of consciousness and states of the brain, its nature must remain completely unknown to us; we do not even know whether this link is causal. The suggestion is deeply unsatisfactory. We can have no conception at all of what it could be for thought, with its essential property of intentionality, to be necessarily linked with brain processes, which cannot have this property. This Cartesian claim has resisted all attempts to undermine it, in my judgment. We cannot decently suppose that, while the contrasting concepts of the mental and the physical are relatively clear, what eludes us is simply the necessary link between them. To entertain the possibility of some sort of monistic view of persons would involve the most radical transformation of our concepts. We cannot take it that anything like our present notions of the mental and the physical would be preserved in this transformation. In spite of all our efforts, we have no idea how to establish such a monistic view, and it is useless to pretend otherwise.

This is even more clearly the case in relation to the divide between 'I' on the one hand and its objective setting on the other. We have no idea what it could be for an item in the objective world, something whose origin belongs to its essence, to be necessarily connected to something which is such that the ascription of such essential properties to it looks incoherent. It seems clear that the very idea that something which has certain essential properties can be necessarily linked to something which is essentially free of such properties involves us in incoherence.

It remains conceivable that future understanding will reveal the apparent dichotomy to be an illusion, but it would be a gross mistake to suppose that anyone who accepts the dichotomy as genuine could be guilty of the 'masked man' fallacy. It is clear that the masked man may well be my father, even though I do not know that he is; and the discovery that he is will not, of course, involve any modification at all to either of the concepts 'masked man' or 'father'. By contrast, it does not appear even intelligible to suggest that the two sides of the objective/subjective dichotomy may be aspects of one and the same entity.

The conclusion we are forced to, then, is that there is no way of entertaining the possibility, that 'I' and its objective setting are anything but contingently connected. There is no eirenic suggestion which will allow us to bridge this divide. I have argued that the impotence of such eirenic proposals is even more obvious in relation to the dichotomy which constitutes the problem of personal identity than it is in relation

Geoffrey Madell

to the divide between mind and body. Our thinking about persons is very deeply dualistic, and we cannot make sense of there being some hidden necessary link between the two sides of the duality. If we cannot countenance the idea that the connection between the two sides of the divide is merely contingent, then, as Nagel has suggested in relation to the mind/body issue, we shall have to accept that the solution to the problem may well have to await an integrated theory of reality which will alter our conception of the universe as radically as anything has to date, but which will probably not arrive for centuries.

I began this paper by observing how curious it is that while the dichotomy which constitutes the mind/body problem has at least been recognized, however superficial have been the attempts at healing it, it is not similarly acknowledged that the problem of personal identity is presented by another subjective/objective divide. I am not at all sure that I have an explanation of this, especially in the light of the fairly evident connection between the two issues. The idea that the notion of a human being should be at the centre of our interest in relation to this problem is the most obvious recent example of this failure to see the issue for what it is. Another view which I have not discussed, but which also epitomizes this failure, is the view that our concept of a person is some sort of social construct, a matter of convention. It is sufficient to point out in response to this suggestion that we do not heal the dichotomy we have been discussing by erecting such a concept, or by supposing that our actual concept exists untouched by this dichotomy. All we would be doing is ignoring all the difficulties I have discussed in any such 'objective' view, without any idea of how it is that our preferred view is untouched by these considerations. I have said nothing on what our final view of the nature of persons and of their identity through time ought to be. What I have done is to enter a plea that we start to recognize what the problem really is.

Imagination and the Sense of Identity

LARS HERTZBERG

Most of us, at one time or another, will have been struck by a thought that we might wish to express in the following words: 'I could have been born in a different time and place, my position in life and all my personal characteristics could have been completely different from what they are; how amazing then that it should have fallen to my lot to live my life, the only life I shall ever live, as this particular individual rather than any other.' This thought need not derive from a sense that there is anything unusual about one's life; what it expresses, rather, may be the sense that there is something gratuitous or contingent about one's being any particular individual at all. This sense of contingency might be connected with a feeling of gratitude, perhaps of responsibility towards others less fortunate in life; or it might be bound up with envy, or pride, or self-pity, etc.

Whatever the attitude taken, the thought seems to be intelligible only from a first person perspective. The idea that one might have this sense of amazement concerning some other person does not seem intelligible. I may be struck by the contingency of some particular aspect of another person's fate or personality (say, an ironic twist of events, a lucky conjunction of talent and circumstance), but his life as a whole, the fact of his being the person he is, is not a thing that could be contingent for me, in the way in which the whole of my own life may come to appear to me to be contingent.

Focusing on this difference will, I believe, help us understand the spirit of Geoffrey Madell's argument. The distinction he makes between a first and a third person perspective seems designed to account for asymmetries like this; to be struck by the contingency of one's being the person one is, it appears, is to become aware of the gratuitousness of the fact that the first person perspective on the world (the only one there is, for me) latches on to the third person perspective at one particular point rather than any other. Where others are concerned, there is no corresponding latching on of perspectives for me to be struck by (though there is for them).

According to Madell, asymmetries like these are essential to our understanding of personal identity. What he takes them to show is that the kind of understanding a person will have of his own identity is irreducibly distinct from the sort of understanding he can have of the

143

identity of any of the things he may encounter in the world. There are two sides to this distinctness, both of which are involved in the thought about the contingency of one's own life. First, that which it is possible for me to imagine concerning myself is not limited in some of the ways in which what I may imagine concerning other things is: thus, I can imagine myself having been born at some other time than I actually was, or the events of my past or present life being wholly different from what they are, but I cannot, Madell claims, imagine some other object to have had an origin different from its actual one, or its history to have lacked the continuity that it has. Second, an account of the world which included only matters as described from a third person perspective would be radically deficient in leaving out the fact that one of the persons described is I.

I must confess that I find both parts of Madell's argument problematic. In my commentary, however, I want to focus on the first part. At the same time, I wish to draw attention to some more general difficulties in the way appeals to the imagination are used in discussions about personal identity.

I

Philosophers frequently speak as if the imagination were a method of inquiry: what we can or cannot imagine, it is thought, shows what kind of thing something is. Madell evidently shares this assumption, speaking as he does about *'exercises of the imagination'* or *'deliverances of the imagination'* having the *power to undermine* a certain conception of persons, or warning us against *'attempts to discredit the imagination'*. But I wish to argue that it is not at all clear what is being presupposed in this way of speaking.

The idea that exercises of the imagination may actually be connected with finding things out will perhaps be resisted on the ground that the word 'imagination' often carries the sense of a contrast with the word 'reality', with what might be called responsible thought. Thus, to call someone's remark a product of his imagination is to say, roughly, that it is completely unfounded or that it shows very poor judgement (compare the German *'Einbildung'*). Or, if someone is said to be living a life of the imagination, this might mean that he tends to indulge in daydreaming or to give his attention to fictitious presentations of various kinds. In this case, the problem may not be his inclination to hold certain kinds of silly beliefs as much as his tending to neglect the concerns of actual life.

To raise this objection, however, is to overlook the fact that there are also what might be called responsible appeals to the imagination. Thus, in the context of solving a practical problem, we may try out various arrangements in the imagination. In making plans we may discuss whether a certain contingency can be imagined. We may blame a person for not being able to imagine someone else's feelings, etc. In contexts like these, a distinction between things that can be and things that cannot be imagined is frequently invoked. My finding it possible or impossible to imagine something is not a question of whether or not I am capable of certain flights of fancy, but is an exercise of judgement, something that may show my knowledge of life and people, or on the other hand my gullibility, my inclination to yield to wishful thinking, etc.[1]

It might be thought that this is the distinction philosophers such as Madell have in mind when they appeal to the imagination as a method for finding out what kind of thing something is. I want to argue, however, that appeals to the imagination cannot in fact be used in order to establish matters of this sort. To see this, let us reflect on the nature of the impossibility that is involved in saying that something cannot be imagined.

II

It might be suggested that what limits our ability to imagine things is a requirement of conceptual coherence. An instance of this might be the claim that time travel cannot be imagined. If someone thought that time travel is imaginable, we could ask him to imagine himself travelling backward in time, and then to put the events that he had imagined in temporal order. In spelling out what he had imagined, he would have to make some contradictory assumptions. He might, I suppose, express this discovery by admitting that time travel 'cannot be imagined' after all. In another sense, of course, that was precisely what he had been doing, but from someone's having imagined an event in this sense it does not follow that such an event *can* be imagined, in the sense we have in mind in distinguishing between what can and what cannot be imagined. The thought experiment would be a kind of imaginative *reductio ad absurdum*.

Now suppose it were suggested that this is the way in which exercises of the imagination can be used to establish what personal identity is.

---

[1] The capacity in question here, I would suggest, is, in fact, closely connected with what Raimond Gaita, in his contribution to the present collection, calls the possession of sense: 'the capacity for sound judgement of what is seriously possible and what is not [which] conditions the intelligible application of such modalities even in the most radical inquiries' (p. 159).

The idea is that we should work out certain imaginary contingencies involving identity, and then see whether or not they can be coherently spelled out.

It is not quite clear, however, precisely what could be shown by the use of this method. Some philosophers have argued that the lives of persons, when regarded from a third person perspective, must have the sort of connectedness that is presupposed by their belonging to the natural kind 'human being'. One might ask what they would make of a story like Kafka's *Metamorphosis*, which tells of Gregor Samsa turning into an insect. Does the story show that one can, after all, remain the person one is even after ceasing to be human (in the story the insect clearly *remains* Gregor Samsa), or should it be discounted on the grounds of conceptual incoherence? Would it be possible to generate logical contradictions here? There seems to be no obvious answer in this case, as there is in the case of time travel.

It might be thought, perhaps, that the sharing of concepts that is presupposed by our ability to use language in communicating with one another should show itself in our agreeing on what our concepts do and do not allow for in specific cases. But in fact the language we use is not circumscribed in this way. After all, it belongs to the life of our language that we tell and listen to stories in which men turn into animals or trees, and statues or wooden dolls turn human, etc. Understanding these stories requires no special preparation: no special sense of the word 'human being' has to be introduced, for instance. In fact, I do not understand a story unless I understand most of the words in it outside the story. And of course, the point of stories like these would probably be lost if they were not taken to be concerned with human beings in the ordinary sense of the words.

Does this mean that these fantastic possibilities are already in some sense provided for in the way these words are used in other contexts, or are we to say that a different way of using these words is involved here? Where does 'one use' end and 'another use' begin? There does not seem to be any determinate answer to this question, and to the extent that there is not, the notion of logical coherence cannot do the work that was required of it in this connection.

III

An alternative view might be that what limits our ability to regard something as an imaginable event, rather than logical coherence, are simply our beliefs about the way things are. Thus, if in the context, say, of a forensic or scientific investigation someone put forward the suggestion that a person had turned into an insect, we obviously could not understand his words as a serious attempt to tell us something, but would take him either to be joking or to be insane. On the other hand, it might be suggested that the reason we regard a story like *Metamorphosis* as intelligible is that it is understood from the outset to be fantastic. In other words, it is not even taken to depict something that might actually happen.

Such, roughly, seems to be the view taken by Kathleen Wilkes in cautioning against the use of thought experiments in discussing questions of personal identity.[2] She draws a distinction between two different forms of imagining: between, on the one hand, what she regards as genuine thought experiments, carried out against the background of the world as we know it (or rather, as scientists know it), and on the other hand, what she regards as fantastic ones, in which the background assumed is indeterminately different from the known world. On Wilkes's view, only the former constitute responsible exercises of the imagination, and hence it is only from them that philosophical conclusions can be drawn (p. 46). The latter kind of thought experiment, it seems, has its place in fiction (where she evidently thinks any thought whatsoever can be entertained provided it is entertaining).

Wilkes rests her distinction on a notion of theoretical possibility, or possibility in principle, which she conceives of as dependent on the current state of scientific knowledge: for a thought experiment to be genuine, it must be clear what theoretical possibilities are taken to be suspended, and in what way. The thought experiment must not involve any impossibilities that are relevant to the outcome: if it does so, it 'fails to establish a phenomenon', and hence is presumably worthless (pp. 17ff.).

There are, it seems, two sides to Wilkes's argument, and I find myself in agreement with one side but not with the other. She is quite right, I think, in focusing on the indeterminacy frequently involved in philosophical thought experiments, in which we are invited to consider some fantastic contingency with no attention paid to the mass of crucial detail that would need to be filled in. (In this connection, she makes some telling points against the facile way philosophers have dealt in brain transplants and other weird operations.)

However, ruling out thought experiments because they fly in the face of well-established scientific positions is quite a different matter from ruling them out on grounds of indeterminacy (we may, in fact, run into problems of indeterminacy even without bringing in the impossible). 'Failing to establish a phenomenon' is, in fact, ambiguous as between 'failing to specify what phenomenon you have in mind' and 'failing to

[2] Kathleen V. Wilkes, *Real People. Personal Identity without Thought Experiments* (Oxford: Clarendon Press, 1988).

show that (under certain conditions) a certain phenomenon would actually occur', and it seems to me that Wilkes does not keep the two notions clearly apart. It is not clear why it should be supposed that succeeding in doing the latter is a precondition for being able to do the former. This ambiguity, once taken note of, seems to me fatally to undermine the plausibility of Wilkes's argument in favour of a close connection between the matter of what can be believed and the matter of what can be imagined.

IV

I would suggest that the question whether something can be imagined or conceived can be fruitfully seen to be connected with people's concern with making sense to one another. Asking whether something can be imagined comes close to asking: does what I am trying to say hold together, or is it in danger of coming apart?

When what someone is saying comes apart, its sense is lost. I no longer understand what he is saying as a way of making the kind of point I took him to be making. I may then fail to see what he is doing, speaking as he does. This may happen in consequence of certain things having been brought to my attention. (Unless I can come to see him making some other point instead, he will then no longer be telling me anything.) And if those things are brought to the speaker's attention, he may no longer want to go on speaking in the same way as before. (Yet he may, perversely, persist in doing so, still hoping that others will be taken in. In a special case, again, the point may be precisely that what is said should be seen to come apart; think of a text like *Alice in Wonderland*!)

Whether what is said holds together or not evidently depends on the *kind* of thing the speaker is trying to get across. It is only in a special range of cases—highly important as they are—that one's ability to make sense to others is directly bound up with questions of factual possibility. If I presume to give a factual report of an event I have witnessed, the intelligibility to others of what I am saying *as* such a report depends on whether they can believe that I believe it, and, if not, whether they can believe that I believe that I can get them to believe it, etc.

Thus, when the defendant in a criminal case gives an account of his whereabouts at the time of the crime, his story obviously comes apart if he can be shown to have involved himself in temporal contradictions. But this does not entail that a story about time travel like H. G. Wells's *The Time Machine* will not hold together even if one realizes that it can be shown to yield contradictory implications. The reason for this, however, is not simply that *The Time Machine* is a piece of fiction, and that in fiction anything goes. Whether a novel does hold together depends on what may broadly be called aesthetic considerations. And these considerations vary depending on the kind of novel it is.[3]

Of course there are other cases, apart from fiction, involving responsible uses of the imagination, in which it makes sense to speak about events without supposing them to be empirically possible: we can imagine a serious discussion of what life would be like if men could live on air or if they had X-ray vision, or what would happen if Christ returned to earth or how I would have acted had I been Napoleon at Waterloo (whether from an interest in appraising his tactical skills, or from a wish to explore my own character), etc. These are all exercises of the imagination from which something may be learnt, though what we may learn and the conditions of our learning it will depend on the purpose of the discussion and the context in which it is carried out. All of them, of course, may suffer from the sort of indeterminacy to which Wilkes has drawn our attention, but this by itself is not sufficient to defeat them; whether and how it does so depends on the nature of the case at hand.

On the other hand, the idea that the facts, or science, determine what can be imagined derives what plausibility it has from the contemplation of cases in which making sense depends on the possibility of being believed. But even in these cases, the nature of the dependence varies according to the nature of the remark being made. What would be unintelligible if presented as a matter of routine, for instance, might still make sense in a context of bewilderment or amazement. (So whether a remark makes sense could depend on the tone of voice in which it is made.)

Thus it may make sense for a scientist confronted with bewildering test results to entertain possibilities that fly in the face of well-entrenched scientific positions. If that were not so, it would indeed be hard to understand the possibility of radical innovation in the sciences. (I do not know whether Kathleen Wilkes meant to exclude this.) Or, to consider rather a different sort of case, if someone's words are to be understood as expressing the belief that a miracle has occurred, the assertion that the event described was in conflict with well-established facts of physics would not tend to undermine the sense of his utterance (in fact this might in some cases be taken to be presupposed by it); what the utterance does require, however, is the context of a life in which belief in miracles has a place.[4]

[3] For a perceptive discussion of these issues, see R. W. Beardsmore, 'The Limits of Imagination', *The British Journal of Aesthetics 20*, no. 2 (Spring 1980), 99–114.

[4] In this connection, consider the discussion between R. F. Holland and Peter Winch on whether it would be intelligible for someone to report an

V

It seems, then, that Kathleen Wilkes's attempt to show what is involved in responsible appeals to the imagination is not successful. On the other hand, it is evident from Madell's critical remarks that his view of the imagination is not to be understood along the lines suggested by her, and so is not open to the same criticism. But this means that we still do not have much of a clue as to the way to understand Madell's notion that 'exercises of the imagination' have the power to support or undermine certain conceptions of identity, or precisely what the error of 'discrediting the imagination' would amount to.

The only positive hint Madell gives of his own view on these matters is in arguing in support of what he calls the necessity-of-origin thesis: 'We do not know what it could mean to say that there is a possible world in which this very same oak tree grew from a different acorn; we have no idea what could pick it out as the very same oak tree' (p. 128). It is as if we had to beware of constructing worlds in which we might be unable to find our way about or unable to re-identify things. But if taken literally this injunction is obviously nonsense: a possible world is not like an unknown continent on which we might conceivably land and where we might have to find our bearings. If talk about possible worlds is to make any sense, it must be understood as a way of spelling out the implications of some possibility we are trying to imagine. It is we who stipulate what will be the case in any possible world we may care to invent. If I imagine an individual entity, whether an oak, a person, or whatever, in different circumstances, the entity as I imagine it must correspond in some way to that individual as it is in the actual world, otherwise it would be hard to see what could be the point of calling it this particular oak, or person. But I see no reason for singling out any particular type of correspondence, such as identity of origin, as essential in all such contexts. On the contrary, whether or not some particular type of correspondence is relevant would seem to depend on the purpose of the exercise.

In fact, both Madell's and Wilkes's account, I would maintain, ultimately rest on the same dubious assumption: both of them seem to suppose that it is meaningful to try to formulate a wholly general answer to the question of what can be imagined, one that does not depend on the particular context in which the question arises. We might call this

---

event which flies in the face of what is generally agreed to be empirically possible. See R. F. Holland, 'The Miraculous', in R. F. Holland, *Against Empiricism* (Oxford: Basil Blackwell, 1980); and Peter Winch, 'Ceasing to Exist', in Peter Winch, *Trying to Make Sense* (Oxford: Basil Blackwell, 1987).

idea, which they hold in common with a great many other philosophers, an absolute notion of imaginability. There is a closely connected idea that Wilkes and Madell also seem to hold in common with a great many other philosophers: that of an absolute notion of possibility. However, in relation to these ideas, they evidently differ in the following respect: in Wilkes's case, the notion of what is possible is apparently taken to determine whether something can be imagined, whereas, in Madell's case, trying to establish whether or not a thing can be imagined is apparently a way of deciding whether it is possible.

On the other hand, on both views the judgement that something is possible or that it can be imagined is taken to be based, in one way or another, on a consideration of the objects or the states of affairs in question. For something to be imaginable is understood as involving a relation, as it were, between our imagination and the world. And this, I would argue, is where the crucial misapprehension lies. For if we attend more closely to the cases in which we actually speak about things being or not being imaginable, we will realize that there is no fixed relation between the imagination and its objects that can determine whether or not something can be imagined; the relation to take into account here is rather that between the imagining and the situation of life in which it takes place. The claim that something can or cannot be imagined, I want to say, is one that is made in our normal dealings with one another, the conditions for making it varying with the context. The task of philosophical discussion, accordingly, can hardly be anything other than trying to make clear what may be meant, in various contexts, in saying that something is or is not imaginable. It is not for philosophy to decide under what conditions saying so would be correct. If this is so, then the 'deliverances of the imagination' cannot meaningfully be invoked in order to settle philosophical disputes.

VI

If the line of thought advanced here is acceptable, this would bar appeals to what can be imagined as a method for settling questions about personal identity. Perhaps it will be thought, however, that Madell's point concerning the asymmetry between the first and third person perspective could be restated by reference to the idea of thought experiments in a way that does not depend on this notion. His argument, if reworked along these lines, might go roughly as follows.

The philosophical literature is full of stories about memories and personal characteristics being 'disconnected' from one body and 'connected' to a different body, about 'brain transplants' partial or complete, about bodies 'dissolved' and 'replicated' on a distant planet, about 'twinning' operations by which two identical persons are made out of one, and various other kinds of weird transformations. In each case, the question we are being invited to consider is: which, if any, of the individuals resulting from this transformation would be identical with the person or persons who were around to begin with? Some philosophers use these thought experiments as part of an attempt to isolate a particular aspect of the person, be it physical or psychological, claimed to be crucial to the preservation of identity, while others are inclined to argue that what they show is that the concept of identity is a complex one and hence will have no determinate application in radically altered circumstances.

Now it has generally been assumed that what determines the outcome of any of these transformations (in so far as it has a determinate outcome) must be some objectively accessible fact about the relation between the initial person and the end-result. When the subject of the transformation is somebody else, this might seem a very natural position to take. However, Madell could be taken to be arguing, all these imaginary exercises miss a crucial point, namely this: if I posit *myself* as the subject of one of these transformations, the outcome would simply be determined by the answer I should give to the question: to which, if any, of the resulting individuals will I have a first person relation? And this does not depend on a physical or psychological connection between me as I was before the transformation and whatever resulted from it: I am, it seems, free to think of myself as having a first person relation to any of the resulting individuals, just as I am free to suppose that any transformation whatsoever could have led up to my being what I am now. It would accordingly be natural to conclude that these experiments can show nothing at all as long as identity is being considered from the first person point of view, since in that case there will be no constraints on what can legitimately be assumed. The reason a third person approach to personal identity must fail, on the other hand, is that it cannot accommodate this freedom from constraints.

This line of argument has the apparent advantage of not necessarily being dependent on appeals to what is possible or to what can be imagined.[5] The thought experiments, we might think, are simply test cases for our concepts: we describe a set of circumstances radically different from those in which we normally apply concepts of personal identity, and then pose the question how our concepts should rightly be applied in those other circumstances. It does not matter in this connection whether the circumstances lie within the bounds of possibility.

Madell's position, then, as against that of most other thought-experimentalists, would be that the answer to this question depends on

[5] I owe this point to David Cockburn.

Imagination and the Sense of Identity

whether we ask it about ourselves or ask it about other people. However, it seems to me to be doubtful whether appeals to thought experiments make any better sense in this connection than appeals to the imagination do. For one thing, it seems clear that some of Kathleen Wilkes's strictures against the indeterminacy of thought experiments are relevant here (indeed I believe her argument might gain considerably by being applied directly at this level, without the detour invoking possibility and the imagination). However, these thought experiments seem to involve an even deeper form of indeterminacy which, I would argue, ruins their usefulness in this connection altogether. (This point is connected with our earlier observations concerning the indeterminacy of the notion of conceptual coherence.)

The use of thought experiments ignores the fact that our language, as it were, is in the world.[6] To the extent to which there is a change in the conditions in which we use our expressions, then obviously the life we live with language will no longer be the same. What we should realize in this connection is that there is no determinate way of separating off, within this life, those aspects of it that are determined by the meaning of our expressions from those that are incidental to it.

When the circumstances for the use of some expression change, we are inclined to think that it should be possible to make a distinction between changes in the use of the expression that merely reflect the change in circumstances, and changes that would show the meaning of the expression to have changed. And accordingly we suppose that there is a definite answer to the question what, in a different set of circumstances, would constitute going on using our expressions with their present meaning. But this is an illusion since it presupposes that there could be something apart from the current practice of our language (something like an underlying structure) to which appeals can be made in discussing what our expressions mean. Of course as speakers of a language we distinguish between right and wrong uses of expressions, but we do so spontaneously, in the course of using language, not by consulting an underlying structure.

Central among the circumstances in which we speak about the identity of individuals are the following two facts: on the one hand, we have a great facility for recognizing and telling apart a large number of different persons by their facial appearance, their bodily posture, even simply their voices, sometimes in spite of the fact that they may have undergone great changes; on the other hand, the identity of the particular

---

[6] The line of argument in the section to follow is inspired by Cora Diamond's paper 'Rules: Looking in the Right Place', in D. Z. Phillips and Peter Winch (eds), *Wittgenstein: Attention to Particulars* (Houndmills and London: Macmillan, 1989).

person someone is, even apart from his or her special talents, traits of character, etc., matters greatly to us in many of our relations to others. Let us suppose instead that one of the following state of affairs were normal:

> There are groups of people whom one cannot tell apart, or whom one can only tell apart with great effort.

> There are several people whose temperaments, experiences and talents coincide very largely, to the extent that one might carry on more or less the same conversation with any one of them.

> People's appearance or their personalities often change radically in completely unpredictable ways.

> The kind of importance people have for one another is such that it rarely matters whom in particular one is speaking to or having dealings with at any given moment.

In any of these altered sets of circumstances the conditions for telling people apart, or the importance of doing so, or both, would be radically different from what they are now. Each one of them could, presumably, be made the subject of a thought experiment (although it is significant that the constructors of thought experiments have almost exclusively concentrated on imaginary *changes in the persons* whose identity is taken to be problematic, rather than on *changes in our attitudes* to people).

But given such radically altered circumstances, it is not at all clear what would count as applying 'our' concepts of personal identity, or what kinds of grounds we could appeal to in trying to settle this. What would living the life we live with our language of identity amount to in those conditions? The important indeterminacy in this connection is not, as Wilkes suggests, that concerning the facts of the situation we are supposed to be describing; the indeterminacy concerns the very question of what we are doing in trying to reach a verdict about the case. (Even simply to say that in those new conditions, questions of personal identity would have become indeterminate, would mean making a commitment the sense of which would be obscure.) What relation is the verdict we might make on one of these fantastic cases supposed to bear to the actual use of expressions of identity by the people who are taken to be in those situations? Are we trying to guess what they would say? But what does it mean to make guesses about something that will never happen? Or are we trying to lay down what they ought to say? If so, by what authority do we presume to be speaking?[7]

---

[7] What lies behind this idea might be the thought that there must be some such explanation of how it is that people are very often able to agree in their use of words in new situations. However, on the one hand it should be clear that people will not always agree (so the suggested theory explains

The idea that thought experiments can help clarify the nature of our concepts of identity presupposes that such commitments would make sense. It is as if our current linguistic practices already contained a procedure for determining the correct application of the concept of identity in all conceivable cases. If this were so, then our language would indeed be unaffected in its essence by the ways in which our life might change, and in this sense it would not be part of the world.

The structure we take ourselves to be exploring by the aid of thought experiments is one I have been arguing does not exist. In appealing to thought experiments involving identity, just as in invoking the distinction between what can and what cannot be imagined, philosophers are presuming, as it were, to measure the shadow cast by our language across 'all possible worlds'. But of course there is no shadow, and so this project is an illusion, and cannot, accordingly, be used for shedding light on the alleged dichotomy between the first and the third person perspectives.[8]

[8] I wish to thank David Cockburn for a number of very helpful comments on an earlier version of this paper.

too much), and on the other hand, the agreement can be most simply understood as due to the fact that people will naturally tend to respond in similar ways to the same instruction. In this respect, the agreement there is in extraordinary situations is no different in principle from the agreement there is in ordinary situations; the latter needs no more of a special explanation than the former.

Radical Critique, Scepticism and Commonsense

RAIMOND GAITA

I

Suppose that someone writes an argument on a blackboard which leads to the conclusion that he may, at that time, be dreaming. He goes over it, considers its validity, the truth of its premises, its assumptions and so on, and then to his dismay, he judges that he is compelled to conclude that he may be dreaming. He goes over the argument repeatedly and carefully, but finds the conclusion 'inescapable'. If reviewing the argument on the blackboard may be taken as an analogue of reviewing thoughts before one's mind, then his condition seems like the condition which Descartes describes at the beginning of the Second Meditation: 'The meditation of yesterday filled my mind with so many doubts that it is no longer in my power to forget them. And yet I do not see in what manner I can resolve them; and just as if I had all of a sudden fallen into very deep water, I am so disconcerted that I can neither make certain of setting my feet on the bottom, nor can I swim and support myself on the surface.'[1]

One could think of this as an example of intellectual purity, of a mind struggling in obedience to Reason's claim upon it; courageously prepared to follow an argument wherever it may go; determined to embrace the truth irrespective of how unpalatable it may be. That is a common way of thinking of it. It can be an edifying representation of philosophical practice which goes with a certain sense of philosophical depth and purity.

We may think of it in another way. We may think that Reason seems to compel him to a conclusion which he cannot seriously conclude because no one could seriously profess it as his belief. He believes that he must conclude that he may be dreaming, because he must put the sentence which expresses it after the 'therefore' sign in what seems to be a piece of valid reasoning. But a conclusion which no one can conclude, in the sense of seriously professing it as one of his beliefs, is a conclusion

---

[1] Réné Descartes, *Meditations on First Philosophy* in *The Philosophical Works of Descartes*, trans. Elizabeth S. Haldane and G. R. T. Ross, (Cambridge: Cambridge University Press, 1975), Vol. 1, 149.

in inverted commas only, a mere 'blackboard conclusion'. What we call reasoning, inferring, concluding, reviewing an argument and so on, stand in non-accidental relations to the possibility of seriously professing a conclusion as one's belief. If a conclusion is one which no one could seriously and unequivocally profess, then it becomes problematical in what sense reasons or considerations have been offered in its favour. The interrelated concepts of a consideration, of a reason, of an argument, of a proof, of a conclusion—all seem to idle when applied to the sceptical professions of the First Meditation. They look like shadows cast by the substantial application of these concepts. If that is true, then the person in my example and the *persona* of the *Meditations* are not exemplars of the exercise of a purified critical intelligence, but false semblances of them. But, now someone might protest that the suggestion that what appears on the pages of the First Meditation is only the shadow play of genuine argument, is as fantastical as the claim that we might suspect that we are dreaming in the kind of circumstances which Descartes describes.

It is always profitable to return to Descartes. His search for a method was prompted by his disillusionment with the state of the sciences. He was shocked by the dogmatism and ignorance of even the most distinguished scholars. Such dismay is not uncommon. However, when we notice the dogmatism and prejudice that has at all times prevailed in the scholarly disciplines, and when we notice that even the best minds are vulnerable to convention and even to fashion, then we do not follow Descartes when we try to diminish these vices in ourselves. It is not part of our understanding of what it is to be thinker who is radically critical of the assumptions of his own discipline, that he first establish that he is not dreaming—not even once in a lifetime as a means to intellectual purification. If we invoke Descartes' distinction between, on the one hand, what one is doing in adopting the *persona* of the *Meditations* and, on the other hand, what he attributes to practice, then we must remember that what we ordinarily call theory, as when we contrast, for example, theoretical with applied physics, is to be included in his extended sense of practice.

The point is stronger than appeal to what we normally do and think. Descartes says in the *Synopsis* of the *Meditations* that 'such things [as are doubted in the First Meditation] have never been doubted by anyone of sense'.[2] If 'sense' is relativized to his extended sense of practice, and if the proper exercise of our critical capacities is conditional upon its possession (as it is conditional upon for example, sanity or sobriety), then it is a condition of serious and critical reflection as we find it in the various disciplines, that a thinker sometimes 'rules

2 Ibid. 143.

things out of consideration' under pain of being, for example, naive, gullible, a crank, or even, insane. What Descartes calls 'sense' is, presumably, not merely a robust practicality, but the capacity for sound judgement, which is a condition of the exercise of those critical concepts which inform our understanding of what it is to think well and badly. Much of this can be summarized by saying that the possession of sense is the capacity for sound judgement of what is seriously possible and what is not: it conditions the intelligible application of such modalities even in the most radical inquiries. However, that prompts the suspicion that the critical categories available to the *persona* of the *Meditations* are inadequate to, or even incommensurate with, those required to expose the complacency and prejudice which so dismayed him in the sciences. They would be incommensurate, if the conditions of life which Descartes presents as obstacles to the purified thinking of the *persona* of the *Meditations*, condition the critical categories which are necessary to any conception of what it is to think well or badly in the sciences, or anywhere else.

II

Can anyone seriously believe that he may be dreaming in circumstances such as Descartes describes in the First Meditation? Descartes sometimes says that one can and he sometimes says that one can't. He says things, in the *Meditations* and elsewhere, which when elaborated, give at least two different accounts of why it seems that one cannot. The first is stated relatively explicitly in the First Meditation. He says: 'For I am assured that there can be neither peril nor error in this course, and that I cannot at present yield too much to distrust since I am not considering the question of action but only of knowledge'.[3] The 'course' in which there can be neither peril nor error is to 'pretend that all these opinions [that he has a body, etc.] are entirely false and imaginary'.[4] He thinks of this as the adoption of a psychological technique which will enable him to hold, at least for some time, to the sceptical conclusions he came to earlier. But even this strategy tends to fail and 'insensibly a certain lassitude leads [him] into the course of [his] ordinary life'.[5] He thinks that the sense in which he (sometimes) *cannot* believe the sceptical conclusions is psychological; which is why he adopts a psychological strategy to try to overcome his incapacity.

The point is explicit in this passage:

[3] Ibid. 148.
[4] Ibid. 148.
[5] Ibid. 149.

And just as a captive who in sleep enjoys an imaginary liberty, when he begins to suspect that this liberty is but a dream, fears to awaken, and conspires with these agreeable illusions that the deception may be prolonged, so insensibly, of my own accord I fall back into my former opinions, and I dread awakening from this slumber, lest the laborious wakefulness which would follow the tranquility of this repose, should have to be spent, not in daylight, but in the excessive darkness of the difficulties which have just been discussed.[6]

Descartes appeals to the common experience that there are truths which we find psychologically difficult to accept, and sometimes especially so if they lead us into uncertainty. He is, therefore, able to treat the sceptical conclusions advanced in the First Meditation as emerging from an inquiry which is naturally prompted by and continuous with his disillusionment with the state of the sciences: the psychological difficulties which threaten his project are of the same kind as undermined the integrity of the sciences: they are species of human frailty. To this we may add that life would be impossible for us if we did not act as though we were certain of things which philosophical reflection teaches us are, strictly speaking, at best probable. Elaboration on such obstacles to pure inquiry is the official doctrine of the *Meditations* and has been the stock defence of the coherence of scepticism.

What, then, can we make of his statement in the *Synopsis* that 'such things never have been doubted by anyone of sense'? If we are told that something has never been doubted by anyone of sense *because* of his sense (which is surely the spirit of Descartes' remark) then we are invited to believe that it *could not* be doubted by anyone of sense. That is less than the claim that no one (not even someone who is insane) could seriously doubt such things, but it is considerably more than is allowed by the official doctrine. The obstacle which the possession of 'sense' poses to the serious profession of such doubts is not psychological.

There is, I believe, an argument implicit in Descartes' criticism of the ancient sceptics which promises an account of the difficulties in seriously professing the doubts of the First Meditation and which is not in such obvious conflict with what he says in the *Synopsis* as is his official doctrine. I will make the argument explicit and for the sake of convenience I will attribute it to Descartes, although I do not stand by the exegetical point. He is worth quoting at length:

My statement that the entire testimony of the senses must be considered to be uncertain, nay, even false, is quite serious and so necessary for the comprehension of my meditations, that he who will not or cannot admit that, is unfit to urge any objection to them that merits a reply. But we must note the distinction emphasized by me in various passages, between the practical activities of our life and an inquiry into truth; for when it is a case of regulating our life, it would assuredly be stupid not to trust the senses, and those sceptics were quite ridiculous who so neglected human affairs that they had to be preserved by their friends from tumbling down precipices. It was for this reason that somewhere I announced that no one in his sound mind seriously doubted about such matters, but when we raise an inquiry into what is the surest knowledge which the human mind can obtain, it is clearly unreasonable to refuse to treat them as doubtful, nay even to reject them as false, so as to allow us to become aware that certain other things, which cannot be thus rejected, are, for this very reason, more certain, and in actual truth, better known to us.[7]

It is difficult to know how much weight to give the tensions in this passage because he is evidently irritable. At first he seems to be saying quite unequivocally that the doubts of the First Meditation may be seriously entertained. However, at the end of the passage he speaks of *treating* such things as doubtful 'so as to allow us to become aware that certain other things, which cannot be thus rejected, are, for this very reason, more certain, and in actual truth better known to us'. To treat things as doubtful as a method of inquiry is less than seriously to doubt them. I will comment later on the common idea that we can defuse the difficulties in the claim that one might doubt such things as are doubted in the First Meditation, by treating the doubt as purely methodological. I want first to concentrate on something else which emerges in this passage.

Earlier I used the phrase 'blackboard conclusion' to pry apart the sincere utterance of a sentence and the sincere belief that one seriously believed it because one felt compelled to mark it as true, from the serious believing or concluding of something. One may read Descartes as rejecting that contrast in the case of the kind of enquiry which he calls 'First philosophy'. Thus although the way a belief shows itself in a person's life is normally a criterion for whether it is seriously held or whether it is, as we say, 'mere words', it cannot be so for beliefs and doubts which could only show themselves in the life of someone who was so 'stupid' that he failed to appreciate the difference between the 'practical activities of our life and an inquiry into truth'. Nothing in one's life as a human being could show whether or not one is serious in

[7] René Descartes, *Reply to Objections V,* in *The Philosophical Works of Descartes,* trans. Elizabeth S. Haldane and G. R. T. Ross, (Cambridge: Cambridge University Press, 1975), Vol. 2, 207.

the profession that one might be dreaming. The ancient sceptics did not prove the seriousness of their scepticism by acting it out. On the contrary, their lives were a kind of category mistake. In the *Reply,* Descartes does not speak of the 'practical activities of our life' as the source of the psychological difficulties which threaten real and sustained doubt, nor does he speak of them to emphasize the pressures they exert on us to act *as though* matters were quite certain. He speaks of them as giving sense to the contrast between a serious profession of doubt and one which is 'mere words', as that contrast is invoked to question the seriousness of the doubts expressed in the *Meditations.* Here, Descartes suggests that reflection on the relation 'between the practical activities of our life and an inquiry into truth', will reveal *conceptual* obstacles to any suggestion that his apparent equivocation about whether he really doubts compromises the seriousness of his project.

The point enables Descartes to put his critics on the defensive. When they ask whether anyone could be serious in his profession that he doubts whether he is awake, then Descartes may challenge them to give a clear account of *what it would be* seriously to doubt such things. That is an advance on the official position which retreated into the implausible claim that it is merely psychologically difficult to doubt such things. However, problems remain. There is an important difference between saying, on the one hand, that there are doubts which, though seriously entertainable by someone of sense, are not to be acted upon by him, and saying, on the other hand, that there are doubts which cannot even be entertained by anyone of sense. Descartes seems to be saying the first in his *Reply to Objections V* and the second in the *Synopsis*, even though he claims in the *Reply* to be commenting on what he meant in the *Synopsis*. The first requires that there be intelligible descriptions of what it would be to act out one's scepticism, albeit, foolishly. The second raises the question whether we can make sense of the idea of a life or of actions as being informed by such scepticism. There are, to be sure, beliefs which cannot even be entertained by anyone of sense but which may be acted upon by those who believe them because they lack sense—the beliefs of a madman for example. But what would count as acting as though one seriously believed that one may be dreaming; or as though it were possible but highly improbable that one might be dreaming; or as though one acted in thoughtless certainty that one was awake because one had never thought about the matter? If a person of sense cannot doubt such things as are doubted in the First Meditation, then it looks as though the meaning of this 'cannot' is not the same as when we say that one cannot doubt such and such unless one is insane, or a crank, and so on.

The point has implications for the common idea that the doubt entertained by the *persona* of the *Meditations* is purely methodological. The method is essentially one of doubting; thus one cannot defuse problems about the coherence of the doubt by emphasizing the method. It needs explaining how doubts which could be entertained only by someone who lacked sober judgement could be the basis of a method to place science on intellectually secure foundations. And if (as may be suggested by our difficulty in conceiving what it would be to doubt such things even if one lacked sense) we find unintelligible the idea that such doubts may seriously be professed, then we have no method. A method cannot survive the judgement that the description of its essence is unintelligible. The belief that the project of radical doubt can be rescued as a method appears to presuppose that it needs rescuing from only the psychological difficulty of entertaining the doubts.[8]

Earlier, I described someone who sincerely believes that he must accept the sceptical conclusion that he may be dreaming. No one has been able to profess such a conclusion unequivocally. We have been exploring different ways of accounting for that equivocation—for the combined sense that one both must and cannot assert that conclusion. The most favoured explanation rests on an appeal to the psychological and practical difficulties in the way of its unequivocal profession. One might say, as did G. E. Moore, that some things could be judged to be doubtful even though it is (psychologically) impossible to doubt them. A more subtle explanation exploits the insight that it is a mistake to think that anything in a person's life could be a criterion for whether or not he is serious in the profession of his scepticism, in order to reveal conceptual difficulties in the denial that he could be serious. Neither of these explanations provide material for a defence of scepticism which is adequate against Descartes' tone in the *Synopsis*, which invites us to acknowledge that no one, not even a madman, could doubt what the *persona* of the *Meditations* claims to doubt. But the second, in present-

---

[8] A fundamental difficulty with this idea is that it is not clear who is applying the method. Is it Descartes or the *persona* of the *Meditations*? Descartes would abandon the method as unfruitful if he found no solution to the sceptical quandry represented at the end of the First Meditation. The same cannot be said for the *persona* of the *Meditations*. It is internal to the *persona* of the *Meditations* that he would be stuck with his doubts if he found no argument to overcome them. Therefore, in whatever sense doubt is a method for the *persona*, it is not of a kind which would enable him to distance himself from it if it proved fatal. Nor can we insofar as we respond to the invitation to adopt that *persona* ourselves. That is one of the consequences of the essentially first personal form of the *Meditations*, which is in that respect, quite unlike the *Discourse on the Method of Rightly Conducting Reason*.

ing a conceptual obstacle to any damaging descriptions of the sceptic's equivocations, contains an insight, which if developed, may be adequate to that task.

III

The concept of commonsense is a critical concept: it is a concept which is fundamental to our understanding of what it is to think well or badly. It does not refer merely to a body of pre-philosophical beliefs. It is a concept which partly conditions our understanding of what can and cannot be seriously entertained. A person who has commonsense in its various forms is one who rules certain things out of consideration, not because they have been proved to be false or improbable, but because to entertain them as possible is to lack that capacity which is a condition of the sober use of concepts like 'it has been proven' or 'it is highly improbable', and so on. There are things which anyone must rule out of consideration, because even to entertain them would be a sure sign that one could no longer trust one's capacity to think. Some things one could think only if one were going mad, and the terror of madness lies partly in the fact that one cannot think one's way out of it: if a person suspects that he is going mad then he can no longer trust his thoughts.[9] Less dramatically, there are beliefs which only a crank could seriously entertain, such as, that the world is flat, or that he can read his future in the stars, or that the Holocaust is a fiction created and sustained by Zionists.

It is sometimes said that no rational person could believe such things, but that is to misunderstand the scope of the concept of rationality. Such people lack something which is not (as is rationality) an aspect or form of our critical capacities but, rather, something which is a condition of their exercise in their various forms. The trouble with cranks and madmen is not that they hold radically unconventional beliefs on insufficient evidence, and it is certainly not that they cannot reason. We call them cranks and madmen because we recognize that the proper exercise of our critical concepts, such as the concept of sufficient evidence, depends upon them not being exercised by cranks and madmen. And it belongs to our concept of a proof that something is a proof only within the ranks of the sane and the sober; those who, as we say, 'are in tune with reality'.

If we have commonsense, certain thoughts never occur to us, not because for practical purposes we treat what is improbable as being impossible, but rather because such facts as its not occurring to us if we

---

[9] Although, clearly, Descartes did not think so.

are sane, condition the sense of such concepts as 'it is possible that . . .', or 'it is probable that . . .' or 'it is impossible that . . .', etc. Such dispositions, in their different forms, to not even entertain certain thoughts, are not consequent upon our belief in probabilities: they condition our ordinary use of concepts of possibility and necessity. Such concepts cannot, therefore, furnish the basis for a root and branch 'strict speech' redescription of our practices. That is why it is foolish to say things like 'We may be dreaming but it is so improbable that we may safely act as though we were awake.'

Descartes could accept all this with one important qualification. The qualification is necessary if his acceptance of this conception of commonsense is to be consistent with his claim that the doubts of the *persona* of the *Meditations* are in some sense seriously professed. He must claim that the concept of commonsense (which, for the purposes of argument, I take to be the same as the concept of sense) is conditioned by particular aspects of our human form of life, and is, therefore, internal to only certain kinds of thinking: these include scientific thinking even in its most theoretical and speculative forms (for scientists assuredly need 'sense'), but they do not include philosophical thinking of the kind found in the *Meditations*.

Descartes' argument can now run as follows. Our actual critical vocabulary is to be divided into two parts. The primary part consists of terms such as 'true', 'false', the names for the various modes of valid and invalid inference and, perhaps, concepts like that of a clear and distinct idea. The secondary part has, in addition to these, the concept of commonsense. We have seen that people lack sense in different ways, some are mad, others are naive, others are gullible, others are incorrigibly sentimental and so on. These critical terms mark out different ways in which we might treat something as beyond consideration. We cannot usually get by with only the primary part even in most intellectual disciplines, but that does not show that there is no kind of thinking for which only the primary part is adequate.[10]

It is natural to think that the sense of the concepts 'true' and 'false' does not depend of the particularities of the lives of those who employ them. The idea that a certain kind of thinking, which is defined by a limited set of critical categories, is unconditioned by any particular form of life, is an idea compatible with materialism. Therefore, when I say that the *res cogitans* is a presupposition of the enquiry initiated in the First Meditation, I do not mean the *res cogitans* as an immaterial substance. I mean the *res cogitans* as defined by critical categories

[10] For the application of this to moral philosophy, see Raimond Gaita, *Good and Evil: An Absolute Conception* (London: Macmillan, 1990), Chapters 15 and 16.

which are unconditioned by the form which life takes for the more substantial creature which is its host.[11]

When we are invited to adopt the *persona* of the *Meditations*, we are invited to recognize that we are thinking beings who are only accidentally thinking beings who live a particular kind of life, in our case, the life of human beings. The *res cogitans* and the *persona* of the First Meditation represent thinking as such, thinking as it would be in its essence in any thinking being. When we adopt the *persona* of the *Meditations*, we try to distill from our humanly conditioned understanding of thought, an essence which is identical for all thinking beings irrespective of their bodily forms and ways of life, and irrespective even, of whether they have a bodily form. The *res cogitans*, the mere 'thing which thinks', which the *persona* of the *Meditations* discovered in the Second Meditation to be his essence, is a presupposition of the intelligibility of the project announced in the First Meditation and of the doubts which are expressed in it.

Is such a conception of thinking intelligible? It seems to be. Do we not find perfectly intelligible the idea of scientifically sophisticated beings on other planets even though we have no idea of their material form? This would be an empty idea if we had no idea of some of the critical categories which defined the operation of their intelligence. We tend to think that they would operate, at least as we do, with concepts of truth and falsehood and with the concepts of valid and invalid inference. But, because of their material form and way of life, they may not have the concepts of sentimentality, or naivete, or even of gullibility or madness: they may not have the concept which Descartes called, 'sense', when he said that no one of sense had ever doubted such things as are doubted in the First Meditation. The point is even clearer if we consider speculation on whether machines could think.

[11] In the Sixth Meditation Descartes tries to give an account of the relation between the *res cogitans* which he believes himself essentially to be, and his body. The account would have to make perspicuous that he was 'very closely united to [his] body and, so to speak, intermingled with it that [he] seems to compose with it one whole'. The problem as he sees it is how an immaterial substance can be so 'closely united' to a material substance so as to seem 'to compose with it one whole', and philosophers have followed him in thinking that this is the primary sense in which the *Meditations* raise a problem concerning the relation between 'mind' and 'body'.

The account I have given of the *res cogitans* does not depend upon it being an immaterial substance, but it reveals I think, the futility of Descartes' hope as he expresses it in the Sixth Meditation. The *res cogitans* as a presupposition of the intelligibility of his hyperbolical doubt, is as serious an obstacle to an adequate account of the relation between mind and body, as is the *res cogitans* conceived of as an immaterial substance.

Radical Critique, Scepticism and Commonsense

I suspect that such a conception of thinking as I have outlined underlies Descartes' protest that there is a sense in which the doubts of the First Meditation can be seriously entertained; and I think that only something like it can rescue him from the cruder remarks he sometimes makes on the relation between philosophical thinking and practice. We can reconcile his claims that there is a sense in which the doubts of the First Meditation may seriously be professed, and his claim that no one of sense has ever entertained them, if we understand him to say that they can seriously be professed only by that part of ourselves which represents thinking as it would be in any thinking thing whatsoever, thinking, that is, which is unconditioned in its critical categories by the particular circumstances of any form of life. Hence the importance of the meditational form of the *Meditations*.

Towards the end of the First Meditation, Descartes says: 'I am forced to admit that there are none of the things I used to think were true which may not possibly be doubted, and not because of carelessness or frivolity, but for sound and well considered reasons (*non per inconsideratiam vel levitatem, sed propter validas et meditatas rationes*).' The Haldane and Ross translation ('. . . for reasons which are very powerful and maturely considered . . .') is misleading because one might wonder what place the concept of a consideration which is 'maturely' considered has in the set of critical concepts which are available only to, and which are indeed, constitutive of, a *res cogitans*. (One might, by the same token, wonder what place the concept of 'frivolity' has.) Bernard Williams has rightly pointed out that the considerations or reasons which the *persona* of the First Meditation offers for his sceptical conclusions, are '*validae* because *meditatae*, sound just because they are well considered'.[12] If we leave aside the complexities of Descartes' epistemological psychology, then in this context 'well considered' basically amounts to repeatedly and carefully checking the argument. For a *res cogitans* seriously to profess a conclusion, just *is* for it to be 'forced to admit it' 'for sound and well considered reasons'; and the sense in which it is 'forced to admit it' is determined by the relatively spartan set of critical categories which mark the primary dimension of our critical vocabulary. That is the development of what is implicit in his criticism of the ancient sceptics.

We may now construct Descartes' answer to my suggestion that the sceptical conclusions of the *persona* of the First Meditation were merely 'blackboard' or inverted commas conclusions because they were conclusions which no one could seriously profess. He could acknowledge

[12] Bernard Williams, 'Descartes' Use of Skepticism', in Myles Burnyeat (ed.), *The Skeptical Tradition* (Berkeley, Los Angeles, London: The University of California Press, 1983).

that a conclusion which no one could seriously profess is a conclusion in inverted commas only, but he would say that there is an ambiguity in the concept of 'seriously concluding' which depends on the distinction between a conclusion which is professed by the *res cogitans* and one which is professed by the creature which is host to the *res cogitans*—in his case, between the meditating *persona* of the *Meditations* and himself as the author of that work. In the latter case, the concept of seriously professing a conclusion is interdependent with concepts which mark the ways in which considerations, beliefs and doubts are ruled out of consideration, and both of these are conditioned by the particular ways of living of the creatures which use such concepts. But pure philosophical thinking is thinking as it is for any thinking thing, and its subject matter is limited to what can be adequately assessed by the limited critical categories which define it. A *res cogitans* could no more lack sense or be mad than it could be drunk.

Bernard Williams calls Descartes' project the 'project of pure enquiry'.[13] The *persona* of the *Meditations* is the 'pure enquirer'. The phrase is apt for the description of the *persona* as I have characterized him. But it is worth noting the important differences between Williams' understanding of what is at issue, and mine.

Williams' conception of the pure enquirer starts from what he calls the 'very basic thought, that if knowledge is what it claims to be then it is knowledge of a reality which exists independently of that knowledge and, indeed, (except for the special case where the reality known happens itself to be some psychological item) independently of any thought or experience. Knowledge is of what is there *anyway*'.[14] He says that this appears obvious at first, but that it has, on closer inspection, the problematic implication that knowledge is possible only if we can conceive of how the world is independently of any perspective on it. Williams calls this 'the absolute conception of reality'. It is a conception of reality which Thomas Nagel graphically expressed when he said that the very concept of objective knowledge seems to require the idea of 'seeing the world as from no place within it'.[15]

My attention has been on something different. It has been on the question whether we can form an intelligible conception of what it is to think critically which is not conditioned by a particular form of life. Descartes assumes that we can extract such a conception from our ordinary understanding of critical enquiry, which would otherwise

[13] Bernard Williams, *Descartes: The Project of Pure Enquiry* (Harmondsworth: Penguin Books, 1978).

[14] Ibid. 64.

[15] Thomas Nagel, 'Subject and Object', in *Mortal Questions* (Cambridge: Cambridge University Press, 1981), 206.

condemn his project as frivolous and lacking 'sense'. Williams is concerned with whether we can form a conception of reality which is not as seen from some point of view. He is concerned with the ontological presuppositions of Descartes project: I am concerned with its logical presuppositions.

The question which I have been asking is, I believe, the more fundamental one, because any enquiry, including an enquiry into whether 'the absolute conception of reality' makes sense, must be an enquiry which reflects upon the critical concepts which condition it. Furthermore, for any finite enquirer, the idea of knowledge is the idea of knowledge as having been arrived at, and that involves critical reflection on the nature of one's journey. There can be no conception of knowledge for a finite enquirer which can bypass reflection on what such an enquirer can seriously profess. And although there has been much discussion of the conception of reality which Williams claims to be the presupposition of Descartes' enquiry, there has been virtually no discussion, in the mainstream of the subject, of how we should understand those concepts which, in my defence of Descartes, I demoted to a secondary status amongst the concepts which condition our understanding of the canons of critical enquiry.

IV

I have been taking what Descartes called sense to be a generic term for the ways we rule things out of consideration, and as meaning much the same as commonsense. The philosophical tradition has usually taken commonsense to be a *body of beliefs* which may be subject to criticism by an enquiry whose critical canons can be specified without reference to the forms of commonsense. I have focused on it, primarily, as a condition of sober, critical judgement. It is true that commonsense refers not only to a capacity for such judgement but also to certain beliefs, and these beliefs may be criticized and abandoned. However, they cannot sensibly be criticized in a spirit which suggests that we can rise above commonsense. But now, if we take sense as a capacity for sober judgement, whose forms are marked by the various ways we rule things out of consideration, then it cannot apply to something which is intelligible to us as thinking only if the categories which mark the forms of sense are inapplicable to it. Thus my earlier conclusion; that a *res cogitans* could no more possess or lack sense than it could be drunk.

A person who claims that he may be dreaming in circumstance such as are described in the *Meditations*, does not lack any of the forms of sense. He is not insane, gullible, naive or a crank. Descartes was, therefore, mistaken when he said in the *Synopsis* that the possession of

sense prevents one from entertaining such doubts. The possession of
sense prevents one from believing that one can bend spoons with one's
mind, or that one can read one's future in the stars, or that the lady in
the cafeteria might be trying to poison one, and things of that kind. It
does not prevent one from entertaining the belief that one may be
dreaming, or that there may be no other minds. Whatever Moore was
defending in his celebrated paper 'A Defence of Commonsense', it was
not commonsense.[16]

It is essential to the grammar of those concepts which mark out what
we must rule out of consideration under pain of madness, gullibility,
naivete and so on, that it is intelligible that someone should seriously
believe whatever inclines us to say he is mad, gullible, naive and so on.
There is no term in our critical vocabulary which names a defect which
is seriously to believe that there is no external world, that one may be
dreaming or that there are no other minds. Such a defect, if we could
seriously conceive it, could not even be a species of madness. We treat
these as merely 'philosophical beliefs' in the unflattering sense which
means that a philosopher's profession of them is 'mere words'. The
philosophical tradition has distorted the concept of commonsense in
suggesting that such doubts are not taken seriously because they conflict so radically with the entrenched beliefs of commonsense.

How then, may the traditional epistemologist, whether he be a
sceptic or an anti-sceptic, convince anyone that his doubt is serious.
The answer is that he cannot. The critical categories which define the
pure enquirer are too limited to allow for the concept of serious judgement and we are, therefore, left without any idea of what would be a
serious and sober profession of scepticism. When, in the previous
section, I said that for a *res cogitans* seriously to profess a conclusion
just *is* for it to profess it because it has repeatedly gone over an
argument, then I was not defining a plausible conception of sober
judgement for a special and restricted domain of enquiry: I was con-
fessing that the conditions for such a conception were absent.

There was never any doubt that the sceptic was sincere in believing
that he must profess his conclusions. But the lesson of the history of
sceptical equivocation is that something must close the gap between the

[16] The point is made especially powerfully by Wittgenstein when he com-
bines it with his radical insight that the reason we cannot doubt such things as
we are invited to doubt by traditional sceptics, is not because we are so
epistemically secure in this region. We do not believe or know that there is an
external world, that there are other minds, that we are now awake: *a fortiori*,
these are not beliefs of commonsense. I know I am awake; I know that there are
other minds: these are pseudo epistemological claims. See Ludwig Wittgenstein, *On Certainty*, trans. Denis Paul and G. E. M. Anscombe (Oxford:
Blackwell, 1969).

sincere profession of scepticism and the serious profession of it, and it cannot be going over the argument, earnestly and carefully, yet again. One can sincerely profess something as one's belief yet it be 'mere words'. The sceptic must convince himself it is not so with him. The paradox of scepticism is that the only way he can even appear to do this, is by invoking a contrast between a concern for truth and 'the practical activities of our life' which, when pressed, must reveal to him the incoherence of his idealization of radical inquiry. The deep lesson is that a seriously professed conclusion of a process of reasoning must be someone's conclusion, in a sense which is more substantial than can be conveyed in the idea of a thinking subject who is purified from some actual subject, living a form of life which determines the critical concepts which mark the forms of sober judgement. That is an anti-transcendental lesson whose implications reach far beyond a concern with scepticism.[17]

[17] I am very grateful to David Cockburn for helpful comments on an earlier draft of this paper.

Getting the Subject back into the World: Heidegger's Version

FERGUS KERR

I

In a footnote to the preface to the second edition of his *Critique of Pure Reason* (1787) Kant remarked that 'it still remains a scandal to philosophy and to human reason in general that the existence [*Dasein*] of things outside us . . . must be accepted on *faith*, and that if anyone thinks good to doubt their existence, we are unable to counter his doubts by any satisfactory proof' (B XL). In *Being and Time* (1927) Heidegger remarks, somewhat less famously, that the scandal of philosophy, far from being the continuing absence of philosophically satisfactory proof of the existence of the world outside human subjectivity, is rather the very idea that such proof need be sought at all: 'If *Dasein* is understood correctly, it defies such proofs, because, in its being, it already *is* what subsequent proofs deem necessary to demonstrate for it' (*BT*, 205).[1]

In other words, the familiar problems of scepticism about the existence of the external world collapse as soon as the place of human beings in the world is properly identified—an attractive thesis, if Heidegger can substantiate it. We need seek no 'proofs'; we need only remind ourselves of the facts. We are, from the outset, beings-in-the-world. There is no problem about the relation between subjectivity and the objective world. How we are is revelatory of the world. Heidegger's choice of the ordinary word *'Dasein'*, meaning 'existence' as in the Kant quotation, to designate the manner of being enjoyed by creatures like ourselves, is of course arbitrary and idiosyncratic, but his purpose is to exploit the word's etymological structure. To say that our way of being is *'Dasein'*, 'being there', is to say that it is a way of *being*, rather than of just *knowing* (as the Cartesian tradition suggests), and it is a way of being already *situated*, rather than of having still to bridge some supposed gulf between subjective consciousness and the external world.

[1] Martin Heidegger, *Sein und Zeit* (1927), trans. John Macquarrie and Edward Robinson as *Being and Time* (London: SCM Press, 1962), cited as *BT*, with the original pagination in the margins.

Fergus Kerr

Whether such terms of art could ever dispose of Cartesian inclinations seems doubtful. But what generates these inclinations in the first place? Why does the Cartesian picture of the subject of consciousness as only contingently related to the external world have any hold on anybody's imagination at all? How far back in the history of philosophy, or how deeply into the genealogy of our culture, do we have to go to discover the source of its power and plausibility?

According to Heidegger, it is Christian theology which bears responsiblity for leading our understanding of ourselves so far off the track that our sense of ourselves as human beings is lost in variations on the myth of the subject as a worldless 'I'. This suggestion is surely intriguing enough to deserve some examination. It would have to be by way of expelling what remains of Christian theology in modern philosophy that we could get the subject of consciousness back into the real world. Philosophers who have long since left theism behind might turn out to have undisclosed theological debts. External world scepticism (the problem of Other Minds) would be secretly trading on a certain theological inheritance. Getting the subject of consciousness back into the world would thus be partly, and perhaps even essentially, an anti-theological task.

II

Heidegger writes as follows:

> [W]hat stands in the way of the basic question of *Dasein*'s being (or leads it off the track) is an orientation thoroughly coloured by the anthropology of Christianity and the ancient world, whose inadequate ontological foundations have been overlooked both by the philosophy of life and by personalism. (*BT*, 48)

Philosophical understanding of what human beings are is thus, at least partly, blocked by theological presuppositions. The very question of the character of the human way of being in the world is confused, so Heidegger claims, by the continuing hegemony of *die antik-christliche Anthropologie*: that conception of what it is to be human in which themes from classical Greek philosophy fuse with Christian considerations to generate a picture of the self by which we are still held captive. That is Heidegger's claim here. Neither Dilthey's *Lebensphilosophie* nor Scheler's personalism succeeded in dislodging this picture, for all their anti-Cartesian efforts, which have been quite positively assessed in the immediately preceding pages of *Being and Time*. Heidegger aims to be more radical.

The picture which we have inherited is composed of two elements, one Greek and the other biblical. In the first place, 'man' is defined as 'something living which has reason': *zoon logon ekhon*. The *logos* is treated as 'some superior endowment', but its ontological character remains as unexamined as that of the *zoon*. What has never been properly noticed, so Heidegger says, is that 'the kind of being which belongs to a *zoon* is understood in the sense of occurring and being-present-at-hand', *im Sinne des Vorhandenseins und Vorkommens*. Reason, animality, or 'the entire entity thus compounded'—everything is envisaged in terms of that which is *vorhanden*. In effect, everything is envisaged on the model of physical objects. We return to this point below.

The second element which distorts our self-conception is the biblical one—'And God said, Let us make man in our own image, after our likeness' (Gen. 1,26). This text, according to Heidegger, is what generates the idea of 'transcendence'—'that man is something that reaches beyond himself' (*BT*, 49). He picks texts by Calvin and Zwingli to illustrate his point:

> Man's first condition was excellent because of these outstanding endowments: that reason, intelligence, prudence, judgment should suffice not only for the government of this earthly life, but by them he might *ascend beyond* (*transcenderet*, Heidegger's emphasis), even unto God and to eternal felicity.

The Zwingli text runs as follows:

> Because man *looks up* [*ufsehen*] to God and his Word, he indicates clearly that in his very nature he is born somewhat closer to God, to something more *after His stamp*, that he has something that *draws him to* [*zuzugs zu*] God—all this comes beyond a doubt from his having been created in God's *image*.

The point of Heidegger's underlinings, in both quotations, is (I think) to suggest that the biblical doctrine that man is created in the image of God encourages the thought of an immediate, or unmediated, relationship between man and God—*cutting out the world*. The idea of the worldless self would thus be the product of a certain obliviousness of the world which the Christian dogma about the creature's relationship to the creator might appear to promote. Heidegger's evidence, effectively limited to these two quotations, may seem thin, but they are presumably intended simply to be symptomatic.

But Heidegger says no more about this. On the contrary, he drops the idea and refers instead to our alleged predilection for seeing everything in the perspective of the *vorhanden*. The theologically generated story might have been to the effect that the Greek definition of human beings in terms of *logos* fused with the biblical notion of the rational creature as God's image to create a sense of the transcendence of the human to the divine which, if not directly involving an ascetical *contemptus mundi*, at least rendered the world something external and occasional. In modern times, as Heidegger says, this description of the self has been 'de-theologized' (*BT*, 49); but the idea of transcendence— 'that man is something that reaches beyond himself'—remains in place, and it is 'rooted in Christian dogmatics'. But Heidegger interweaves a quite different story:

> The two sources which are relevant for the traditional anthropology—the Greek definition and the clue which theology has provided—indicate that over and above the attempt to determine the essence of 'man' as an entity, the question of his being has remained forgotten, and that this being is rather conceived as something obvious or 'self-evident' in the sense of the *being-present-at-hand* [*Vorhandensein*] of other created things. (*BT*, 49)

The intriguing suggestion that Christian theology might have prompted and propagated such a deep sense of the intimate communion of the soul with the divine that the world would fall into oblivion and the worldless 'I' come to prominence, gives way to the more prosaic-sounding thesis that we are inclined to see human beings, and everything else, in terms of *Vorhandenheit*. That is the notion which we need to explore, and it appears to have little to do with theology.

III

Yet the myth of the worldless 'I' *is* one of the nefarious effects which Christian theology has bequeathed to modern philosophy—so Heidegger insists (*BT*, 229). There are, as he says, 'residues of Christian theology within philosophical problematics which have not as yet been radically extruded'. Once again, then, he makes the intriguing suggestion that certain problems in modern philosophy might owe their form, or even their existence, to unacknowledged and unexpunged theological considerations. Once again, might it not be the case that certain of the more inveterate problems in modern philosophy would resolve themselves once a hidden theological agenda had been discovered and disavowed?

Heidegger offers two examples of alleged theological residues in philosophy, the first of which is the contention that there are 'eternal truths'. The discussion need not detain us here. Heidegger's point is simply that there can be no truths—no true principles or propositions—without human beings to hold them. 'All truth', he says, 'is relative to *Dasein*'s being' (*BT*, 227). Before Newton's day, to take Heidegger's own example here, his laws were neither true nor false—

they simply did not exist. This does not mean that what his laws showed
to be the case did not exist until he formulated them. On the contrary,
the entities, states of affairs, and so on, which Newton's laws
'uncovered', as Heidegger puts it, certainly existed. But for his laws
certain things about the world should not have come to light. That is all
that Heidegger means. If there were no *Dasein*, if there were no beings
in the world in the way we are, things would be just as we suppose them
to be but it would not be true or false that they are so—unless there is an
'ideal subject', enjoying a God's eye view.

This brings us to the second remnant of Christian theology in
modern philosophy—'the jumbling together of *Dasein*'s phenomenally
grounded "ideality" with an idealized absolute subject' (*BT*, 229). This
may be spelled out as follows. The mindedness which human beings
enjoy is embedded in the various phenomena in which the human way
of being in the world is displayed. These phenomena can be
described—indeed the greater part of *Being and Time* is an attempt at
such description. Heidegger's claim here is that we are inclined to
misconceive our mindedness ('ideality') because we are bewitched by
the notion of an 'ideal subject'—*ein phantastisch idealisiertes Subjekt*,
an illusory construction, a conception of the subject which is a fantasy,
in effect the myth of the worldless 'I'.

The motive for this illusory conception, Heidegger says, lies in the
requirement that philosophy should deal with the '*a priori*' and not with
'empirical data'. It is for scientists to deal with empirical data; philosophers are concerned with the transcendental conditions of experience.
There is something in this requirement, Heidegger allows. But the
philosophers with whom he is familiar, and against whom he inveighs
here, assume that the *a priori* of subjectivity is secured by notions such
as 'pure I' and 'consciousness as such'. (I take it that Husserl is his chief
target, but the tradition goes back through Fichte and Kant to
Descartes.) For Heidegger, however, when the subject of consciousness is redescribed as *Dasein*, the *a priori* of subjectivity turns out
to be familiar facts of life. Far from capturing the *a priori* conditions of
subjectivity, notions such as 'pure I' and 'consciousness' simply obscure
the realities in which the human way of being is grounded. In effect, it
does not protect the distinctive character of human subjectivity to
remove it from the ordinary everyday world. When philosophers try to
grasp the essence of something such as that which distinguishes human
beings from other creatures, they have been inclined to postulate
metaphysical entities like 'pure I' and 'consciousness'. Heidegger rec-
ommends that such notions be eschewed and that we rediscover the
transcendental conditions of being human in facts of life such as he has
already been describing in his phenomenology of *Dasein*.

Fergus Kerr

But what has this to do with residual theological considerations? Nothing, at least in so many words. Throughout *Being and Time*, however, Heidegger repeatedly mocks the notion of the Cartesian self in such terms that it gradually becomes clear that his implication is that only a god would fit the picture. The 'knowing subject', whose way of being is customarily left unexamined in epistemological discussions (*BT*, 60), is plainly *'das Geistding'* (56), the 'isolated subject' (118), *'das Ichding'* (119), and, above all, the 'bare subject without a world' (116)—for short, the 'worldless subject' (206). In *Being and Time*, after all, Heidegger is out to show that our way of being (as he would put it) is essentially a way of being in *time*. He starts from the conviction, that is to say, that, in traditional epistemological discussions, we set aside, or tend simply to forget, the historical and temporal nature of the cognitive subject. What he is suggesting, in effect, is that the subject of consciousness which dominates epistemology (including external world scepticism and so on) is the image of the only being who putatively exists outside the world and time, free of history and independent of all other beings—none other than the deity, as traditionally conceived.

IV

The notion of transcendence—'that man is something that reaches beyond himself' (*BT*, 49)—plays a considerable role in Heidegger's work. One might even say that his work is an attempt to show that, when human beings go in for this kind of reaching beyond themselves, their goal is not the deity but the world. In a sense, then, he wants to free the notion of transcendence from theological associations.

One version of Heidegger's story goes as follows. The notion of transcendence—surpassing, going beyond—implies that there is something transcendent: 'that toward which the surpassing takes place, that which requires surpassing in order to be accessible and attainable, the beyond, that which is over against' (*MFL*, 204).[2] But the concept of the transcendent has a history: it has always been contrasted with notions of the immanent and the contingent.

The concept of the transcendent which has the immanent as its contrary gives rise to epistemology, so Heidegger maintains. The immanent, as he starts by saying, is 'that which is in the subject, within the soul, remaining in consciousness'. This is surely not the definition

[2] Heidegger, *The Metaphysical Foundations of Logic*, trans. Michael Heim (Bloomington: Indiana University Press, 1984), cited as *MFL*, the text of a lecture course at Marburg in 1928.

which would immediately occur to most philosophers. Heidegger seems to be working with the distinction, familiar in Scholastic philosophy, between an act which is performed entirely within the mind of the subject, and produces no external effect, and is in that sense *immanent*, and an act which, in this jargon, is *transient*, in the sense that it makes some difference in the world. At any rate, the transcendent is 'that which does not remain within but is without, what lies *outside* the soul and consciousness'.

Heidegger at once reformulates this, exposing the metaphor in the definition: 'What is outside the borders and encompassing wall of consciousness has then, spoken from the inmost yard of this consciousness, surpassed the enclosing wall and stands outside'. Speaking from inside (how else, since the first person point of view is being taken for granted), the transcendent is what lies beyond the enclosure wall. 'Here the subject', as Heidegger goes on to say, 'is thought of [*vorgestellt*: pictured] as a sort of box with an interior, with the walls of a box, and with an exterior'. Of course, as he says, nobody supposes that our minds are really in any kind of box—but the analogy prevails: '[it] belongs to the very conception of the transcendent . . . that a barrier between inner and outer must be crossed'. We remain strongly inclined to picture our minds as having to break out of some kind of enclosure to reach the world outside. (Compare Wittgenstein's remark: 'The idea of thinking as a process in the head, in a completely enclosed space, makes it something occult', *Zettel* 606, retranslated.) Getting to know the world outside the subject's consciousness seems to mean 'leaping over or pressing through the wall of the box', 'crossing a barrier or border'. But all this depends for plausibility on the picture of consciousness as encapsulated: *die Kapsel-Vorstellung vom Subjekt* (*MFL*, 205).

The transcendent, then, when subjectivity is pictured as somehow encapsulated, has to be something external and objective: 'something on hand outside' which is at the same time 'that which stands over against'.

The transcendent is also contradistinguishable from the contingent: 'The contingent is what touches us, what pertains to us, that with which we are on the same footing, that which belongs to our kind and sort' (*MFL*, 206). In contrast with this, then, the transcendent is 'what is beyond all this as that which conditions it, as the unconditioned, but at the same time as the really unattainable, what exceeds us'. That to which transcendence transcends, as Heidegger now says, is 'what lies beyond the contingent'. This need not be God 'as understood by Christians', but it 'always means the unconditioned, the Absolute in some form or other'—and this means, in effect, 'the divine'.

179

Fergus Kerr

Thus, in Heidegger's view, there are two notions of transcendence and of the transcendent. The first trades on the picture of consciousness as encapsulated and gives rise to traditional epistemological problems about knowing the external world. The second sees everything as conditioned by the absolute. Historically, so Heidegger suggests, without adducing any evidence at this point, these two notions of the transcendent keep becoming entangled with each other. Evidence is not needed here because he clearly believes such entanglements are inevitable:

> For once the epistemological conception of transcendence is granted, whether expressly or implicitly, then a being is posited outside the subject, and it stands over against the latter. Among the beings posited opposite, however, is something which towers above everything, the cause of all. It is thus both something over against [the subject] and something which transcends all conditioned beings over against [the subject]. The transcendent, in this double sense, is the Eminent, the being that surpasses and exceeds all experience. So, inquiry into the possible constitution of the transcendent in the epistemological sense is bound up with inquiry into the possibility of knowing the transcendent object in the theological sense. (*MFL*, 207)

Indeed, Heidegger concludes, it is the question of having rational knowledge of God which motivates interest in epistemology: 'The problem of the existence of the external world and whether it can be known is implicated in the problem of the knowledge of God and the possibility of proving God's existence'.

It is difficult not to feel that Heidegger's connections have been made much too quickly. That epistemology (external world scepticism and so on) might be tied up with natural theology (theistic proofs and so on) seems an interesting and not implausible proposal; but, as so often, Heidegger leaves it tantalizingly sketchy. The most notable point theologically is, however, that God as 'cause of all' is said to appear 'among the beings posited opposite' the subject—towering above them admittedly, but still 'among' them. It is true that, in our culture at least, people are strongly inclined to take God to be one item among the others with which we have to do (although the supreme and eternal one, no doubt)—whether or not they are theists. It is equally clear, on the other hand, that the greatest efforts of such central Christian thinkers as Augustine, Thomas Aquinas, Luther, and so on, have gone into insisting that God is *not* one being among others—something which Heidegger must surely have known, from his interest in Eckhart if from nowhere else.

Thus, even if the linkage between epistemology and natural theology had not been settled too rapidly, it might in any case be a misconception of God with which Heidegger operated here. The theology which continues to distort philosophy, as he thinks, might be exactly what the classical theologians sought to eliminate from theology.

V

But Heidegger's attitude to Christian theology, although hostile at one level, is also proprietorial. Time and again, in *Being and Time*, he appropriates some Christian theme. Almost every conceptual innovation in the book may easily be traced to a theological source.

Heidegger does not conceal these Christian sources. The phenomenon of *Angst*, of which he makes so much, while it may never have been properly acknowledged by philosophers, has received attention in Christian theology: he refers us to passages in Augustine, Luther, and Kierkegaard (*BT*, 190, footnote). The even more important notion of 'care', *Sorge*, is related to the Stoic notion of *merimna* but also to the New Testament notion (*BT*, 199, footnote): 'The way in which "care" is viewed in the foregoing existential analytic of *Dasein* is one which has grown upon the author in connection with his attempts to interpret the Augustinian (i.e. Helleno-Christian) anthropology with regard to the foundational principles reached in the ontology of Aristotle'. Thirdly, and most significantly of all for Heidegger, it is in Christian theology— 'from Paul right up to Calvin's *meditatio futurae vitae*'—that the phenomenon of mortality has been brought to bear upon (philosophical) anthropology (*BT*, 249, footnote).

That does not exhaust the list of key Heideggerian notions which owe a great deal to Christian inspiration. The three just mentioned do, however, characterize human beings in a way that undermines the conception of the self as a centre of rational consciousness. To insist on affectivity, involvement and finitude—on human beings as in (or out of) tune with their situation, inescapably concerned (even if seeking to take flight), and living under the shadow of death—is to shake off the myth of the self as a purely rational, disengaged and timeless entity. The notion of the 'transcendental ego' collapses under pressure from the New Testament.

But it is above all the idea of 'world', and thus of 'being-in-the-world', which Heidegger develops from theological sources. That this is so is barely visible in *Being and Time* itself, but other writings of the time make it clear. In effect, it is the Christian notion of being *in* this world but not *of* it that enables Heidegger's anti-Cartesian project to get going. If it is the Christian anthropology that generates the misunder-

Fergus Kerr

standing of the human way of being which is the myth of the isolated worldless subject (as we have seen Heidegger claim), then it turns out, somewhat paradoxically, that it is reflection on primitive Christian language and experience that supplies the notion of 'being-in-the-world' which so easily deflates that myth. The (allegedly) theologically generated fantasy of the worldless subject is thus subverted by the theologically rooted notion of the subject as always already being in the world.

In *The Essence of Reasons*[3] Heidegger tells the following story about the notion of 'world' as he wants us to understand it. Invoking the work of the classical scholar Karl Reinhardt, he first tells us that, in ancient philosophy, the word for 'world'—*kosmos*—means neither some particular entity nor the sum of all entities. But his airy allusion to fragments of pre-Socratics carry little conviction. His relief is perceptible when he turns to the New Testament:

> It is no accident that in connection with the new ontical understanding of existence that appeared in Christianity the relationship of *kosmos* to human *Dasein*, and so even the concept of world, was focused and clarified. This relationship was experienced so profoundly that *kosmos* thereafter came to signify a basic type of human existence. In Paul (cf. I Corinthians and Galatians), *kosmos houtos* ['this world'] means not merely, or even primarily, the condition of the 'cosmic', but the condition and the situation of *man*, the character of his stance *with regard to* the cosmos and of his evaluation of what is good. (*ER*, 51)

In other words, when Paul refers to 'this world', he means the human condition as such, rather than the universe as the subject of cosmology, geography, and so on. With New Testament Christianity, so Heidegger is claiming here, a new sense emerged of the place of man in the world—a new sense, rather, of how the things of this world *matter* to human beings.

Heidegger clearly thinks that Christianity introduced a new sense of the human condition which prepares the way for his notion of human beings as moral agents who are always already 'in-the-world'. The reference to the Epistle to the Galatians is not much help: the phrase 'this world' does not occur. Heidegger must be thinking of the phrase 'the present evil age (*aion*)', which appears once (Galatians 1,4): it comes to much the same thing as 'this world'. In the First Epistle to the Corinthians, however, there are several references to 'this world'—for

[3] Heidegger, *The Essence of Reasons*, trans. Terrence Malick (Evanston: Northwestern University Press, 1969), cited as *ER*, from *Vom Wesen des Grundes*, first published in a *Festschrift* for Edmund Husserl (1929).

182

example: 'the wisdom of this world' (3,19), 'the fornicators of this world' (5,10), and 'the form of this world' (7,31). In context, and backed up by more than a dozen references to 'the world' *tout court*, nobody could doubt that Paul here develops a profound sense of 'the world' as the network of interests, opportunities and temptations in which human beings find themselves.

Heidegger goes on to cite the Fourth Gospel, with the following conclusions:

> The Gospel of John uses the concept of *kosmos* with uncommon frequency—particularly in contrast with the Synoptic Gospels—and at the same time in a very central sense. 'World' stands for the basic form of human *Dasein* as estranged from God or, more simply, the *character of being human* [*Menschsein*]. 'World' is also, then, a regional term for the whole of mankind [*alle Menschen zusammen*], without distinction of wise men and fools, righteous men and sinners, Jews and Gentiles. The central meaning of this wholly anthropological concept of world is expressed in its function as an opposing concept to the divine filiation of Jesus, which is itself conceived as life, truth and light. (*ER*, 53)

Nobody would doubt that the word 'world' is of central importance in the Fourth Gospel, nor that it means the world as it is related to human beings as moral agents, rather than simply the physical universe. The world becomes identified, particularly in the second half of the Gospel, with those men who turned against Jesus, and a note of hostility attaches itself to the word. But it is clear that the Johanine concept of 'world' is 'anthropological' in the sense that it refers to the world as always already morally significant.[4]

Heidegger continues for several pages with his history of the concept of 'world'. This New Testament coinage, as he claims it to be, becomes standard usage in Augustine and Thomas Aquinas—and the evidence provided seems sound. By the early eighteenth century, however, in such authorities as Baumgarten and Crusius, in the wake of Christian Wolff, the concept loses its anthropological connections and comes to mean 'the entirety of natural things'. In Kant's work, then, while the word 'world' ordinarily means the physical universe, the 'existential' meaning reappears—'without its peculiarly Christian nuances' (*ER*, 61). The specifically Christian sense of the world as a permanent temptation to sin (although of course not intrinsically evil) drops away, so Heidegger says, leaving the purely anthropological sense of 'world' which he wants to exploit.

[4] See *The Gospel according to John*, trans. with an introduction and notes by Raymond E. Brown (New York: Doubleday, 1966), Volume 1, 508–9.

It is thus from Christian sources that Heidegger develops the anthropological concept of 'world' which enables him to characterize human beings as being always already engaged as moral agents in a public order of common interests, needs and attachments. The self no longer appears as a worldless consciousness which has occasionally to negotiate a relationship with objects in a physical universe. That picture ceases to be plausible. Rather, human beings are revealed from the outset as so absorbed in a humanly significant world that detachment has to be a rare and difficult enterprise.

Paradoxically, then, the residue of Christian theology in modern philosophy which is the conception of the worldless subject begins to disappear as soon as we remember the Christian notion of 'this world': the network of values, opportunities and temptations with which human beings always have to cope. The fantasy of the unrelated subject which Heidegger claims to be a theologically motivated creation collapses when we attend to the central New Testament notion of our 'this-worldly' condition. What theology is it, then, that has to be eliminated from modern philosophy to clear the way for a proper understanding of what it is to be a human being?

VI

Heidegger's suggestions, as he was the first to say, often turn out to be *Holzwege* (the title of one of his most important collections of essays): tempting paths in a forest which finally lead nowhere. The intriguing idea with which we started, that the Cartesian self might be the residue of a Christian disregard for the world, led to nothing: we were left with some unfinished business about the apparently quite non-theological notion of *Vorhandenheit* (Section II). On the other hand, Heidegger repeatedly mocks the worldless self in such terms that it becomes the mirror image of a transcendent being, free of space and time—something remarkably like God (Section III). Heidegger's analysis of the notion of the transcendent includes an unwary reference to God as a being among the others with which the subject has to do—a conception which makes one wonder what theology it is, precisely, that needs to be expunged from philosophy (Section IV). Paradoxically, it is to the New Testament notion of the world as the morally significant order in which human beings are always already involved that Heidegger appeals to subvert the myth of the worldless subject (Section V).

In short, it begins to look as if Heidegger's project to rescue human beings from the illusions of the Cartesian myth draws on Christian theology as much as it seeks to eliminate it. Brief discussion of two further notions in *Being and Time* will confirm this ambivalence.

Getting the Subject back into the World: Heidegger's Version

The human way of existing is, according to the anthropological view of the world, always already a multiplicity of ways of evaluating things, whether as opportunities, obstacles, temptations or whatever. Once we give up 'the naive supposition that man is, in the first instance, *ein Geistding* which subsequently gets misplaced "into" a space', we can see the ways in which our being is essentially responsiveness, involvement, concern, *Sorge*: 'having to do with something, producing something, attending to something and looking after it, making use of something, giving something up and letting it go, undertaking, accomplishing, evincing, interrogating, considering, discussing, determining . . .' (*BT*, 56). There are also 'ways of concern' which are 'deficient'—such as 'leaving undone, neglecting, renouncing, taking a rest'. And one way of disengaging from involvement with things is the fateful move in which we learn to see them simply as objects of contemplation rather than as obstacles or opportunities. There is a way of relating to things which unhooks them from their connections with one another and with everything else, allowing us to objectivize them as isolated particulars in a neutral space. We might say that this is the most decisive feature of our culture: the possibility of acquiring an impartial spectator's point of view, submitting ourselves as self-effacingly as possible to things as they must be, independently of human interests and needs.[5]

The fateful side to this modification of the human way of dealing with things in the world, according to Heidegger's story, is that we are tempted to picture ourselves as most characteristically impartial spectators in a hurly-burly of bare particulars. The attractions of such atomism have to be resisted—with such considerations as this:

> What we 'first' hear is never noises or complexes of sounds, but the creaking waggon, the motor-cycle. We hear the column on the march, the north wind, the woodpecker tapping, the fire crackling. It requires a very artificial and complicated frame of mind to 'hear' a 'pure noise'. The fact that motor-cycles and waggons are what we proximally hear is the phenomenal evidence that in every case *Dasein*, as being-in-the-world, already dwells *alongside* what is ready-to-hand [*zuhanden*] within-the-world; it certainly does not dwell proximally alongside 'sensations'; nor would it first have to give shape to the swirl of sensations to provide the springboard from which the subject leaps off and finally arrives at a 'world'. *Dasein*, as essentially understanding, is proximally alongside what is understood.' (*BT*, 163–4)

[5] See Charles B. Guignon, *Heidegger and the Problem of Knowledge* (Indianapolis: Hackett, 1983).

This 'anthropologistic pragmatism', as Ryle called it in his famous review of *Sein und Zeit*,[6] is by now a familiar strategy in the retreat from atomistic conceptions.

The difference between things as they affect us (as opportunities or obstacles, and so on) and things (the same things often) deliberately disengaged from their human context for impartial study or contemplation is, in Heidegger's jargon, the difference between what is 'ready-to-hand' (*zuhanden*) and what is simply 'present-at-hand' (*vorhanden*). In his most famous example, the hammer which the craftsman judges to be too heavy or too light in this or that situation can become 'a corporeal thing subject to the law of gravity' (*BT*, 361).

Heidegger's campaign against the myth of the worldless subject of course includes an attack on the notion of the isolated 'I'—'To avoid this misunderstanding we must notice in what sense we are talking about "the Others". By "Others" we do not mean everyone else but me—those over against whom the "I" stands out. They are rather those from whom, for the most part, one does *not* distinguish oneself—those among whom one is too' (*BT*, 118). We are always already responsive to one another, with detachment, aloofness, solitariness, and so on, as 'deficient modes' of our initial solidarity. Other people—other minds— are not 'proximally present-at-hand as free-floating subjects along with things' (*BT*, 123). No doubt, people can be removed from their morally significant context, for example to be weighed and measured in various ways, and thus they become *vorhanden*. But initially and normally— 'proximally'—others are disclosed, as Heidegger says, 'in concernful solicitude' (*BT*, 124).

Heidegger thus sees the need to warn us against treating other people as if they ordinarily fall under the description of being merely *vorhanden*. More remarkably, however, he also finds it necessary to warn us that *Dasein* is not, as presumably we might be inclined to think, *ein Vorhandenes*, 'something present-at-hand', to which certain mental capacities might then be ascribed (*BT*, 143). So powerful is the temptation to treat everything as if it first appeared bereft of all human significance that even the expression specially invented to protect human existence from being so reductively conceived might be contaminated. Still more interestingly, in his discussion of how the subject receives its bearings in the humanly significant world, Heidegger remarks that what is ready-to-hand (*zuhanden*) 'is certainly not present-at-hand (*vorhanden*) for an eternal observer exempt from *Dasein*' (*BT*, 106). He at once again insists that human *Dasein* is not 'a corporeal thing which is present-at-hand'—some *vorhandenes Kör-*

---

[6] Originally published in *Mind 38* (1929), reprinted in Gilbert Ryle, *Collected Papers* (London: Hutchinson, 1971), Volume 1, 197–214.

perding. But what is this *Dasein*-exempt eternal observer but God? Why does Heidegger feel obliged to warn us against thinking that the *zuhanden* in our human world might appear as something *vorhanden* to an eternal observer? What notion of the deity do we have to have if we are to be inclined to think any such thing? Who needs to be warned against the idea of a neutral deity with a perspective on the world and the relationships and states of affairs within it which deprives them of all human significance?

Heidegger's warning here may seem casual and insubstantial, but is it not such apparently negligible stray remarks which reveal—betray—a philosopher's private agenda? In this instance, at any rate, whatever the theology with which Heidegger is operating here, it has nothing to do with Christianity.

VII

No doubt we need to remember the priority of the *zuhanden* over the *vorhanden*: impartial and objective procedures come late. If we are inclined to forget this, and Heidegger starts from the assumption that we are so inclined, then it cannot be from *Christian* theology that our inclination draws strength and plausibility. Whatever the attractions of a notion of the deity as an eternal observer who brackets out the human contribution to the cosmic scene, and it would not take much ingenuity to fill out some such notion, it could not be described as Christian. Christianity seems, rather, to have an obsessively anthropocentric notion of the deity.

In *Being and Time* Heidegger introduces one further notion which we need to consider—that of 'falling', *Verfallen*. Ryle, before declaring that 'the fog becomes too thick', perceptively suspects that, by this stage, Heidegger is 'reviving important Augustinian theses which lead one to wonder if the second [never published] part of this work will not be a sort of Eckhart philosophy in phenomenological clothing'.[7] Heidegger scornfully repudiates the thought that his new-found 'ontological' notion of 'falling' might be reduced to Christian talk about the 'corruption of human nature', whether man is 'drunk with sin', and suchlike (*BT*, 179–80). As with the expression 'this world' (cf. Section V), Heidegger clearly thinks that the notion of 'falling' can be disentangled from its connections in the Christian religion and put to work in what Ryle calls his 'anthropologistic metaphysic'. What were originally themes in a religion which people professed and practised now become available for *non*-religious purposes. It may be hard to believe that the

[7] Ibid. 210.

notion of humankind as 'fallen' could be freed of its theological matrix, but, in the extensive thought-experiment which is *Being and Time*, Heidegger clearly does try to revive certain Christian theses, radically secularizing them, in order to develop a phenomenology of the human condition in which no theological residue would remain.

'Falling', about which Heidegger writes a great deal, refers to an inescapable tendency which he thinks we human beings have to overlook or deny our place in the (anthropologically conceived) world, as this is provided by our necessarily having 'projects' and by our being irreversibly 'cast' in unchosen circumstances. Our lives are constituted by 'thrownness', *Geworfenheit*—roughly speaking, our being conditioned by our past; and by 'projection', *Entwurf*, our having to keep pressing forward one way or another. It is a simple idea. Aristotle (we may say) sought to show that the mind is both active and passive; Kant, in turn, tried to hold together a theory of knowledge which treated learning about the world as a finding, with one that regarded such learning as also a construction. Heidegger, then, moving from epistemology to philosophical anthropology, reminds us that our lives, as well as our knowledge, are constituted by what we do, given what we have inherited, with the possibilities open to us. The idea is so simple that it comes to no more than that we can, and indeed cannot but, make something of ourselves—but always within inescapable limits. (What we inherit may of course free us, as well as restrict our possibilities.)

Where falling comes in is as follows, according to Heidegger's story.[8] There is something frustrating about being an inheritor:

> As being, *Dasein* is something that has been thrown; it has been brought into its 'there', but *not* of its own accord. . . . As existent, it never comes back behind its thrownness . . . In being a basis—that is, in existing as thrown—*Dasein* constantly lags behind its possibilities. It is never existent *before* its basis, but only *from it* and *as this basis*. Thus 'being-a-basis' means *never* to have power over one's ownmost being from the ground up. This 'not' belongs to the existential meaning of 'thrownness'. (*BT*, 284)

What that ugly set of remarks—little less rebarbative in the original German—comes to is simply that we are never in a position to begin our lives from scratch. The negative aspect of our having a history is that we are never the ground, or cause, of our existence.

In the structure of 'projection, as in that of 'being thrown', there is another negative element:

---

[8] See John Richardson, *Existential Epistemology: a Heideggerian Critique of the Cartesian Project* (Oxford: Clarendon Press, 1986).

> *Dasein* is its basis existently—that is, in such a manner that it understands itself in terms of possibilities, and, as so understanding itself, is that entity which has been thrown. But this implies that in having a potentiality for being it always stands in one possibility or another: it constantly is *not* other possibilities . . . Freedom . . . *is* only the choice of *one* possibility—that is, in tolerating one's not having chosen the others and one's not being able to choose them. (*BT*, 285).

Again the thought is simple enough. As we pursue this course of action rather than that, make this choice instead of the alternative, realize this possibility rather than some other one, we necessarily waive innumerable unrealizable options.

'Falling', according to Heidegger's story, is our inveterate tendency to ignore or deny these negative aspects to our lives. In particular, we immerse ourselves in our present concerns, ignoring our debt to the past as well as our vulnerability as regards what is to come. Many pages of *Being and Time* are devoted to describing, in considerable detail, the many strategies which we adopt in everyday life to avoid acknowledging how contingent our lives are. We should of course now have to dip into these pages to see how true to life Heidegger's observations might be. It suffices for our purposes here, however, just to note that what our putative tendency to 'fall' amounts to, in Heidegger's story, is our skill at overlooking our historical character and our limited possibilities. What he is saying, in effect, is that, if we commonly live obliviously of our contingency (and that is a big 'if'!), it is because we entertain secret aspirations to divinity. To say that one is never ground of one's own being (*causa sui*) and that one is never the total actualization of all one's possibilities (*actus purus*) is, in traditional theological language, to say that one is not God. Our way of being in the world could seem so defective only because we compare it, unwittingly no doubt, with the way of being and knowing appropriate only to God. There may indeed be a subject who is unbound by the world but that would have to be a subject so omnipotent that he created himself *ex nihilo* and so infinite that he actualized all his possibilities.

Heidegger's version of getting the subject back into the world thus displays a deeply ambivalent attitude towards Christian theology. He may say that the myth of the worldless subject would collapse if the last remnants of theology were expelled from philosophy, but the notion of the deity with which he operates seems quite un-Christian (Sections IV and VI). On the other hand, when he sketches the philosophical anthropology which he offers as the alternative to the Cartesian myth, he appropriates, naturalizes and develops certain manifestly Christian themes—'this world' (Section V), and 'falling' (Section VII). It is not so much a matter of ridding modern philosophy of residual theology, then, as of naturalizing some ancient theological themes in order to develop a philosophical anthropology which takes better account of the human condition.[9]

[9] I am grateful to David Cockburn for his comments on an earlier version of this paper.

Incarnational Anthropology

JOHN HALDANE

1. Introduction

The renaissance of philosophy of mind within the analytical tradition owes a great deal to the intellectual midwifery of Ryle and Wittgenstein. It is ironic, therefore, that the current state of the subject should be one in which scientific and Cartesian models of mentality are so widely entertained. Clearly few if any of those who find depth, *and truth*, in the Wittgensteinian approach are likely to be sympathetic to much of what is most favoured in contemporary analytic philosophical psychology. Finding themselves in a minority, they might well look elsewhere for support, hoping to establish the idea that opposition to scientific and Cartesian ways of thinking is by no means philosophically eccentric. Perhaps this partly explains the increasing British and North American interest in 'continental' thought, particularly as it bears (as most of it does) on the nature of human beings. Husserl, Heidegger, Merleau-Ponty and Sartre are obvious enough subjects for such attention.

In his interesting essay 'Getting the Subject Back into the World', Fergus Kerr joins a growing group of English-speaking writers attracted by the work of Heidegger.[1] Untypically, however, Kerr's attention has been caught by Heidegger's speculations about the involvement of *theological* ideas in the development of a view of persons as somehow set above, against or apart from the world of subjectless *things*. I am not a Heidegger scholar and I shall not raise any questions about Kerr's speculative interpretation of his subject. Indeed, I shall not be greatly concerned with Heidegger at all. I will, however, consider Heidegger's explicit claim that Christian theology has bequeathed to modern times an entirely misconceived account of human beings, and in connection with this suggestion I will discuss some issues in the area of theology and philosophy of mind. The latter conjunction of topics is now rarely encountered. I regard this as unfortunate, for there may lie within it the possibility of achieving a better understanding of what we are and how we differ from other things—be they *subjects* or *objects*—and how such differences are made possible. Before proceed-

---

[1] See Fergus Kerr, 'Getting the Subject back into the World: Heidegger's Version', in this volume, 173–190.

John Haldane

ing to Heidegger and theological anthropology, however, I need to review something of current philosophical psychology and to identify certain features of it.

2. Contemporary Philosophy of Mind

Anyone who reads extensively within contemporary philosophy of mind and reflects upon what they have been studying should feel the discomfort of intellectual claustrophobia. Notwithstanding that the subject is widely and actively pursued its content is remarkably confined. The boundaries of possibility are taken to stand close to one another and the available options are correspondingly few and, I believe, unappealing. They are, basically, one or another form of *physicalism*, reductive or not, and one or another form of dualism. Even this characterization suggests a wider range of possibilities than is actually favoured. Most contributors to contemporary discussions assume some version of *property dualism*, the main point of difference being over the question of how the relevant properties (and perhaps all properties) are to be regarded, i.e. projectively or detectively, reductively or non-reductively, nominalistically or realistically, and so on.

Recent times have seen a renaissance of realist versions of dualism, though the small, frail and uncertain offspring do not match the robust products of Platonic, Augustinean and Cartesian conceptions. For the most part, however, philosophy of mind has gone *anti-realist*—in various related senses of that term. Two such approaches are especially prominent and correspond to similar traditions in metaethics, *viz.*, *relativism* and *error theory*. A commonly held version of the former, which again is easily described by way of its parallel application in ethics, is *projectivism*. According to this, we are (for whatever reason) disposed to ascribe to human beings, and to some other things, a range of characteristics which they do not in fact possess. As one might say, following Hume:[2] 'Take any bodily behaviour allowed to be an utterance, examine it and its causes in all lights, and see if you can find that matter of fact, or real existence, which you call *meaning*. In whichever way you take it, you find only bodily movements. There is no other matter of fact in the case. The meaning entirely escapes you, as long as you consider the object. You never can find it, till you turn your reflection into your own breast, and find a response, which arises in you, towards this behaviour.'

[2] The original passage comes in Hume's *Treatise of Human Nature*, Book III, Part I, Section I.

Many people who hold this sort of view, such as Dennett, are projectivists only in respect of certain classes of phenomena.[3] They advocate realism with regard to constitutive features of the ground upon which the response-dependent characteristics are imposed. Indeed, the very metaphor of *projection* seems to force realism at some level, for it does not seem possible that what faces us is simply layer upon layer of projections, images all the way through.[4] On the other hand, there are those, including Hilary Putnam, who think that the conjunction of projectivism and realism, with regard say to psychology and physiology respectively, fails to register the full implication of at least some of those considerations which might have moved one in the direction of projectivism in the first instance.[5] It is often supposed, for example, that no coherent account can be given of the idea that objects are possessed of properties independently of our conception or experience of them; or similarly that it makes no sense even to think of the world as delineated apart from particular theories or practices within which talk of things and their characteristics features. Thus, some hold that any *philosophical* distinction between the real and the projected is misconceived. For present purposes it will be sufficient (though not uncontroversial) to characterize views of this sort as instances of wholesale *conceptual relativism*. On this account one need not accord priority to one domain over another (though one is not necessarily prohibited from doing so). It is easy to see, therefore, why those who take everyday psychology seriously, but who are repelled by ontological dualism, are attracted to some version of this view.

By contrast with accounts which regard the subject matter of intentional psychology as partly (or wholly) constituted by our affective responses and practical interests, advocates of *error theories* consider psychological concepts as products of mistaken hypotheses and insist that there are simply no phenomena to which they are properly applicable. Quite literally *nothing* is an intentional state or process. In view of this conclusion one might suppose, with Paul Churchland for example, that *eliminativism* is the only reasonable option; but, in fact, one could allow that, notwithstanding the vacuity of everyday (and theoretical) psychology, we cannot or should not abandon our erroneous assumptions.

[3] See D. Dennett, *The Intentional Stance* (Cambridge, Mass.: MIT Press, 1987).

[4] In this connection see C. McGinn,, 'An *a priori* Argument for Realism', *Journal of Philosophy* **76**, No. 3 (March 1979), where a similar line of thought is pursued in response to one version of global anti-realism.

[5] See Hilary Putnam, *Reality and Representation* (Cambridge, Mass.: MIT Press, 1988) and for some discussion of this J. Haldane, 'Putnam on Intentionality', *Philosophy and Phenomenological Research* **52** (1992).

For various reasons which I have set out at length elsewhere and will not now repeat, I regard eliminativism and error theory as entirely misconceived and ultimately unintelligible.[6] I am in sympathy with their proponents to this extent, however, that if projectivism or total conceptual relativism are the best that can be hoped for by way of securing the position of our common view of ourselves as persons, then it would be better to say that our self-conception is a delusion—for all that it may be inescapable.

This is not the occasion to pursue the issue but it is appropriate for what follows to register my opposition to this form of anti-realism also. One reason for doing so is that such views involve a generalized version of *compatibilism* which suffers from the same weakness as the restricted versions introduced in connection with freedom and determinism. Given the metaphysics of the projectivist, for example, we are invited to believe that while an event may be wholly determined in its causes it may be conceived of in a fashion which allows it to be a free action. Certainly it is believable that what is determined may be *thought of* as being free, but thinking does not make it so and in the circumstances this belief would be false. Of course the projectivist may reply that on his view our taking something to have a psychological character may be sufficient for its possessing it, for responses *constitute* the phenomena. But then I think we would do better to view things as they really are and say that so far as what *occurred* is concerned it was determined, notwithstanding that we may regard it in ways that take no account of this.

Considering these rejections of *relativism* and *error theory*, one might expect enthusiasm for recent versions of *realist* property dualism. Once again, however, I cannot see that these come close to being coherent never mind convincing. Admittedly they accord reality where other views elevate delusion but they give no intelligible account of how mental properties are related to physical ones; more precisely, they give no adequate account of how the two sets of properties are *integrated*. Some authors take the view that the two sets cannot be brought together in any way that accords with such common assumptions as that thought may be causally efficacious, and so they retreat to some form of epiphenomenalism. It is difficult to see that this is anything other than a defeat so far as concerns the attempt to give account of ourselves in accord with the testimony of experience and reflection. If the existence of psychological phenomena makes no difference to the course of events, then we are more than half way in to the position occupied by

[6] See J. Haldane, 'Folk Psychology and the Explanation of Human Behaviour', *Proceedings of the Aristotelian Society, Supplementary Volume* **62** (1988), 223–54.

the error theorist. But this conclusion, like that of the unrestricted error theory, is so far at odds with the evidence which continues to motivate philosophy of mind that it is barely intelligible as an answer to the question: what is our nature as thinkers and agents? Moreover, current versions of property dualism are wont to combine it with substance monism of a physicalist type. This encourages an emphasis on 'our' in the previous question, for reflection suggests that there is a continuing psychophysical subject of thought and action. The neo-dualist is apt to cite the human body or some part of it, i.e. the brain, as being that with which this subject is associated, but these suggestions are fraught with conceptual and epistemological difficulties and we are no nearer to understanding how subjectivity could be a characteristic of an entity whose sortal or substantial identity is given by its physical nature.

3. Heidegger, *Dasein* and the Image of God

In the light of these difficulties it is appropriate to step back and consider how the current condition arose and also what options might be available beyond those already discussed. I presume that it is partly in this spirit that Fergus Kerr, having previously made a commendable study of Wittgenstein,[7] has turned to consider the historical analysis and philosophy of mind of Heidegger, and it is clear why some of what Heidegger has to say is likely to be received sympathetically by those already attracted by Wittgenstein's work on similar themes.

In *Sein und Zeit*,[8] Heidegger takes on the task of showing how being embedded in the world is a precondition of our mindedness in general (*Dasein*) and hence, ironically, of those concepts and thoughts which seem to suggest an independently constituted subjectivity, and so give rise to the familiar problems of modern philosophy; most obviously, external-world scepticism and solipsism. He writes as follows:

> From what we have been saying, it follows that Being-in is not a 'property' which Dasein sometimes has and sometimes does not have, and *without* which it could *be* just as well as it could with it. It is not the case that man 'is' and then has, by way of an extra, a relationship-of-Being towards the 'world'—a world with which he provides himself occasionally. Dasein is never 'proximally' an entity which is, so to speak, free from Being-in, but which sometimes has

[7] Fergus Kerr, *Theology after Wittgenstein* (Oxford: Blackwell, 1987).
[8] Martin Heidegger, *Being and Time*, trans. John Macquarrie and E. Robinson (Oxford: Blackwell, 1978). Subsequent references are to this volume. The page numbers are those of later German editions as indicated in the margins of the Macquarrie & Robinson translation.

the inclination to take up a 'relationship' towards the world. Taking up relationships towards the world [whether cognitive or sceptical] is possible only *because* Dasein, as Being-in-the-world, is as it is.[9]

Later Heidegger applies this conclusion directly to the issue of scepticism and considers the idea of the subject as this has been developed within the western philosophical tradition:

> We *must* presuppose truth. Dasein itself, as in each case my Dasein and this Dasein, *must* be; and in the same way the truth, as Dasein's disclosedness, *must be*. This belongs to Dasein's essential thrownness into the world . . . even when nobody *judges*, truth already gets presupposed in so far as Dasein is at all.
>
> A sceptic can no more be refuted than the Being of truth can be 'proved'. And if any sceptic of the kind who denies the truth, factically is, [*sic.*] he does not even need to be refuted . . .
>
> [W]ith the question of the Being of truth and the necessity of presupposing it, just as with the question of the essence of knowledge, an 'ideal subject' has generally been posited . . . Is not such a subject *a fanciful idealization*? With such a subject have we not missed precisely the *a priori* character of that merely 'factual' subject, Dasein?[10]

Forgetting the unattractive pretension and self-indulgence that is characteristic of Heidegger's writing, there are easily identifiable parallels between the thoughts indicated above and Wittgenstein's central ideas with regard to human nature and knowledge,[11] and between both of these and the recent work by Davidson on subjectivity and cognition.[12] It is not altogether clear, however, what precise positive view, *if any*, Heidegger offers in place of those he dismisses. The expressions 'Dasein', 'Being-in-the-worldness', 'factual subjectivity', etc., are possibly suggestive of something congenial to those seeking to 'get the Subject back into the World', but they are terms of art whose meaning requires further articulation and whose application has to be shown to be illuminating. I am not myself confident that these tasks can be accomplished, or that if they were to be then anything genuinely novel would be revealed.

[9] *Being and Time*, Division I, ch. II, sec. 12, p. 57.

[10] *Being and Time*, Division I, ch. VI, sec. 44 (c), pp. 228–9.

[11] For a relevant account of these see F. Kerr, *Theology after Wittgenstein*, Part Two.

[12] See especially 'A Coherence Theory of Truth and Knowledge', in E. LePore (ed.) *Truth and Interpretation*, (Oxford: Blackwell, 1986) and 'What is Present to the Mind?', in J. Brandl and W. Gombocz (eds) *The Mind of Donald Davidson*, (Amsterdam: Rodolpi, 1989).

One might, nonetheless, find value in Heidegger's critical ideas about the origins of the supposedly false dualism of (worldless) subject and (subjectless) world. As Kerr observes, Heidegger claims to identify two central sources for this—located, as one might say, in Athens and in Jerusalem. The first is the idea that there is an important difference between Man (Subject) and the rest of nature (World) inasmuch as he possesses and it lacks, rationality—*zoon logon ekhon*. The second is the Judaeo-Christian doctrine that man is made in the image of God—*imago Dei*. On the same page as the last of the passages quoted above Heidegger goes on to write as follows: 'Both the contention that there are eternal truths and the jumbling together of Dasein's phenomenally grounded 'ideality' with an idealized absolute subject, belong to those residues of Christian theology within philosophical problematics which have not as yet been radically extruded.' However, the main locus of his case for identifying the supposedly pernicious influence of theological ideas comes in the section titled *How the Analytic of Dasein is to be Distinguished from Anthropology, Psychology, and Biology*.[13] It is there that he writes of the Christian idea of transcendence, according to which 'man is something that reaches beyond himself . . . [being] more than a mere something endowed with intelligence', and cites as specimen texts passages from Calvin and Zwingli. Setting aside questions of evidential support (seven lines of text from two authors both belonging to the Reformation), and questions of historical interpretation, an issue arises concerning Heidegger's philosophical competence.

Kerr quotes the following passage from *Metaphysische Anfangsgründe der Logik*: 'The problem of the existence of the external world and whether it can be known is implicated in the problem of the knowledge of God and of the possibility of proving God's existence.'[14] The nature of this implication and of its direction is not adequately explained. At one point it looks as if the problem of the external world (*epistemological transcendence*) is taken to be the source for the idea of an ultimate object set against the plurality of cognitive subjects, but elsewhere it seems that it is the idea of an unconditioned absolute being outside the world (*theological transcendence*) which gives rise to the general notion of objects outwith the mind and then, by a further stage, to the idea that there is a problem as to how, if ever, the cognitive subject makes contact with the world.

[13] See *Being and Time*, Division I, ch. VI, sec. 44 (c), p. 272; and Kerr, 'Getting the Subject back into the World: Heidegger's version', this volume, 177.

[14] See Kerr, 'Getting the Subject back into the World', 180.

John Haldane

Evidently Kerr is in some measure of agreement that Heidegger does not put up much of a show when it comes to substantiating the claim that Christian theology is the source of a troublesome conception of human beings from which philosophers must free us. But his interest is caught by the idea that elsewhere Heidegger draws upon scriptural and other Christian writings in the development of an account of *Dasein*. The questions which then arise are: what exactly is the element of Christian thought which must be 'extruded' from philosophy if we are to arrive at a correct account of our nature? and what are the acceptable theological notions which may help us to effect the necessary extrusion?

Drawing in part on recent work by John Richardson,[15] Kerr proposes that for Heidegger the essence of our subjective alienation is the result of a movement from practical engagement with the world to (broadly) scientific contemplation of it. (*Im anfang war die tat?*). This movement brings with it the notion of an objective view which in turn is associated with the idea of a transcendent status, a possessor of which would be unlimited in cognitive capacity, unconditioned by any historical context, and unrestricted in power to realize all possibilities. Such a status is of course that classically ascribed to the Deity. In brief, then, the idea is that like Lucifer we strive to be God. To this, someone might reply that in the myths of the eternal damnation of Satan and the expulsion from Paradise of Adam and Eve the religious tradition provides means enough to deflate delusions of divine grandeur, and to induce gratitude for whatever condition Providence has bestowed. That reply is not considered, but I suppose the thought is that so long as the idea of a transcendent status remains around we are always going to aspire to it, or at least to regard our own condition as, by comparison, defective. In this way, then, the elimination of un-naturalized Christian anthropology becomes the precondition of a true account of 'the being of *Dasein*'.

Heidegger's thought on these issues is strikingly facile and I suspect that Kerr has done more work than his subject in order to fashion the latter's fragmentary remarks into some kind of coherent whole. Even so the conclusions he attributes to him are open to objection. As Kerr remarks: 'The Christian God is already in the world'. Instead of taking issue with the details of Heidegger's story, however, I want to develop a theme touched on by Kerr and consider whether rather than Christian anthropology darkening reflection about our nature it is not a possible source of illumination. I shall argue that if one takes seriously certain central Christian doctrines, even if only as possibilities, and thinks about how they might be accommodated within metaphysics, then

---

[15] John Richardson, *Existential Epistemology: A Heideggerian Critique of the Cartesian Project* (Oxford: Clarendon Press, 1986).

198

interesting prospects for progress in philosophy of mind may come into view.

4. Theology and Philosophical Anthropology

Consider the following three ideas.

(i) Traditional Christians believe that, in the person of Jesus Christ, God became a man. The doctrine of the Incarnation finds expression in the words of the Nicene Creed: 'For us men and for our salvation he came down from heaven: by the power of the Holy Spirit, he became incarnate from the Virgin Mary and was made man.' (*Qui propter nos homines et propter nostram salutem descendit de caelis: Et incarnatus est de Spiritu Sancto ex Maria Virgine, et homo factus est.*) It is heretical to hold that Jesus Christ was a union of two persons, one Divine the other human (*Nestorianism*), or that Christ had only a Divine nature (*Docetism*) or that he had only a human nature (*Arianism*).

(ii) In Genesis 1: 26–28, we read the following: 'Then God said, "Let us make man in our image, after our likeness . . . So God created man in his own image, in the image of God he created him; male and female he created them."' In his First Letter to the Corinthians 11: 7, St Paul is concerned with implications of this doctrine for liturgical practice, advising 'that a man ought not to cover his head, since he is the image and glory of God'. This injunction presupposes a theological anthropology but does not articulate it. That task was begun by the Church Fathers and continued in the middle ages by the scholastics. In his *Commentary on the Sentences*, Aquinas repeats the claim that man is made in the image of God (strictly, that he *is* an image of God—*imago Dei*). As was seen, this is the sort of endorsement by a Christian philosophical theologian which, together with the original Genesis text, Heidegger blames for alienating us from our natural environment. Anyone disposed to agree with him, however, would do well to consider what exactly Aquinas means by this phrase as used of human beings. He writes as follows: 'Similarity is considered with regard to the form. Now the form of the human body is the rational soul, which is an image of God (*imago Dei*); for this reason the human body not only enjoys the similarity of a vague general copy (*vestigium*) but also the similarity of a specific likeness (*imago*), inasmuch as it is informed by the soul.'[16] Admittedly, the sense of this is not transparent, but it could hardly be

---

[16] *Commentary on the Sentences* (of Peter Lombard), III, d. 2., q. 1., a 3. The translation is taken from B. Mondin S.X., *St Thomas Aquinas' Philosophy in the Commentary on the Sentences* (The Hague: Nijhoff, 1975).

thought that the insistence upon the body's participation in the 'image' encourages a dualist reading.

(iii) Returning to his First Letter to the Corinthians 15: 35, we find St Paul teaching that Christ is raised from the dead and that resurrection awaits those whom he chooses to save. Towards the end of his Epistle Paul writes as follows:

> But some will ask, 'How are the dead raised? With what kind of body do they come?' You foolish man! What you sow does not come to life unless it dies. And what you sow is not the body which is to be, but a bare kernel, perhaps of wheat or of some other grain. But God gives it a body as he has chosen, and to each kind of seed its own body . . .
>
> So it is with the resurrection of the dead. What is sown is perishable, what is raised is imperishable. It is sown in dishonour, it is raised in glory. It is sown in weakness, it is raised in power. It is sown a physical body, it is raised a spiritual body. If there is a physical body, there is also a spiritual body (*soma pneumatikon*). Thus it is written, 'The first Adam became a living being; the last Adam became a life-giving spirit.'

In each of these three cases interpretation is called for, but it is worth remarking in advance that dualistic readings are not inescapable and indeed there are philosophical and theological difficulties standing in their way.

5. The Incarnation

Consider again the doctrine of the Incarnation: the claim that the son of God—co-eternal with the Father—became a human being. This is often charged with contradiction but I cannot see that these charges have been made out. Suppose, for example, that an objector observes that the doctrine commits one to the claim that in so far as He was God Christ was uncreated but in so far as he was a Man he was a creature. This, it is supposed, yields the contradictory claim that *Christ was and was not a creature*.

One reply to this challenge is to deny the commitment ascribed to the doctrine. Certainly God is uncreated, and Christ being God is thus an uncreated being; but while it may be that most men have been created it is not part of what it is to be a man that one have been created.[17] Creatureliness is not of the essence of humanity. If this is right then

---

[17] This point is made by Herbert McCabe in published correspondence with Maurice Wiles. See 'The Incarnation: an exchange' in H. McCabe, *God Matters* (London: Chapman, 1987), 70.

there is, so far at least, no contradiction (and perhaps not even the appearance of one) in the claim that Christ had Divine and human natures—even if possession of the former rules out the possibility that Christ was a creature.

This first sort of response, however, is inadequate as a *general* reply.[18] The orthodox believer *may* be willing to allow that Christ was an uncreated man but he certainly wishes to assert that he was none the less *born* of human kind (*et incarnatus est . . . ex Maria Virgine*), and the latter is an attribute which, as it stands, *is* incompatible with being Divine—at least as divinity is understood in the Christian tradition. Thus the orthodox Christian seems committed to the following two claims:

(A1) Christ was born.
(A2) Christ was not born.

How might this difficulty be resolved? It has long been the practice of some theologians—the more thoughtful ones—to refer the characteristics of Christ to the relevant aspects of His person, i.e., the distinct human and divine *natures*. Thus, instead of (A1) and (A2) one might say the following:

(B1) Christ *qua* Man was born.
(B2) Christ *qua* God was not born.

This, however, may not seem any advance if one supposes that the correct logical form of this second pair of statements is given by first-order predicate calculus. For according to that they would be represented as follows:

(C1) Fa & Ga.
(C2) Ha & ~Ga.

This then yielding

(C3) (Fa & Ha) & (Ga & ~Ga).

But there is good reason to suppose that (C1) and (C2) do *not* give the correct logical form of the statements about Christ and to think this for quite general reasons to do with the logic of what I shall term *aspect-involving predications*, i.e. ones involving such expressions as

---

[18] To judge from the discussion in chapter 9 of his *Understanding Identity Statements* (Aberdeen: Aberdeen University Press, 1984) this is the response favoured by T. V. Morris. However, I have not yet had the opportunity to read his monograph on the Incarnation, *viz. The Logic of God Incarnate* (Ithaca: Cornell University Press, 1986) which may depart from this approach, though I doubt it.

John Haldane

'inasmuch as it is', 'in respect of its being', 'under the description', 'as', etc. (these giving rise to what the scholastics termed reduplication; the relevant Latin expressions being *inquantum* and *secundum quod*).[19]

Consider first the following example. My status as a resident and community-charge payer in St Andrews does not entitle me to use the University Library; however, my position as a member of the University does so entitle me. Thus, it seems that the following are both true:

(D1) J.H. is entitled to use the University Library.
(D2) J.H. is not entitled to use the University Library.

The apparent contradiction is avoided by observing that these predications are in fact aspect-related and hence that the perspicuous form of representation is:

(E1) J.H. *qua* University member is entitled to use the Library.
(E2) J.H. *qua* resident is not entitled to use the Library.

Here the appearance of conflict is dissolved and we are left with perfectly compatible statements. The question is whether this solution will serve for the Christological statements (B1) and (B2) above. One might think that it will not since the cases are not analogous. The predicates 'is entitled to use the Library' and 'is not entitled to use the Library' clearly stand in opposition to one another but the exact form of this opposition is a matter for further specification. The expression 'is not entitled' admits of a weaker and a stronger reading which yield, respectively, a contradictory and a contrary to the predicate 'is entitled'. The universe is dividable into those things which are entitled to use the Library and those which are not. Among the latter complement, however, are those who are merely unentitled (the 'contradictory complement') and those who are disentitled, i.e. prohibited (the 'contrary complement'). Accordingly, the suggestion might be that in the example introduced above—of my being entitled and not entitled—the latter is only a matter of *unentitlement* and not one of *disentitlement*, and hence a reconciliation is possible in this case (by means of (E1) and (E2)) though it would not be were I, as a resident, to be *disentitled* to

---

[19] In *Providence and Evil* (Cambridge: Cambridge University Press, 1977) Peter Geach offers a brief discussion of reduplicatives in connection with Christological predications. At one point he writes: '[C]learly, this predicate [is as P, Q] entails the simple conjunctive predicate "is both P and Q" but not conversely' (27). I agree that the latter does not entail the former but nor, I believe, does the former imply the latter. If 'A is both P & Q' is equivalent to 'A is P & A is Q' then the contradictions which Geach and I both want to avoid would be one elimination step away. The only statements derivable from 'x *qua* F is G' are (i) 'x is F', and (ii) 'x is G *qua* F'. But the second of these is obviously just a syntactical variant of the original.

202

use the library. In this second case an inescapable contradiction results; and, the thought continues, it is this case which is the proper counterpart of the claim that Christ was born and Christ was not born. Being unentitled in one capacity leaves open the possibility of being entitled in some other. Being disentitled does not. The Christological case is like the latter, both sets of predicates cannot be simultaneously satisfied.

One reason for thinking this to be the case in the library example is that entitlement and disentitlement are concerned with licensing and prohibiting actions and processes and it is clear that these procedures are not compossible. But this is a problem for action (a practical conflict) and it does not obviously follow that there is a strict contradiction. Whatever about that, however, the foregoing line of objection does not demonstrate the derivability of a contradiction from the *qua* analysis of the reduplicative Christological claims. Consider again the question of the logical form of these statements taking first a generalized version of the library entitlement/non-entitlement claims:

(F1) Anyone *qua* member of the University, is entitled to use the Library.
(F2) Anyone *qua* resident and charge payer, is not entitled to use the Library.

Applying the orthodox analysis these will be represented as follows:

(G1) $(x) (Fx \rightarrow Gx)$.
(G2) $(x) (Hx \rightarrow \sim Gx)$.

This implies that nothing can satisfy the predicates F and H, for if it did a contradiction would be directly derivable. But something *does* satisfy F and H (many things do) hence this cannot be the correct analysis. So, my preferred schema makes essential use of the *qua* construction to introduce aspect-involving predication. Recall that non-entitlement admits of two readings yielding mere unentitlement (the straight contradictory complement) and disentitlement (the contrary complement). This gives us two sorts of cases:

(H1) x *qua* F is entitled.
(H2) x *qua* H is not (i.e. is un)entitled.

and

(I1) x *qua* F is entitled.
(I2) x *qua* H is not (i.e. is dis)entitled.

If (H2) does not imply that x is unentitled, *simpliciter*—and it does not—then neither does (H1) imply that x is entitled, *simpliciter*. Thus, x *qua* F is G does not entail that x is G, *simpliciter*. If this inference were valid then a contradiction would be derivable but we know from the actual case which (H1) and (H2) represent that it is not. But since the general schema 'x *qua* F is G → x is G' is not a valid one it cannot be used in respect of (I1) and (I2) either in order to derive a contradiction.[20] In neither interpretation of the entitlement/non-entitlement

[20] Needless to say, this claim will be regarded as controversial. The following two objections may occur to readers (the first was put to me by Graham Priest).

(i) The analysis of 'x as f is not (i.e. is un)entitled' presented above is not that which an objector to my reduplicative account would give. For he could observe the ambiguity in claims of the form 'it is not the case that x is f' between *external* and *internal* readings of the negation, i.e. involving the sentence or the predicate respectively. So, the claim (H2) above should be represented as ~(x) (Hx→ Gx), and not as (x) (Hx→ ~Gx). This then unsettles the proposed identity of logical form. Recall that my thesis is that the following inferences are valid but since they yield a contradiction their antecedent conditionals cannot give the correct analysis of the entitlement/non-entitlement claims:

> (x) (Fx → Gx), Fx ⊢ Gx.
> (x) (Hx → ~Gx), Hx ⊢ ~Gx.

The counter-proposal is that since the correct logical form of the second conditional is ~(x) (Hx→Gx), then ~Gx is not validly derivable, and one is not forced into a contradiction: Gx *simpliciter* does follow, ~Gx *simpliciter* does not.

My reply is as follows: ~(x) (Hx→ Gx) is equivalent to (∃x) (Hx & ~Gx). If we assume, however, that the predicates F and H are co-extensive, i.e., in the example discussed above, that all members of the university are also community-charge payers, then the latter is clearly false since everyone is both a rate-payer and entitled to use the library. Thus, in the case where F and H are co-extensive the claimed existential consequence is false while the premise 'Anyone who is a resident is not (i.e. is un)entitled' remains true. So far as concerns the present issue, therefore, the wide scope reading of the negation fares no better than did the narrow one.

(ii) A second response argues that one may detach non(i.e. un)entitlement *simpliciter*, while capturing the sense of the *qua* construction in a standard logical form analysis. Consider the generalized non-entitlement claim (F2) above:

> Anyone *qua* resident and charge payer is not entitled to use the Library.

This, it is supposed, may be represented as follows:

> (x) (Hx & ~Ix & ~Jx & ~Kx, etc. → ~Gx).

Here I, J, K, etc. stand for various entitling properties; thus we have:

> Anyone who is a resident and charge-payer and is not a member of the University and is not a visiting scholar, etc., is not entitled to use the Library.

The problem with this proposal, as I see it, is that the reduplicative 'x *qua* H is not G' is semantically determinate in the way that the counter proposal is not.

opposition is it *demonstrated* that there is a strict contradiction. In the one case the reduplicative analysis reveals why this is so, in the other it shows it not to be, and I have added to this an explanation of our intuition that here there is a real (and not merely an apparent) contradiction, i.e. the suggestion that it generates a practical impossibility.

Returning, then, to the doctrine of the Incarnation I am suggesting that some of the supposed contradictions are eliminable by means of ascribing to Christ *qua* Man the very same attribute as is possessed by Christ in his Divinity, and that others are treatable by the reduplicative analysis. This is not to suggest that the latter explains how something can be born *qua* Man, and not born *qua* God, but the want of such an explanation is part of what lies behind the orthodox claim that this and other doctrines are *mysteries*.

Let me next advert to another feature of the favoured reduplicative analysis. It is important to see that in the schema 'x *qua* F is G' the proper subject term is 'x' and not 'x *qua* F'.[21] '*Qua* F' is part of what is predicated, and this accounts for my introduction of the phrase 'aspect-involving predicates'. (Indeed, this favours using the form x is F-*qua*-G.) One good reason to parse things in this way is that otherwise falsities result. Since it is one and the same *thing* that is and is not entitled to use the library, if the subject of the non-entitlement were 'x *qua* resident and charge-payer' then it would be true that 'x *qua* resident and charge payer is entitled to use the library', but this is false. More pertinently, in the Christological case it would license the statement 'Christ as God was born' which again is false—and heretical (compare the case of 'Christ as God died on the Cross'—*Theopassionism*). The term 'Christ' is a proper name designating a single individual in all of its occurrences: 'Christ', 'the man Christ', 'Christ as man', 'Christ as God', etc., all refer to one eternal person possessed (at different times) of two natures; 'the humanity of Christ' and the 'Divinity of Christ' signifying these natures or aspects themselves. What all of this indicates, then, is that a minimally adequate logical treatment of attributions to Jesus Christ, the Incarnate Word of God—i.e. one which avoids contradiction—implies that there is but *one subject* of Divine and Human attributes. This is a happy result from the point of view of orthodoxy: Chalcedon and Nicea are vindicated and Nestorianism is avoided, but it also bears upon the treatment

[21] The importance of this point was first impressed upon me by reading 'Nominalism', in P. Geach, *Logic Matters* (Oxford: Blackwell, 1973).

One could grasp the sense and determine the truth value of the first without being able to do the same for the second—indeed, the 'etc.' barely conceals that as it stand there is no articulable sense to grasp nor truth to determine. Given this fact the proposal fails as an analysis.

John Haldane

of the *imago Dei* and resurrection doctrines, as well as upon the project of mundane anthropology.

6. Humanity and Existence

So far as concerns the latter there is one point which is important to discuss here. In recent times it has again become fashionable to argue that questions of personal individuation and identity must and can be resolved by reference to an account of human subjects which sees them as instances of a natural kind or species. This brings with it the idea of real or *de re* essences. There is much to be said for this sort of account, not least that it saps the power of the mind/brain-transfer thought experiments so beloved of English-speaking philosophers from Locke onwards. A natural-kind theory which eschews individual essences will hold that there is nothing necessary for the individual save what is essential to the species. If it is necessary for men to have hearts, then it is essential that I have a heart but *not* that I have the heart I do have, or indeed any particular other one. Likewise for brains. No metaphysically special status attaches to any given brain. If someone were to achieve the Brown/Johnson brain-exchange a species-essentialist should stand firm in the face of odd co-donor behaviour, knowing all the while that so far as individual *identity* is concerned the operation was of no greater significance than had it involved an exchange of hearts.

The previous thought yields the advice: keep track of the human beings and you will know who is who—*up to a point, that is*! This qualification may need to be added because of an implication of the theological doctrines listed above—most obviously those associated with the Incarnation. Consider the following sentence;

(J) It is necessarily true that if J.H. is a man then J.H. is a man.

This admits of two familiar readings:

(J₁) *De dicto:* Necessarily, if J.H. is a man then J.H. is a man.
(J₂) *De re:* If J.H. is a man, then necessarily J.H. is a man.

But a further separation needs to be made. The *de re* claim can be associated with two distinct metaphysical views, as follows:

(1) If J.H. is a man then necessarily J.H. has certain features, such that J.H. could not cease to instantiate these and still be a man.
(2) If J.H. is a man then necessarily J.H. has certain features, such that J.H. could not cease to instantiate these and still exist.

De re readings of J are compatible with each of (1) and (2). If, however, one were to take seriously the doctrine of the Incarnation then

206

one would want to accept (1) but deny (2). Christ as God existed from all eternity but one and the same person took on a human nature at a given moment in history. At the point of incarnation and thereafter Christ as man possessed a human essence, but the existence of the subject of that essence—the person Christ—existed before assuming it. So notwithstanding that *Jesus of Nazareth* was a human being and as such could not have failed to possess certain attributes, it was not essential that *Christ* be a man, i.e. *his* existence was not tied constitutively to this nature.

This may suggest to some readers a duality of substances: a Divine person inside a human one, analogous to the Cartesian duality of a mind inside an organism. But I have already indicated why the former view is not forced upon the believer and noted that Christian orthodoxy set itself against any such dualism. Suppose then one were to accept the *one person/two natures* theological formula and to review the metaphysics of human personhood in the light of it, what might emerge? Clearly not Cartesianism and possibly not an essentialism which makes J.H.'s existence depend upon his being human. Recall in connection with this the other theological ideas listed earlier: the *imago Dei* doctrine and St Paul's eschatology—to which it would also be appropriate to add, in respect of Jesus, the Transfiguration: '[A]s he was praying the appearance of his countenance was altered ['his face shone like the sun' (Matthew 17: 2)] and his raiment became dazzling white.' (Luke 9: 29), and the mysterious post-Resurrection appearances:

> [S]he turned round and saw Jesus standing, but she did not know that it was Jesus . . . [He] said to her, 'Do not hold me, for I have not yet ascended to the Father' . . . the disciples were again in the house, and Thomas was with them. The doors were shut but Jesus came and stood among them . . . he said to Thomas, 'Put your finger here, and see my hands; and put out your hand, and place it in my side.' (John 20: 14–28)

It has been common to draw connections between the transfigured Christ of the 'high mountain' and the generally unrecognizable condition of the resurrected Christ. As was noted, a yet more direct link is forged by St Paul between the risen Christ and the condition of those who will be raised in glory; we are to have 'spiritualized bodies'. Some writers have taken the occasion of St Paul's enigmatic phrase to challenge the doctrine with a dilemma: are they *spirits* or are they *bodies*? But this may be viewed as much as a symptom of the commentators' intellectual limitations as it is that of St Paul's. The point of the phrase, as of that section of the Epistle, is to indicate that a glorifying transformation awaits those whom God will save. My interest here is in whether this can be fitted into any coherent metaphysical scheme.[22]

[22] For some related discussion of the Christian idea of a bodily afterlife see J. Haldane, 'A Glimpse of Eternity?', *The Modern Churchman* **30**, No. 3 (1988).

John Haldane

7. Incarnational Anthropology

When reviewing the currently favoured options in philosophy of mind I remarked that most projectivists and (realist) property dualists are inclined to be monistic with respect to the ground or bearer of psychological attributes. This monism is materialistic in the sense nowadays intended by the term 'physicalism'. When reading the work of philosophers of these sorts, and indeed most other writers in the field, it is difficult to resist the thought that, to some degree or another, they are working under the influence of corrupted versions of two Aristotelian ideas. The first is the *substance/attribute* distinction, the second the *form/matter* one.

It is sometimes said, e.g. in connection with discussions of the doctrine of transubstantiation, that the medieval scholastics thought of properties as being metaphysical skins enveloping the objects which possess them. This is historically quite inaccurate and badly misrepresents the view they actually held and had derived from their reading of Aristotle. From Locke onwards, however, there has been a growing tendency, especially among English-speaking philosophers, to think about substances and properties in something like the object/envelope way.

Given the materialist presumption, one might more aptly liken the relationship to that between an object and skins or coatings which cover its surface. Just as one may add further layers and the character of the surface will change in various ways depending partly on the nature of the previous surface; so, in this way of thinking, properties are laid (by Nature) one upon another atop an underlying bearer, and the character of any given layer is determined in part by what lies beneath it. This simple picture best makes sense of much of the contemporary discussion of *supervenience*, especially in connection with the psychological aspects of human beings. It is as if there is a something covered in a chemical coating which contributes to but does not exactly determine the character of the animalistic coat, which in turn affects the psychological layer settled upon it. Put another, but no more satisfactory, way, the psychological 'supervenes' upon the biological which 'supervenes' upon the chemical. (Here the etymology suggests that the term fits exactly the relationship it is now employed to describe, one layer 'coming upon' another.)

I shall not dwell upon what is wrong with this picture nor the current uses of the idea of supervenience; it is worth remarking, however, that had they been able to make sense of them Aristotle and Aquinas would very likely have been amused. Certainly this way of regarding the substance/attribute relation is not at all what they had in mind. For them, to be a substance is to be a kind of thing some of the characteristics of which are (metaphysically) constitutive of it but others of which, including, for example, location and volubility, may be possessed at one time but not at another. Clearly, in the Aristotelian tradition it makes no sense, save in special cases, to think (even metaphorically) of characteristics, whether essential or accidental ones, as lying in layers over the surface of the things which possess them.

A further mark of the difference between a sophisticated neo-Aristotelian such as Aquinas and many contemporary writers is revealed by the ways in which each speaks of *matter*. Possibly both might say that a human being is materially composed but what this would be likely to mean in the mouth of each is importantly different. I said earlier that, as currently employed, the substance/attribute distinction suggests that if one could uncover the underlying bearer of the psychological, biological and chemical layers exhibited by a human being one would be left with a 'something'. The question 'What?' might now be met with the answer 'a lump or other quantity of matter'. This way of speaking reveals that the original *philosophical* concept of matter as co-relative with form or nature, has undergone a change leaving in its place (or, more confusingly, lying alongside it) an *empirical* notion. For Aquinas, by contrast, matter is best thought of (when philosophical questions are at issue) not as a kind of experientially encounterable stuff but as a metaphysical aspect of substances, be they countable things or measurable quantities of certain kinds. The only sense in which it is unarguably true for Aquinas that a human being is materially constituted is that the substance, i.e. the individual J.H., is an actual living nature operating in various ways—as opposed, that is, to a mere possibility of a life which we might envisage if invited to consider human nature as such.

Conceived of in the abstract, matter is the potentiality for the instantiation of form, and form is the actualizing principle, that which makes something to be the kind of thing it is. Neither matter nor form can exist outside the individual substance whose concrete existence they mutually determine. Consider in this connection the following passage from Aquinas' discussion of the metaphysics of the creation:

> As to formation, the argument is clear. For if formless matter preceded in duration, it already existed; for this is implied by duration; since the end of creation is being in act. But act itself is a form. To say, then, that matter preceded, but without form, is to say that being existed actually, yet without act, which is a contradiction in terms. Nor can it be said that it possessed some common form, on which afterwards supervened the different forms that distinguish it . . . Hence we must assert that primary matter was not created

altogether formless, nor under any one common form, but under distinct forms.[23]

In the metaphysical sense matter is the potentiality for the instantiation of form. (This claim is comparable to the idea that space is the condition of the existence of material objects.) Clearly, it does not follow from this alone that every individual substance which realizes this potentiality is material in the modern sense. This being so we might entertain the prospect that empirical matter involves but one mode of potentiality and that the same form of determining principle may be realized in distinct (but related) ways corresponding to different species of possibility. And furthermore that it may be realized in each of these simultaneously.[24]

Needless to say all of this is highly speculative and stands in need of much more investigation; but what it encourages me towards is the thought that an account may be available of how one person, Christ, could have two natures: the Divine form actualizing one species of potentiality as the *Logos* and another as *Jesus of Nazareth*. Such an account might also be expected to explain how a created person could be at one time a rational animal incarnate in an empirical medium, and at some later stage possibly be transfigured by translation into a different mode of being. In neither case is there need to be drawn back into a form of dualism. It is one and the same person that is actualized through all eternity in the manner appropriate to the Son of God and is realized also in the empirical mode as a human being, and following the Resurrection in a further manner possibly not imaginable by us but in relation to which St Paul speaks of the *soma pneumatikon*. Likewise, one may entertain the possibility of sharing in that glorified form of life, and perhaps thereby warranting the description *imago Dei*, while not doubting for a moment that one's life as a mortal rational animal *is* one's present mode of existence and more likely than not one's only one.

These final thoughts combine a recognition of present immanence with a prospect of future transcendence. I cannot see that Heidegger's rejection of the latter as an unsettling legacy of Christian theology

[23] *Summa Theologica*, Ia, 1.66, a. 1, ad 1. The translation is that of the Fathers of the English Dominican Province (London: Washbourne, 1912).

[24] The idea of different modes of potentiality, different kinds of 'matter', also has application in connection with the question 'how is thought possible?' For discussion of this see J. Haldane, 'Brentano's Problem', *Grazer Philosophische Studien* 35 (1989); and 'Mind/World Identity Theory and the Anti-Realist Challenge', in J. Haldane and C. Wright (eds) *Realism, Reason and Projection*, (Oxford: Oxford University Press, 1992).

places him in any better position to explain the former. On the contrary, the only prospect I see for explaining the subjectivity of *Dasein*, and its very existence, involves the sort of incarnational anthropology discussed above.[25]

[25] I am grateful to my colleagues Peter Clark and Anthony Ellis for discussions of issues raised in this essay.

How Many Selves Make Me?[1]

STEPHEN R. L. CLARK

Back Before Descartes

Cartesian accounts of the mental make it axiomatic that consciousness is transparent: what I feel, I know I feel, however many errors I may make about its cause. 'I' names a simple, unextended, irreducible substance, created *ex nihilo* or eternally existent, and only associated with the complete, extended, dissoluble substance or pretend-substance that is 'my' body by divine fiat. Good moderns take it for granted that 'we' now realize how shifting, foggy and deconstructible are the boundaries of the self; 'we' know that our own motives, feelings and intentions constantly escape us; 'I' names only the current speaker, or the momentarily dominant self among many fluid identities.

Kathy Wilkes has observed that the ancient Greek picture of human life, though nothing like as dissociated as some over-eager commentators have pretended, is hardly Cartesian.[2] The Aristotelian synthesis proclaims 'us' as social animals, with distinctive, inter-related faculties that do not rely on one-same 'Cartesian Consciousness' for their existence and activity. This more fluid, extended, organically grounded conception of human (and other) being is truer to our experience, and to the discoveries of modern psychobiology, than any semi-Cartesian vision can be. Wilkes professes herself quite unable to grasp what it is that philosophers like Nagel think is left out of neo-Aristotelian science. I in my turn find it very difficult, or impossible, to take reductive or eliminative materialism seriously as an account(?) of my experience(?) or of the world that houses it. Wilkes herself would deny that she is an eliminativist of the Churchlands' kind, but what she declines to eliminate, it seems, is only the *language* of folk-psychology. Where the Churchlands advance an 'error theory', to the effect that folk-psycho-

[1] Earlier versions of this paper were read to the Philosophical Society at Stirling University, and to the conference at St David's. I am especially grateful to Kathleen Wilkes, David Cockburn, Andrew Brennan, and to Barry Dainton, currently of Liverpool University, for their comments. My conclusions were brought more strongly into focus by Ramchandra Gandhi's comments at the second Anglo-Indian Convivium held in East Sussex in September 1990.

[2] Kathleen V. Wilkes, *Real People* (Oxford: Clarendon Press, 1988).

Stephen R. L. Clark

logical language embodies a false theory (that we have minds and effective purposes), Wilkes only denies that it embodies any particular theory, and agrees that such a theory would be false. I share Patricia Churchland's suspicion that instrumentalist interpretations of our mentalistic concepts are a last ditch attempt to avoid the pain of radical correction, the realization that we were simply wrong, that our language was not 'cutting the world at its joints'.[3] By the same account, calling someone a witch was never a factual error, but simply a declaration of intent, quite compatible with its not being true that she could ill-wish cows or fly unseen to naked festivals, and serving important social interests. On the other hand, I also share Wilkes' view, but for other reasons, that our mentalistic language is *not* theoretical. Our language, any language, embodies any number of theories, or of theoretical terms: some of them are probably false or foolish. But it is not a *theory* that I am conscious, and intend to write this paper: not a theory, because there is nothing at all that I have better reason to believe and that is best explained by guessing that I'm conscious and intent upon my task. On which more below.

All dualistic theories, that distinguish the stuff of consciousness from the stuff of merely material motion, are, by many modern accounts (including Wilkes' and Churchland's) false: being conscious is either being (behaviourally) alert in variously complex ways, or nothing that we have any reason to believe in. The notions that make up our present idea of personhood (of self-reflectiveness, responsibility and the like) do not require us to believe in single, simple substances, Cartesian egos. Instead we are faced by complex arrays of lesser elements, struggling to keep in step. Neither identity through time, nor unity at a time, are all-or-nothing affairs—a doctrine seemingly confirmed by stories of 'multiple personalities', recently discussed by Wilkes and Brennan.[4] My argument will be that those stories, and the admitted multiplicity of human personality, do not have quite the moral they suppose, and that a return to pre-Cartesian consciousness is not well represented by non-dualist Aristotelianism.

'"Know Yourself" is said to those who because of their selves' multiplicity have the business of counting themselves up and learning that they do not know all the numbers and kinds of things they are, or do not know any one of them, nor what their ruling principle is, or by what they are themselves.'[5] Thus Plotinus, greatest of late pagan phi-

[3] See Patricia S. Churchland, 'Replies to Critics', *Inquiry* **29** (1986), 241–72.
[4] Wilkes, op. cit. (n. 1); Andrew Brennan 'Fragmented Selves and the Problem of Ownership', *Proceedings of the Aristotelian Society* (1989–90), 143–58.
[5] Plotinus, *Ennead* VI 7. 41, 22f.

214

losophers in the treatise on Forms and the Good, described by Armstrong as 'perhaps the greatest of the single works of Plotinus.'[6] Those who seek to follow the Delphic instruction—so Hesychios was to say—find themselves, as it were, gazing into a mirror, and sighting the dark faces of the demons peering over their shoulders.[7] Descartes left us with the impression that self-knowledge was our normal, and necessary, condition: the earlier tradition makes it clear that such knowledge is difficult, and our 'single-heartedness' a distant, luminous goal. We are the conduit for gods, the battleground of competing spirits, the multiply refracted, broken images of a single soul.

So fractured memories, discordant motives, concealed causes are not anomalies: they are the ordinary human condition, and only the saint, hero or philosopher has tamed and transformed the squalling horde of impulses so far as to 'know herself' as single. The rest of us do not know why we do things, are not 'the same' from one foolish moment to the next and constantly misidentify even our most 'present' and 'immediate' feelings. It does not follow that there is no single self to be uncovered.

The Case Against Multiplicity

'Nearly all those perplexing reports of two or more people in one body, so to speak, that arouse a unique interest in the classroom are reports of observations made in a relatively distant past.' So Thigpen and Cleckley,[8] comparing such sightings to reports of centaurs and the like, before going on to describe their own discovery, 'Eve and her Three Faces'. There are of course, by now, more cases from more recent history to think about, but it is worth recalling how those earlier cases were first reported. If we take investigators seriously when they report their sense that they have been dealing with two or more distinct personalities, typified by the differences in verbal response, gesture and whatever quality it is that enables us to recognize people whom we cannot adequately describe, perhaps we should also take seriously their sense that they were dealing with quite distinct persons, some of them

---

[6] A. H. Armstrong *Enneads* (London: Heinemann, Loeb Classical Library, 1988), vol. 7, 78.

[7] G. E. H. Palmer, P. Sherrard and K. Ware (eds), *Philokalia* (London: Faber & Faber, 1979), 186.

[8] Corbett Thigpen and Harvey M. Cleckley 'A case of Multiple Personality', *Journal of Abnormal and Social Psychology* **49** (1954), 135–51 (reprinted in I. G. Sarason (ed.), *Contemporary Research in Personality* (Princeton: Van Nostrand, 1962), 367–83; see also *The Three Faces of Eve* (London: Secker & Warburg, 1957), 50.

Stephen R. L. Clark

discarnate spirits. If we believe Sally's claim to be co-conscious, aware of all the Misses Beauchamps' doings in waking life and dream, why not believe claims to be dead Spaniards? Maybe a supposedly 'alternate' personality is only a faintly more plausible medium, telling tales of night-club successes rather than Martian landscapes? The cases of Miss Beauchamp and of Doris Fischer, for example, were extensively discussed in the Proceedings of the Society for Physical Research, and McDougall, its one-time President, seemed to suspect at one time that Sally (in the Beauchamp case) was a distinct, discarnate person.[9] Sidis and Goodhart[10] move from the Beauchamps to a case of mediumistic possession referring to Martians. 'Spanish Maria', investigated by C. E. Cory in 1920,[11] believed herself to be the soul of a long dead Spaniard. 'Patience Worth' employed Mrs John Curran as her medium: or the latter allowed Patience an influence as a dual personality.[12] Prince[13] employed the evocation of visions in crystal—a technique known as scrying. A good many of the cases—to come closer to this modern day—uncovered in Crabtree's therapeutic practice were self-identified as cases of possession, or reincarnational reminiscence. The therapy of taking those identifications calmly and literally seems to have been just as successful as a therapy of 'dissociated states' (and perhaps less harmful than Morton Prince's efforts, or those of Thigpen and Cleckley).

Tales of multiple personalities, in short, took shape within a highly, even vulgarly, spiritistic view of things, and not the naturalistic or materialistic view that is now axiomatic for would-be serious researchers (though for no clear reason). I have no prejudice in favour of the occult interpretation, but some things can be said for it. McDougall was right to think that there was something odd about the Sally/Beauchamp case on any straightforwardly physicalist account: 'Sally', you will recall, had complete access to the various states and actions of all other Beauchamp personae, but none of the latter had direct knowledge of Sally. How could this be if they were sustained by the self-same brain? Crudely: if Sally is the brain-in-question, and so are the Beauchamps, then Sally and the Beauchamps are identical. But

[9] W. McDougall, 'The Case of Sally Beauchamp', *Proceedings of the Society for Psychical Research* **19** (1905–7), 410–31.

[10] B. Sidis and S. P. Goodhart, *Multiple Personality* (New York: Appleton & Co., 1909), 65.

[11] C. E. Cory, 'Spanish Maria', *Journal of Abnormal Psychology* **14** (1920): A. Crabtree, *Multiple Man* (Eastbourne: Holt, Rinehart and Winston, 1985), 41f.

[12] Cory, *Psychological Review* **26** (1919).

[13] M. Prince, *The Dissociation of a Personality* (New York: Longmans, Greene & Co., 1908), 78ff.

216

Prince was adamant that 'Miss Beauchamp' could be reintegrated only by Sally's disappearance. I remark in passing that other early cases were resolved (it seems) by the gradual victory of the *livelier* personality: thus Mary Reynolds (1811–?) had two 'entirely separate' lives and personae, neither knowing anything of the other, and Felida X (1858–88) remembered in her 'secondary condition' all that had happened in the life with which she did not identify.[14] In both cases 'the gradual pushing out of the neurotic personality by the healthy one had all the appearance of a self-cure'. In effect, Prince thought of Sally as a demon or possessing ghost, and attempted exorcism. In fairness it should be added that Prince had more reason for suspicion than Hawthorn[15] implies: as 'Sally', his patient lacked tactile and kinaesthetic sense, any grip on the passage of time and a marked refusal to think that her health and survival depended on Miss Beauchamp's body.[16] But was Sally's self-identification as a spirit[17] really incompatible with her being the proper governing spirit of that body? 'He cannot bring himself to admit [despite his opening maxims] that what Sally stands for is a disintegrated part of a "normal" young woman.'[18] Wilkes comments that certain unacknowledged prejudices (not shared by all Prince's contemporaries) were at work in his therapeutic practice. As Hawthorn[19] says, 'Prince's description of the three personalities he isolated as "the Saint, the Woman and the Devil" tell us a lot about Prince.' Thigpen and Cleckley operate to an identical stereotype.

If we choose not to take the occult conception seriously, and the associated psychodrama of reincarnational reminiscence, table-rapping and clairvoyant perception, perhaps it is worth being a little more sceptical about the other stories. Where so much depends upon the reliability of witnesses our view of their general credulity or prejudice must colour our view of what they say. It is at least a little naive to accept one set of stories at face value while dismissing the other as obvious fictions, a naivity not greatly diminished by appeals to supposedly 'objective tests' to validate some theory-laden descriptions and not others. How much of what Prince and the others record would have been described like that without a prior belief in occult happenings, or a prior readiness to tell such highly coloured stories? 'It is highly likely that role-playing, whether conscious or unconscious, whether in child-

[14] Crabtree, op. cit. (n. 11), 39ff.
[15] J. Hawthorn, *Multiple Personality and the Disintegration of Literary Character* (London: Edward Arnold, 1983).
[16] Prince, op. cit. (n. 13), 147ff.
[17] Prince, op. cit. (n. 16), 489.
[18] Hawthorn, op. cit. (n. 15), 18.
[19] Ibid. 8.

hood or in the surgery, is an essential element in the aetiology of the condition.'[20] In fact, there is even more to be said about the influence of therapists. Prince elicited personae, through hypnotherapy and conversation, and insisted on giving them names. There may indeed be 'naturally occurring' fugues (like the often cited Ansel Browne's studied by William James) but cases of 'multiple personality' of the Beauchamp, Eve or Milligan kind do seem to be produced with the very active assistance of the therapist. 'Relatively few patients manifest clear signs of multiple personality at the beginning of therapy. Instead such signs tend to become increasingly evident as therapy progresses.'[21] It is no necessary reflection on the integrity of Prince and the others to ask whether such behaviour is perhaps largely a social construct. Thigpen and Cleckley, to do them justice, recognize the danger and seek to exculpate themselves.[22] This is also Crabtree's opinion (though he remains inclined to suspect clairvoyant or reverant influence in some cases): 'when a client walks into the therapist's office and sits down, the expectation framework of the therapist immediately comes into play'.[23] On the one hand, role-playing and 'dramatic personation' may give people the chance to speak and behave in novel ways that have been excluded by their normal (or therapeutic) expectations; on the other, those same dramatic roles may be elevated to the status of supposedly independent loci of conscious agency. Patients may 'fall in with' what serves their interests (as an exciting and sometimes liberating game), or simply comply with what the therapist, an obvious authority-figure, seems to require of them. Crabtree remarks on the surprising excellence of role-players who had no previously shown gift for acting. The roles people thus play may begin as fairly stereotypic, but acquire life and detail before an appreciative audience of other role-players (and therapists). This 'sceptical' conclusion is also drawn by the social psychologists, Spanos, Weekes and Bertrand, who elicited distinctly multiple personalities from college students required to role play an accused murder on remand (using the interview technique employed in the accused 'Hillside Strangler' of 1979). Pace Wilkes[24] it does not seem to be very difficult to induce differential results even in supposedly 'objective' tests (which is why we cannot rely upon such tests to prove that the preferred descriptions are correct). And Eve Black was *not* allergic to nylon (she only *said* she was).

[20] Wilkes, op. cit. (n. 1), 110.
[21] N. P. Spanos, J. R. Weekes and L. D. Bertrand, *Journal of Abnormal Psychology* **94** (1985), 362–76.
[22] Thigpen and Cleckley, op. cit. (n. 8), 165.
[23] Crabtree, op. cit. (n. 11), 211f.
[24] Wilkes, op. cit. (n. 1), 111.

My initial move, then, is to question the reliability of the reports of genuinely multiple personalities, cases where one single human being is revealed to be housing, or be alternately controlled by, several distinct selves who cannot be held mutually responsible for each other's doings. The point is not that the patient is suspected of fraud (although Kenneth Bianchi might well be suspected of that, with a strong incentive to feign irresponsibility), but that patients may be as compliant as the rest of us, as eager to indulge an authority figure. It is still easier to do so when even mistakes are given an instant justification. In a court of law someone professing deafness who replied 'No, I can't hear you' to the whispered question 'Can you hear me?' would be a proven liar; in a consulting room, such a reply is evidence of 'deep hypnotic trance', provided by an 'inner self' distinct from the one who 'really' cannot hear. 'I want to talk to the one who heard me' then elicits a different range of allowable response, and a new persona. Compliance and excitement are not the only driving forces: as I have already hinted, people may be 'possessed' in order to speak or act in ways not normally allowed, given due licence because they briefly incarnate a god, or a secret, interesting character. Some of those later labelled 'multiples' began simply as ordinarily day-dreaming, literary children.[25] While playing that character they may 'genuinely' ignore or forget all sorts of things likely to rush back upon their ordinary consciousness when the game is over.[26] 'Popular accounts of the role of multiple personality appear relatively attractive by portraying the protagonist as a person with a dramatic set of symptoms who overcomes numerous obstacles and eventually gains dignity, esteem and much sympathetic attention from significant, high status others'.[27] Slightly more responsible accounts, such as that of Thigpen and Cleckley, remain, by any normal standards, profoundly unscholarly: stories and suspicions are reported without adequate reference; unnamed witnesses are adduced for this or that piece of exotic behaviour. This seems to be as true of their contributions to learned journals as of their admittedly popularizing (and exploitative) book. We are told, for example, 'that there is reason to suspect that at least once [Eve Black] convinced a tipsy dancing companion that she had achieved distinction in Saville as a female matador',[28] without being told what that reason is, or who the compa-

---

[25] See Hawthorn, op. cit. (n. 15), 11ff. It is also widely claimed that such 'multiples' were often or always victims of sexual and other abuse as children. It is not surprising that such victims should exaggerate the normal tendency to forget unpleasant or disgraceful episodes.

[26] See I. M. Lewis, *Ecstatic Religion* (Harmondsworth: Penguin, 1971).

[27] Spanos *et al.*, op. cit. (n. 21).

[28] Thigpen and Cleckley, op. cit. (n. 8), 195.

nion. Aldridge-Morris has commented that 'frequently there's no corroborative evidence to prove that what the patient is saying bears any resemblance to reality'.[29] Thigpen and Cleckley pour justified scorn on the interpretative freedom enjoyed by Reichians, Freudians and Scientologists, but leave me with an almost equal distrust of their own methods. Anyone who can assess the success of Eve's 'reintegration' by the judgment that '[Evelyn] was unquestionably a better-looking, a far more attractive woman than we had ever seen her before'[30] ought to put himself through a period of self-analysis! I do not wholly endorse Hawthorn's judgment that it is the impossible double standard socially enjoined for women that breeds multiples. Sylvia Plath's heroine, seeing her 'life branching out before [her] like the green fig-tree in the story', and faced by an impossible choice between mutually exclusive futures,[31] is an image of the human condition, not just the 1950s female. As the Buddha is said to have realized, 'the root of all evil is the desire to live all one's possible lives'.[32] But there is indeed an element of male oppression, and collusion, in the stories of Beauchamp, Eve, Sybil and the rest. The victims were constrained to distinguish some moods and impulses as 'not really them', to focus on others as 'properly' their own, to forget what they had thought and done, because the therapists themselves colluded in oppressive stereotypes.

The Beauchamp case, in particular, remains quite unresolved, and my chief impression from Prince's account is of a man who merited Sally's devastating rebuke: 'it's always your theories you have in mind—not at all the people. . . . You've treated me like Hell'.[33] It is a mark of Prince's imperviousness that he prints this as 'a [childishly] wrathful letter' in Appendix P. The complacency with which he welcomes a 'reintegrated Miss Beauchamp', 'just a normal, healthy-minded person',[34] to the exclusion of Sally and the extinction of 'emotional idealism' and assertive anger alike, leaves him, as far as I am concerned, as a deeply flawed witness. How much of what he said and did was a response to his own, unexamined needs, not hers?

Human beings have an enormous capacity for personation, falsification, compliance and willed forgetfulness. I have yet to read of a

[29] Ray Aldridge-Morris, *Multiple Personality: an Exercise in Deception* (London: Lawrence Erlbaum, 1989), cited by Jean Snedegar, *The Independent*, 20 March 1990, p. 15.
[30] Thigpen and Cleckley, op. cit. (n. 8), 271. It may be they have other, better, reasons for their conclusions: how could we tell?
[31] Sylvia Plath, *The Bell Jar* (London: Faber & Faber, 1966), 80; cited by Hawthorn, op. cit. (n. 15), 117.
[32] J. S. Dunne, *The City of Gods* (London: Sheldon Press, 1974), 125.
[33] Prince, op. cit. (n. 16), 560.
[34] Ibid. 514.

genuinely convincing case of 'multiple personality' in the sense imagined by popularizers and fantasists such as Wyman Guin. The latter's story 'Beyond Bedlam'[35] conceives a world where all of us display alternate personalities with wholly distinct legal and civil obligations. The one unforgiveable adultery[36] is an 'affair' with one's spouse's alternate self. In brief, I am much less sure than Wilkes that these cases are distinctly 'real' as distinct from contrived, fictional or literary![37] One might as well call on Carlos Castaneda's testimony to his experiences with an Amerindian magician. I am especially critical of Thigpen and Cleckley, for reasons at which I have already hinted. First, the trio of Eve White, Eve Black and Jane are suspiciously reminiscent of BI, Sally and BIV in the Beauchamp case (though Eve Black lacks some of Sally's odder characteristics, and it is Jane rather than Eve Black that claims acquaintance with *both* the other personalities). Secondly, Thigpen and Cleckley's story is a swamp of unattributed anecdote.

The Case for Multiplicity

But this is not to say that cases of 'multiple personality' are wholly unreal, nor that they pose no fascinating questions for philosophers. There is a case for saying that human existence is essentially a fictive one, that the stories we tell have an ineradicable role in creating who and what we are. 'To ask what a person is, in abstraction from his or her self-interpretations, is to ask a fundamentally misguided question, one to which there couldn't in principle be an answer.'[38] In that sense, these stories are no more fictional, and no less significant, than the more familiar story of the heroic ego.[39] We can use them as imaginative fictions even if we doubt that anyone has ever been physically compelled to live like that. That someone tried, or is thought to have tried, to live out the story adds a certain weight to what might otherwise be merely abstract possibilities.

McDougall[40] pointed out that the phenomenon of co-consciousness rebutted the equation of memory-chain and identity. Sally 'remembers'

[35] Wyman Guin, *Beyond Bedlam* (London: Sphere Books, 1973), 150ff.

[36] As Eve White apparently thought: Thigpen and Cleckley, op. cit. (n. 8), 206.

[37] Daniel Keyes, who wrote *The Minds of Billy Milligan* (New York: Random House, 1981), is better known as the author of the science fiction story, *Flowers for Algernon*. They are both touching stories, but I prefer the latter.

[38] Charles Taylor, *Sources of the Self* (Cambridge: Cambridge University Press, 1989), 34.

[39] See 'On Wishing there were Unicorns', *Proceedings of the Aristotelian Society* (1989–90), 247–65.

[40] W. McDougall, *Outline of Abnormal Psychology* (London: Methuen, 1926), 541f.

all that Miss Beauchamp feels and does (allegedly, better than Miss Beauchamp) but resolutely denies any *identity* with those personae (Prince castigates her for this, but seems actually to believe her claim). Perhaps it is not 'true' that Sally is not Miss Beauchamp. But the mere possibility that she can sensibly *deny* identity with what she remembers emphasises that self-identification is something more than reminiscence. Conversely, a refusal to admit that one has really and truly performed some abominable act (which has, admittedly, been performed by someone, with the connivance of one's very own body) does not prove that one didn't: but it does raise the question, 'what could settle the claim?'.

'Sally was the Ireland of Miss Beauchamp's body politic.'[41] The comparison of 'individual human being' with the fractured unity of a social group or empire regularly excites derision when students consider Plato's *Republic*. But what is so absurd about the comparison? All biological organisms are hierarchically organized systems of systems: 'in reality the individual is an aggregate of systems of simpler individuals'.[42] Similar architectural solutions appear at many different levels of organization. Is a termite nest one individual or many? It depends what we are counting, and what is most usefully adduced as a cause. So what could be less surprising than the discovery that 'I who address you am only one among several selves or Egos which my organism, my person, comprises. I am only the dominant member of a society, an association of similar members',[43] or an occasionally symphonic chorus of ordered parts? It does not seem to me that physicalists can really object even to treating *nations* as single organisms, with 'wills' and 'understandings' of their own. Saying that nations are bigger, or less tightly organized, is no reply: however tightly organized a nation was, common sense (or such remnants of archaic theory as we retain) would reckon it an extra and unlikely thesis that there was someone (some national spirit) intimately acquainted with and conscious in the national doings. Physicalists seem to be committed to the view that 'being a someone' only means being sensibly spoken of as doing or thinking this or that. So nations and multinationals are as much and little 'persons' as we are, and someone larger than we individually know already knows as much. On this account it is not wholly surprising that psychic, as well as physical, organization should sometimes break down, that a hitherto subordinate monad should begin to act in ways not licensed by central authority, or seek to usurp-control entirely. The surprise is rather that 'we' usually

41 Ibid 546ff.
42 Sidis and Goodhart, op. cit. (n. 10), 4.
43 McDougall, op. cit. (n. 40), 546f.

manage to communicate as well as we do: even a little encouragement to rebellion or faction will usually succeed.

But is there then any 'right' answer to questions of identity? There is no merely geographical, geological datum to say whether the Falkland Islands are a 'part' of British territory or Argentinian (and certainly not: 'they're physically *closer* to Argentina than to Britain'). Their identity and the national identity of their inhabitants are functions of natural justice or international law, not physical fact. Analogously, personal identity is a moral, or legal, or civil matter, and not a straightforwardly biological one. We can, as it happens, provide relatively clear criteria for the identity of single human organisms from conception to decease: but even those criteria leave many grey areas (as we should expect), and do not require us to adopt any particular criteria of personal identity. The first occupants of a piece of land *may* have permanent title to that land, but if they or their descendants do it is not because they have retained ancestral ways, nor because physical fact determines moral or socio-legal reality. Prince's assumption that BI might turn out to be 'a pathological entity . . . having no right or title to existence' if she were not 'the first Miss Beauchamp'[44] is just as fallacious, as is his talk about 'the law of psychology' that condemned Sally to extinction'.[45]

The parts of which individual human organisms are compounded are not well-differentiated pieces (as if we were Empedoclean chimeras): a 'part' may be an entire working system spread through the larger organism, or a colony of creatures living their life alongside the more centralized structure of cerebro-neural networks. Dual personalities— pseudo-science aside—are *not* clearly associated with 'left' and 'right' hemispheres (where did the other personalities come from?). But they may still be conceived as elements in the struggling congregation of souls. Maybe neither Sally nor Miss Beauchamp is that single brain, but each a neural network spread throughout the brain. Is it then a mere convenient fiction to insist on 'personal responsibility' for oath and act? That this body here once uttered words of promised loyalty, which the presently dominant monad disowns, is no affair of 'mine': Jane and Eve Black deny that they owe any loyalty to husband or child. If there is no 'really binding loyalty' there is equally no 'real self' to discover: at best the therapist and multiply dissociated client should aim for an endurable consensus among the struggling clans, a consensus bearable to its members and to the families and friends with whom their life is lived. If such a condition is achieved it will be easy to project it backwards, to suppose that 'it was always really there'. Just so, nationalist historians may read current characteristics back into their own prenational past,

[44] Prince, op. cit. (n. 13), 186–240.
[45] Ibid. 399.

forgetting that what is now one nation might very well have been absorbed in several others.

Is that last possibility such as to reveal a real disanalogy between nations (or termite nests) and human animals? Surely there is no way (in fact as distinct from fantasy) that my own body (what is now the vehicle, we hope, of a more or less coherent strategy) could have turned out to belong to others? It might have turned out differently, of course, but however it turned out would have an unrivalled claim to own the whole of its history, and none of anyone else's. I suspect that this, for committed physicalists, must be an illusion. It is not obvious that this thing here, 'my body', must have just the extension whether in space or time that conventionally it does. Banal reliance on bodily identity as indisputable is only a failure to remember differences of scale, and the many actual alternatives that have, historically, been devised. But that is another story.

National or personal consensus need not involve an absolute unanimity. There is a case for relaxing our demands for consistency, unity and hierarchic control, both for the sake of personal peace, and to avoid the epistemic error of so fearing self-contradiction as never to want to change one's mind! If we are simply telling stories, there might be merit in a less heroic tale than philosophers have fancied. But there might, contrariwise, be disadvantages to such a fashionable recognition of our multiplicity and social relativity. Might it not be better to reconsider older theories, as well aware as any modern is that we are opaque and pluralistic beings? Do the stories I have been sketching give us any real reason to abandon tradition? Do they not confirm tradition?

Stepping into the Light

Billy Milligan, whom American courts—briefly—excused for rape and assault on the plea that he suffered from a seriously multiple personality, described the process whereby different personae moved out into control of their shared body as one of 'stepping into the light (of a spotlight) from a dark room'.[46] Perhaps, despite my earlier warnings about the quality of the evidence, that is the right way to describe the case; different homunculi gain control of the lumbering organism (as invading viruses displace the control mechanisms of our cells), and all of us may suddenly find that we are similarly multiple. I am conscious that doctors have often assumed too readily that this or that uncomfortable condition is the byproduct of social or personal unease, a convenient story to make sense of troubled times, only to discover a little later

---

[46] Crabtree, op. cit. (n. 11), 52, after Keyes, op. cit. (n. 37).

that there is a simple physical explanation, and that they have been patronizing the victims of viral infection or biochemical upset. Maybe tales of multiple personality are real, and really products of the complexity of our animal organism. Therapists who believe in the syndrome hardly seem to think so, since they make so much of their clients' often having been abused as children.[47] Schism is a strategy, and not an imposition. But this may be false.

Let us suppose that there really are such cases. If there are, whether they are socially or biochemically explicable, there may still be a better way of describing what goes on. Instead of believing that separable homunculi step into a metaphorical light, why not suppose that it is the *light* that successively illuminates relatively separate memories and behavioural syndromes? That there is only one self, though many syndromes? That, after all, is how the victims often seem to speak.

The story of Thomas Hanna, recounted by Sidis and Goodhart, culminates in an intense struggle to determine the fate of his two personalities: 'each of them was the "I" of Mr Hanna, and still they differed from each other. He could not choose one, because each was of the same nature as the other; they could not be joined because they were quite different personalities . . . He felt that the two lives were his and that they had to be synthesized into an ego.'[48] The verbal confusions may be Hanna's, or his therapists'. On the one account two selves competed: but who was it who had to choose? Is the 'choosing self' yet another personality in dispute with the first two? On the other, one same self must organize his memories and impulses after a period when that same self was periodically denied access to one or other set of memories. If selfhood is defined by memory-chain there are two selves here—but I have already pointed out that 'co-conscious' cases show that sameness of memory is insufficient to establish self-identity. If selfhood is not defined by memory, then one same self is the light that plays over this memory chain or that, or selects one fig among many. Hanna's chief problem was simply to work out what chronological order his memories should form.[49] This is ill-described by saying that he needed to 'synthesize his ego': his ego, so to speak, was there already and needed to synthesize the story of his life.

My proposal is as follows. In one sense, Sidis is correct that 'multiple consciousness is not the exception, but the law. For mind is synthesis of

[47] It is a clumsy methodological error to suppose that—if there are real multiples at all—they must all end up requiring therapy. It is therefore quite wrong to claim that we know that all or most multiples (if they exist) must have been abused as children.
[48] Sidis and Goodhart, op. cit. (n. 10), 193.
[49] Ibid. 199.

many systems, of many moments of consciousness'.[50] Most of the
thoughts that float across the sphere of my attention are disconnected,
or loosely associated, fragments. More powerful thought-complexes
emerge periodically, of very various kinds, relatively oblivious of their
cousin-complexes. Anyone who doubts this should attempt the simple
task of trying to think of one simple thing for the space of ten seconds.[51]
The ordering attention of the light can sometimes control, constrain
and discipline those thoughts to remain present for examination, but
only with great difficulty. It is an important step in self-knowledge to be
made to realize (most easily perhaps at three in the morning) just how
fluid and uncontrolled our ordinary thinking is. 'Whence came the soul,
whither will it go, how long will it be our mate and comrade? Can we tell
its essential nature . . . Even now in this life, we are the ruled rather
than the rulers, known rather than knowing . . . Is my mind my own
possession? That parent of false conjectures, that purveyor of delusion,
the delirious, the fatuous, and in frenzy or senility proved to be the very
negation of mind.'[52] And again: 'it is a hard matter to bring to a
standstill the soul's changing movements. Their irresistible stream is
such that we could sooner stem the rush of a torrent, for thoughts after
thoughts in countless numbers pour on like a huge breaker and drive
and whirl and upset its whole being with their violence . . . A man's
thoughts are sometimes not due to himself but come without his will.'[53]
What we cannot control is not our own: even my mind is not my own.[54]

But on the other hand, it is quite wrong to ignore the self-sameness of
the attention itself. That light is not identical with any of its passing
objects, nor are any more or less fractured personalities the same thing
as that self. I frequently forget what I am doing or have done, and find it
difficult to retrieve that epistemic package. As frequently I lose my grip
on the behavioural mode or mood that is needed to make me function as
a party-goer, parent, or philosopher. As Midgley remarks: 'some of us
have to hold a meeting every time we want to do something only slightly

[50] Ibid 364.

[51] During discussion at the Conference I inflicted this elementary exercise on
my audience, and concluded (from their unanimous failure to achieve a ten-
second thought) that we could hardly be said to control our thoughts at all.
Ilham Dilman responded that he had at least thought of the thing I had asked
them to, and so must have controlled his thinking at least for a moment. True
enough: but now (if you control your thoughts) *don't* think of a white mare.

[52] Philo, *On Cherubim*, 114f.: *Collected Works*, trans. F. H. Colson, G. H.
Whitaker *et al.* (London: Heinemann, Loeb Classical Library, 1929), vol. II,
77.

[53] Philo, *De Mutatione*, 293f: ibid., vol. V, 265f.

[54] Sangarakshita, *Survey of Buddhism*, 6th ed. (London: Tharpa Publications, 1987), 196f.

difficult, in order to find the self [that is, the personality] who is capable of undertaking it'.[55] This does not tempt me to deny the sameness of my self, which is no particular personality.

All I have said so far could easily be read as Aristotelian (in Wilkes' sense). We need not suppose that there are many real subjects in a victim of 'multiple personality' or fugue. There is one subject, the single human being, who forgets or puts aside or dramatizes what is going on. The goal of self-awareness is always hard to reach, and sometimes made more difficult by the need to behave in radically different ways in differing circumstances. A child who is required to hide from others and herself what happens by night must play any number of parts: but there is still one child only who may at last retrieve *her* memories. But I see no real reason to equate the subject of those experiences with a human being. As far as the phenomenon goes we only need to speak about the light of consciousness itself. Nor am I convinced that appeal to a supposed simplicity and objectivity in the identity of 'one human being' is more than rhetoric. We think there are human beings, as discrete individuals of a single kind (not to be reduced to multicellular colonies, nor yet incorporated in hive-organisms), because we first experience selfhood.

The extraordinary difficulty that, I find, some commentators experience with this conception rests upon two errors. The first is to suppose that my talk of light was metaphorical. It is commonly assumed, without much thought, that our first ancestors began by naming 'physical realities' and only later used 'the same terms' for real or imagined mental properties. But it is surely obvious that our first ancestors had no such knowledge of the physical. What they called 'light' (or rather what they called by such words as have developed into 'light' and its cognates) was the experience of finding things becoming clear and distinct and colourful, of distinguishing themselves from the world they dwelt in, of dwelling under heaven. That experience has gradually encouraged us to think that there are physical realities outwith experience, and to use experiential terms (by metaphor) to refer to them. The light of attention is the primary phenomenon, not some occult hypothesis described by empty simile. The final absurdity is reached by those who, having postulated a world outwith the mind and pretended that thereby they could explain the mind, now deny that the primary reality, of mind, exists at all.[56]

[55] Mary Midgley, *Wickedness* (London: Routledge & Kegan Paul, 1984), 123.

[56] I have discussed some of the difficulties in attempts to explain the existence or nature of consciousness by referring only to such things as can supposedly exist without consciousness in *From Athens to Jerusalem* (Oxford: Clarendon Press, 1984), ch. 7.

The second error is to assume that what one finds within or with the mind is what one is. Neither psychological nor physical continuity determine personal identity as a moral or socio-legal reality. If those continuities are all that we can *find* then we must conclude either that self-hood is something not to be discovered like that, or that personal identity is of the same kind as national identity, a truth-by-convention, a product of the human story. The latter hypothesis (combined as it usually is with a rejection of any belief in objective morality) leaves us adrift. The former is the one that I prefer, and here seek to re-establish as a genuine option.

Hawthorn, citing a story of Jean Rhys that describes a cold, clear commentary on her heroine's action, then inquires 'why is it that the cold, clear, rational, logical part of a woman's brain [sic: why?] should be forced to be merely a "hidden observer"?'[57] My reply is that such an internal commentator is not unknown to males as well: the medieval term for it was 'synderesis',[58] from which both 'consciousness' and 'conscience' take their start. This point is not, or not exclusively, that social pressures make it difficult for *women* to identify themselves whole-heartedly with a rational overview of their own and others' lives. We *all* find it difficult so to do, and usually fail to focus our attention with sufficient clarity to recognize that we must be distinct from the silly, struggling animal or the complex of personalities that perhaps are grounded in that animal's physical being. What I here call the overview is the attention become aware of its own being, its own distinctness from the fabric of the life it judges. Whereas most forms of knowing are of an object distinct from the knower, self-knowledge is of another kind, but arises from and issues in a knowledge (and perhaps control) of the various moods, epistemic packages and personalities that compose the human aggregate.

Some ages, no doubt, make it easier for the overview to take shape, and perhaps to gather to itself all kinds of fantasies. On the one hand, the crowd of merely human characters; on the other, an angel, Martian or possessive ghost that can hardly at times contain its scorn of the human comedy. Such are the 'inner helpers' (or hindrances) on which Allison[59] or Crabtree sometimes rely. Prince's own account of Sally's assaults upon BI can easily be read as the attempt of an exasperated intellect to arouse a weak-minded, self-important, hypocritical and slavish ('unstable' and 'suggestible' are Prince's words) character to an awareness of the human comedy. 'I must not spare the rod, for by it you

[57] Hawthorn, op. cit. (n. 15), 34.
[58] T. C. Potts, *Conscience in Mediaeval Philosophy* (Cambridge: Cambridge University Press, 1980).
[59] R. Allison, *Mind in Many Pieces* (New York: Rawson, Wade, 1980).

[BI] may be saved yet.'[60] The fact (if it was one) that 'Sally' lacked Miss Beauchamp's 'culture',[61] namely her knowledge of French and shorthand (*sic*), does not necessarily imply that Miss Beauchamp was 'superior' or (still less) 'saintly'! BI, he says, was never rude, vengeful, jealous, envious or malicious: perhaps, but 'saintliness' is not to be equated with feebleness. His account also suggests, covertly, that it was BIV that better deserved the title 'Devil' (she was after all arrogant, selfish, irascible, a liar and contemptuous of BI's prayer-life). 'How can one disown oneself, how hate oneself, or how exult in one's own destruction, one's own undoing?'[62]—a genuine piety or culture would have no difficulty in answering these questions.

But the overview is not the same thing as a fantasized Martian, or timetravelling Neputunian:[63] that too is only a fleeting character. Nothing that can be thus described and fixed is to be strictly identified with the Self, yet that Self is, as the continuing focus of attention, real. Some moderns imagine that their deconstruction of the self captures the Buddha's intention, reducing each supposedly substantial thing to a disconnected sequence of moments (with the apparent moral that no future or past moment can be worth fearing or desiring). My own suspicion is that the reductive analysis—which must go on to deconstruct those very atomistic moments—was simply intended to isolate attention, consciousness itself, the light that transcends all moments, thoughts and impulses. The self is indeed not 'like' anything. 'This consciousness is luminous.'[64].

An intrusive question: alternating personalities are compatible with this story, but what of supposed cases of co-consciousness (now largely disregarded by psychotherapist believers in the syndrome)? Sally claimed constant awareness of BI's and BIV's thought and action, though without identification. Was there anyone attentive to BI or BIV *with* identification? Were there, in brief, two genuinely distinct selves attendant on Miss Beauchamp? Prince, as I have said, speaks incoherently on this matter, sometimes blaming Sally for not accepting her real identity with BI and BIV, and sometimes working toward the

[60] Sally: Prince, op. cit. (n. 13), 166.
[61] As ibid. 150.
[62] BI: ibid. 209.
[63] As in Olaf Stapledon, *Last Men in London* (Harmondsworth: Penguin, 1972; first published 1932).
[64] *Anguttara-Nikaya* 1, 10: cited by Sangarakshita, op. cit. (n. 54), 104. Edward Conze emphasizes that Humean comparisons are deeply misleading: whereas Hume 'understood our personality after the image of inanimate objects, which also have no "self", or true inwardness of any kind . . . the Buddhist doctrine of *anatta* invites us to search for the super-personal' (*Thirty Years of Buddhist Studies* (Oxford: Clarendon Press, 1967), 239f).

Stephen R. L. Clark

elimination of an intrusive presence. Sally's own testimony, as reported, emphasizes the distinctness of selves (and the real identity of BI and BIV). 'BIV is *not* a person. Why do you insist that she is?'[65] On the other hand when Sally attends too closely to the thoughts typed as BI's she vanishes into BI: 'If Sally is directed to concentrate her mind on a mathematical problem, or other similar subject, Sally tends to change to Miss Beauchamp.'[66] Prince seems to have been absolutely convinced that Sally—whom he regarded as 'childish'—could not possibly be 'the original Miss Beauchamp' or 'a normal person',[67] though it would not be difficult to write her story in just that sense. In Sally alone a clear, rational awareness of Miss Beauchamp's largely self-induced troubles can be seen;[68] as 'Sally' loses that overview (translation: 'as the self is absorbed in contemplation of one memory track'), one of the fragmentary characters emerges. When 'Sally' re-emerges it is with a critical memory of what passed before she waked, a realization that she is *not* what she had been condemned to attend upon. Sometimes she has that doubled consciousness of which most of us have some knowledge: knowing that she does (qua BI/IV) what she cannot approve. But if it *was* true that Sally nonetheless retained a co-conscious reality *alongside* 'Miss Beauchamp' then perhaps the hypothesis of (largely beneficent) possession should be accepted as a serious one. Or perhaps it is BI/IV that is the intrusive, debilitating presence. Neither hypothesis is a joke.

The Plotinian Self

So what is the older theory that I would hope to see brought back into the light of philosophical conversation? One of its most familiar versions is the Kantian, but Kant was actually reproducing something far older.[69] Not all of that older theory is strictly relevant here, but I must sketch its outlines before offering my own conclusions. The Aristotelian synthesis, in Wilkes' interpretation, identifies us unproblematically as social, language-using animals. But Wilkes thereby (and quite consciously) omits one of the oddest features of Aristotle's analysis, and ignores the treatment that Aristotle had from his successors for over a thousand years.[70] *Nous*, the undying intellect,

[65] Prince, op. cit. (n. 13), 316.
[66] Ibid. 152; see also 221.
[67] Ibid. 234.
[68] Ibid. 238.
[69] See Philip Merlan, *Monopsychism Mysticism Metaconsciousness* (The Hague: Nijhoff, 1963).
[70] See H. M. Robinson, 'Aristotelian Dualism', in J. Annas (ed.), *Oxford Studies in Ancient Philosophy*, vol. I (Oxford: Clarendon Press, 1983).

has no bodily organ, and (qua *nous poietikos*) actualizes what would otherwise be mere potential, as light brings colours into light and being. *Nous*, strictly so called, is intellectual, but Aristotle does not mean that it 'thinks things through': rather is it the sheer awareness of its proper objects, and may even, loosely, be named as the subject of sensory awareness. Whatever Aristotle's intention in this, the later Platonists had no difficulty with the concept. *Nous* is mirrored or shadowed in soul, sentience, multiplicity. Thus: awareness, attention, is in its ordinary form irreducibly polar, a union of subject and object. Awareness of a wider realm than that immediately given to the struggling animal-self may be present to us, exactly, as a presence, a 'higher self'. As that grips our attention 'we' are elevated to that higher level. What had been an invading or guiding '*daimon*' is revealed as our very self, and a wider self and realm becomes faintly visible to us.[71] So by successive rises 'we' (all, so far, at the level of 'Soul') may find ourselves identified with *Nous*, properly so called, the intellectual vision of a rationally ordered whole in which Thinking and Being are the same. Without such a union, as I have argued elsewhere, our hopes of cognitive success are small. Beyond Thought-and-Being, for Plotinus, lies the One: that One is not subject to any rational analysis, but it is perhaps reflected—for us—in the glimpse we may have of a non-polar awareness, where the object, fully tamed and recognized, drops out of sight, and 'unfocused' or 'unprojected' awareness stands free, as the very Self. 'The Self is identical with unprojected consciousness.'[72]

Wherein lies the unity, the sameness, of that Self? Not in the sameness of an object, nor any particular character. *Nous* as such has no character (for else it could not 'receive', could not attend upon, just any object). Those who mistakenly identify themselves by what they have so far 'attended on', whatever project, memory chain or passion, are understandably startled and adrift when that object is removed, when they find themselves 'they know not where', released from the chains of their own forging. It is easy for them to conclude, especially with the aid of a helpful psychotherapist, that 'they' must be someone else. 'Lawks a mercy on me! This is none of I!' The banal response that they inhabit, by public testimony, 'the same body' is of no help at all, since the sufficiency of bodily continuity (even if that notion could be given any secure foundation) for the sameness of selfhood is exactly what such experience calls in question. But they are, nonetheless, mistaken. The sudden realization of Jane that she is Eve White, or of the 'real Miss

---

[71] Plotinus, *Enneads* III 4.3; see my 'Reason as Daimon' in C. Gill (ed), *The Person and the Human Mind* (Oxford: Clarendon Press, 1990), 187–206.
[72] C. O. Evans, *The Subject of Consciousness* (London: Allen & Unwin, 1970), 144.

Stephen R. L. Clark

Beauchamp' that she is BI or BIV ('These different states seem to her to be very largely differences of moods'[73]) was flawed—it seems to me—just in the apparent failure to realize that the self is one thing and the mood it briefly endures another. 'Learn therefore, O Sisters, to distinguish the Eternal Human that walks among the stones of fire in bliss and woe alternate, from those States or Worlds in which the Spirit travels.'[74]

This realization—and it may well be that few of us can hold it steady for more than a moment, and most easily mistake for it what is no more than a slight shift of mood—is gestured at in other traditions than the Plotinian. Once the ox is caught and tethered and the oxherd quiet in contemplation of a wider world than that defined by local projects, the mere light of unprojected consciousness may dawn.[75]

The Self is the *same* self because that is what it is: what other self could it be? In our moments of awakening we are quite untheoretically aware of the identity of what wakes here and what woke then (from which experience, more theoretically, we may infer the possibility of transcending time). To wake up is to know ourselves, so far. By the same token it may well occur to us, in ratiocinative mood, that the Self in me is just the same as that in you; that only the One Self attends on parallel and successive states of mind and action, separating itself out as One in Many. What makes my self is no other than what makes yours, and the differences between us lie at the level of what that attends on, or how it is—as it were—refracted. That is indeed an inference that Averroistic interpreters of Aristotle (and non-dualist Vedantins) have preferred; there is one *nous* only, and that the divine mover.[76] But at the level of particulars, the Self here and the Self over-there *are* differently reflected.

So how many selves make me? In one way, indefinitely many: for any mood or memory track or organic part or member of my squabbling congregation may move into the light. In another way, one only, and that only one the very same that finds itself continually renewed, as the moon's reflection in the trembling of the water's surface. By physicalist accounts there is no 'real Miss Beauchamp', but—at best—some practicable amalgam of diverse systems (which may well not be what Prince compelled into existence). By Plotinian accounts the character

[73] Prince, op. cit. (n. 13), 525.
[74] W. Blake, 'Jerusalem', 49.72f, in G. Keynes (ed.), *Collected Works* (Oxford: Clarendon Press, 1966), 680.
[75] See D. T. Suzuki (ed.), *Manual of Zen Buddhism* (New York: Grove Press, 1960).
[76] There is a related doctrine in Augustine, on which see R. H. Nash *The Light of Knowledge* (Lexington: University Press of Kentucky, 1969), 94ff.

(exactly) called 'Miss Beauchamp' is at last a figment, and any Enlightenment that broke out in 'her' story would have recognized in Sally's tricks and moral lessons a cheerful brutality of much the same kind as is practised by Zen masters. We are not merely or only social animals formed from ancestral colonies of protozoa (as they from colonies of mitochondria and procaryotic cells): they, and most likely many other organisms, are the mirrors in which the Self is fractured and reflected.

And why accept my, Plotinian, story? For at least three reasons. First, that without some such story we have warrant neither for supposing that we shall ever find out how things really are, nor for endorsing the vision of individual worth that lies at the root of our political and moral liberalism. If we are no more than colonies, adventitiously united, why suppose either that there is one right way to truth, or that we should protect and preserve mere human individuals? Second, that the story's abandonment by enlightenment philosophers rests upon bad arguments (for example, Hume's claim not to have found the self by looking). Third, that it is true to experience: not the experience, perhaps, that we lazily call our own, but the experience available to anyone who seriously seeks enlightenment. At the very least the story is compatible with all the tales of multiple personality and fugue that Wilkes, apparently, thinks lend support to her own rewriting of the Aristotelian theme.

And what about human beings, just as such? There are no such things, any more than there are fish or creepy-crawlies: that is to say, such classes are merely socio-legal ones, dependent on the values that we story-telling entities have severally given them. There are no such things as fish, because that word covers creatures of at least three different biological orders (*agnatha*, *osteichthyes* and *chrondichthyes*), and because such biological groupings themselves are not natural kinds.[77] But 'being human', in another sense, is still an important character, for it amounts to the presence in an animal organism of the self itself in so far as that self can become aware of its own being. We have no grounds in biological science for thinking that all and only our conspecifics are thus 'human'. Without the conviction that some are we shall have lost our reason for treating them as 'persons'. And that too is another story.

---

[77] See my 'Is Humanity a Natural Kind?', in Tim Ingold (ed.), *What is an Animal?* (London: Unwin Hyman, 1988), 17–34.

How Many Selves Make Me?[1]

KATHLEEN V. WILKES

1. Preliminaries

The answer to the title question which I want to defend in this paper is 'none'. That is: I doubt strongly that the notion of 'a self' has any use whatsoever as part of an *explanans* for the *explanandum* 'person'.

Put another way: I shall argue that the question itself is misguided, pointing the inquirer in quite the wrong direction by suggesting that the term 'self' points to something which can sustain a philosophically interesting or important degree of reification.

I am not of course suggesting that the term should not exist in the everyday language; I propose no linguistic reform. Instead I suggest that it is in some respects like 'sake', or 'will'; or indeed (but these would be more contentious) 'mind', 'soul', or 'conscious/consciousness'.[2] What links all these notions, to my mind, is that they do not pick out phenomena which repay systematic study: that is, what we need and want to study—scientifically or philosophically—is best described in terms that abandon talk of all of these.

Evidently we use (and need to use) all these terms in daily discourse. After all, in the previous paragraph I wrote 'to my mind'; and I can talk of problems weighing on my mind, can say that I am in two minds; I can comment on the strength of will of a child struggling against having his hair brushed; I can wonder whether fish are conscious of pain; I can do something for your sake; and believe in something with all my soul. We say and need to say many things which we do not expect to be taken literally. Consider how even the Astronomer Royal might comment on the beauty of the sun's setting; how we describe something as on the tip of the tongue, and we do not mean a flake of chocolate; how we use noun-terms that we

---

[1] This is an entirely different paper from that delivered at the Lampeter meeting. At Lampeter I was concerned to reply to Clark, because he had been kind enough to take my discussion (in *Real People*: Oxford: Clarendon Press, 1988) as a springboard and foil for his own thesis. It rapidly became clear from the discussion there that there were more general issues that deserved exploration—in particular, the very notion of 'a self'.

[2] I have attempted to defend this view of 'consciousness' and 'mind' in *Real People*, and in K. V. Wilkes, '. . . , Yishi, Duh, Um, and Consciousness', in A. Marcel and E. Bisiach (eds), *Consciousness in Contemporary Science* (Oxford: Clarendon Press, 1988).

do not intend to refer, such as 'sake'; consider too how even those who deny the truth of Freudian theory find comments like 'he's Oedipal', or 'she's suffering from penis envy' usefully insulting from time to time.

So, similarly, we all talk of 'myself', 'himself', and so forth. Note, though, two interesting features of 'X-self' talk. First, the terms 'self', and 'selves', *without* the prefix, are relatively *in*frequent—at least in non-philosophical daily discourse. Ordinary language is and should be a *guide* to what seems to matter, even if not an infallible guide. Second, the term 'itself', referring to inanimate objects, is at least as popular as are the *'animate'* 'X-self' locutions. This second point might invite us to consider whether 'X-self' talk is indeed something specifically distinctive about persons. So the indispensability of 'self' or 'selves' talk (almost always prefaced by 'my-', 'your-', 'him/her-', 'it-', 'our-', 'their-', 'them-') is not *obviously* a mark of its utility in philosophical discourse about personal identity.

Nor, to finish the account of what I am *not* saying, do I attack the philosophical utility of the term 'self' solely because it is hard to say where one self begins and another takes over. That is a fair criticism of the term 'self' (indeed, it is perhaps the most recurrent complaint of undergraduates meeting the views of Parfit in 'Personal Identity', or *Reasons and Persons* for the first time). Insofar as some of my difficulties with the notion may suggest or imply the 'how do we count selves?' problem, they do not use that as a premise; they should stand independently.

Enough of preliminaries.

2. The Unity of Consciousness

Where Clark and I clearly agree is that it is no longer possible to sustain the idea that a tight, all-or-nothing, 'unity of consciousness' is either necessary or sufficient for something to be 'a self', or to be me. It was never possible to defend this proposition: there is often little 'strong' unity, and what 'strong' unity there is need not always be conscious. But (at least in Britain) philosophy, and to a lesser extent psychology, spent a long time hoping that it was defensible. The authority-figures for this myth were Descartes and Locke in chief, and it was Descartes' *innovation*: before him, few if any would have dreamt of saying anything so implausible. The myth lasted a long time but is now dead. Indeed, if it has residual motility (to paraphrase a memorable remark of Koch's about behaviourism[3]), it is because the corpse is unable to understand the arguments.

[3] See S. Koch, 'Psychology as Science', in S. C. Brown (ed.), *Philosophy of Psychology* (London: Macmillan, 1974), 4.

This claim is very easy to defend. Weakness of will (*akrasia*) and self-deception are familiar examples of times at which we are disunited, at odds with ourselves (note: with *ourselves*). Even if some akratics are well-aware of their disunity, the self-deceived may not be conscious of theirs. There are many other examples. Someone may be glad his father has died (his last months were spent in great pain) and also sorry (he loved him and misses his company). The first of these thoughts might be suppressed, not conscious. Or: it is easy to believe that p and also that not-p, just when the inconsistency is not brought to attention; for example, I was once asked which king succeeded William II. I remember my reply: 'I am very bad on early medieval history—no idea'. Only later did I remember that I knew well the school jingle 'Willy, Willy, Harry, Steve, Harry, Dick, John, Harry Three . . .' Or: we have inconsistent attitudes: tolerant of our childrens' faults ('so active and energetic'), but intolerant of the neighbours' children ('noisy troops of hooligans'). Or: we can do some things of which we supposed ourselves incapable, such as a problem in set theory, or driving a car in a barely-known city in Yugoslavia. Or: we are strong parent-figures in one context, dependent and anxious authority-seeking hypochondriac patients in another; consider Berne's *Games People Play*. Or: our moods and emotions puzzle us; for instance:

> In sooth, I know not why I am so sad;
> It wearies me, you say it wearies you;
> But how I caught it, found it, or came by it,
> What stuff 'tis made of, whereof it is born,
> I am to learn;
> And such a want-wit sadness makes of me,
> That I have much ado to know myself.
> (*The Merchant of Venice.*)

Indeed, Heraclitus was there first:

> You will not find out the limits of the *psuche* [usually
> translated 'soul'; but 'mind' or 'self' would be equally
> good or bad: KVW] by going, even if you travel over every
> way—so deep is its nature.[4]

All this is adequately familiar.

That is enough alone to refute the hope that 'I' am a 'self' held together by a strong 'unity of consciousness'. But since this topic is introduced in Clark's paper by the phenomenon—or, if you prefer, alleged phenomenon—of multiple personality, and since indeed I used multiple person-

[4] H. Diels and W. Kranz (eds), *Die Fragmente der Vorsokratiker* (Dublin and Zurich: Weidmann, 1968), vol. i, Fragment 45, p. 161.

ality myself in *Real People* as something that presents insuperable difficulties for the concept of a person, I shall allow myself to use this and other 'clinical', or 'experimental' examples to ram the point home.

Multiple personality is one. So is commissurotomy: the operation sometimes carried out (to a greater or lesser extent: the corpus callosum is rarely severed completely) on patients with intractable epilepsy. Commissurotomy often throws up cases where patients have a 'divided consciousness'; thinking and writing, for example, with the right hemisphere and left hand that they have just held in the left hand a pipe, and simultaneously thinking and writing with the left hemisphere and right hand that the object held was a pencil. More problem-cases abound with such phenomena as fugue states, and states of transient or long-lasting amnesia. Hypnosis is evidently another source of examples of division: consider the hypnotically-anaesthetized subject who *says* he feels no pain when his left arm is immersed in a stream of icy water, while at the same time he writes busily with his right hand that he is in anguish. A more depressing, but unfortunately very familiar, example is clinical depression itself (as distinct from everyday depression, which might be due to something like a hangover), when that is endogeneous or menopausal. Or of course consider the truly *extraordinary* cases of hemisphere neglect, of pure alexia,[5] of the various agnosias, and so on through a long list. As for the neuroses and psychoses: psychoanalysts of whatever persuasion can select their own preferred examples of psychological disunity, breakdowns in self-knowledge and the unity of consciousness, and so forth.

I used Shakespeare to show how everyday phenomena militate against any 'strong' unity, just above. Geschwind can be used to underline the way in which psychologists often need to drop any assumption of 'strong' unity:

> ... these cases [the alexias—KVW] should give us pause in accepting a point of view which had a powerful influence in all the behavioral sciences, particularly in the period between the wars. Workers in these areas were enjoined to look at the patient as a whole man and not to view him as compartmentalized. I would not question the value of looking at the whole man under certain conditions, but it is clear that there are circumstances in which this approach cannot only be inappropriate but

[5] Hemisphere neglect, and the agnosias, are relatively well-known. But pure alexia may not be: it is a rare, but well-documented, condition. Briefly: pure alexics can write but cannot read (although they can sometimes read numbers). All visual objects except letters and words can be recognized, *except* colours. However, the pure alexic can say *that* the sky is blue, bananas yellow, blood red, etc.; and they can sort red and orange colour-chips into the appropriate piles. There is an explanation for this (see *Real People*, 158–60); but what is beyond doubt is that the normal inter-linkage of competences has broken down in a way difficult for common sense to grasp.

actually actively misleading to the investigator. To look at the patient as fragmented may be extremely fruitful under certain circumstances of disease. Indeed, perhaps even the normal intact person is not so much of a whole as we have been led to believe. This may be particularly true in early childhood . . .[6]

As usual, the psychologists are ahead of the philosophers. It seems that the mind is, to some considerable extent at least, 'modular'—whatever we read-in to that over-used term.

The overall point is that *except* in the dramatic case of multiple personality (where opinions can and do differ), we seem to believe that we have one and only one person—maybe ill, maimed, in trouble, mixed-up, forgetful, immature, self-deceived, damaged, menopausal, or whatever; and we take the appropriate attitude. People just are like that. Common sense attitudes, uncontaminated by philosophical musings, need to be taken and considered seriously, even though they may prove to be in some respects misguided; or so Aristotle thought, and here at least I can say with confidence that Clark and I agree: both of us have the utmost respect for Aristotle.

If we think in terms of 'selves', then it is clear that we need to accept the idea that we are not 'unified' in the strong sense demanded by Descartes, Locke, and many others. We must have some unity, at pain of breakdown, insanity, or the bafflement of the observer (which is why extreme instances of multiple personality present *such* a problem). But the degree of unity is unclear; a single person can ride over and survive a very substantial degree of disunity.

Thus we cannot and should not rest the integrity of the notion of 'a self' on the tempting idea of a unity, consistency, or coherence of consciousness. Or, if we do—weakening the stringency of our demands on unity, coherence, and consistency—the ascription of 'same self' amounts to nothing more or less than the ascription of 'same person', and so cannot help to explain it.

3. Multiple Personality

So: we should accept the fact that 'strong' unity is a will-o'-the-wisp. In other words, *that* cannot serve to pick out 'selves'. How then could we make sense of this notion?

It is clear that a unified consciousness might be a good start, even if that unity has holes, gaps, puzzles. Most of us, most of the time, can

[6] N. Geschwind, 'The Development of the Brain and the Evolution of Language', in C. I. J. M. Stuart (ed.), *Monograph Series on Language and Linguistics*, (Washington: Georgetown University Press, 1964). Reprinted in N. Geschwind, *Selected papers on Language and the Brain.* Boston Studies in the Philosophy of Science 16 (Dordrecht-Holland: Reidel, 1974), 321.

remember many of our past actions, and can intend to do things in the future. Where we find such coherence and consistency, then we would have no difficulty in proclaiming sustained identity—of selves, and of persons. This is a boring claim, though, because it describes most of us for most of the time; and few would wish to argue that there are many people who are different 'me's over time. The claim I wish to underline here, however, is that what goes for 'selves' goes equally for 'persons'. We have as yet no reason to suppose that 'self' should be *preferred* to 'person' as an *analysandum*, or is useful as an *analysans*.

It has to be the abnormal cases that challenge us.

Multiple personality cases challenge us because there are some instances which *apparently* throw up personalities each of which could, when treated in isolation from their competing personalities, fit the profile of a 'real person'. I think that neither Clark nor I need to go over the data that purport to establish independent personalities. Whether it is fiction (as I think Clark believes) or whether it is fact (as I am reluctantly driven to believe)—that is, whether it is a thought-experiment or whether it is a real datum—we have a problem for personal identity here.

The problem arises from the possibility that of the several personalities in a full-blown case of multiple personality, some or several might have no access to each other (so no continuity of consciousness or memory across personalities) and may each have the sort of complexity that characterize normal people. Whatever Clark's reservations about the objectivity and accuracy of Prince's account of Miss Beauchamp,[7] I shall continue to refer to this case, for the reasons spelled out in the chapter of *Real People* which discussed her case;[8] and occasionally to that of Jonah/Jusky.[9]

---

[7] M. Prince, *The Dissociation of a Personality* (London: Longmans, Green and Co, 1905).

[8] But why should any reader of this volume have read *Real People*? Perhaps it would be as well to repeat, in a footnote, the burden of my preference for Prince over the cases described in *Sybil* or *The Three Faces of Eve*. First: Prince was writing for his colleagues and not for the popular market. Thus his tome is less 'sensational', less aimed at startling and intriguing the reader (although it does both), and goes into considerably more dry detail. Second, he is laudably sceptical about some of the more extreme claims of some of the personalities (or alleged personalities) with which he thought himself confronted. Third, he wrote before Freudian psychoanalysis had swept the US, and so his work is relatively free from the strong influence of Freudian and neo-Freudian analysis. Fourth: although he did not have to hand the psychological and physiological tests now available—and which were used to good effect to distinguish between the personalities of Jonah/Jusky, as well as in several more cases—he unearthed a whole host of differences in tastes, preferences, atti-

In other words: BI, BIV, and Sally, the three main alternate personalities of Miss Beauchamp, were capable of self-deception, inconsistent attitudes, weakness of will, and many of the other psychological ills that flesh is heir to. They could change their minds, regret a course of action, deceive Prince and also themselves. They themselves took on and put off roles: BI could play the role of patient with Prince, the role of (slightly sanctimonious) believer when in church, and was a reliable and trusted friend in other contexts. Put paradoxically: it is precisely *because* they were so 'rounded', so capable of inconsistency, that they present more of a challenge—to the philosophical and common sense understanding or personal identity—that do any of Jonah's stablemates.

Jonah had three main alternates. One, Sammy, was 'specialized' for diplomatic work. If one of the family of alternates had done something violent, such as breaking a car window, Sammy would usually turn up to apologize and to be tactful. King Young usually appeared to rescue (or to exploit?) Jonah when a pretty girl was in the vicinity. Usoffa Abdullah arrived when things became dangerous: a hard and vicious street-fighter. Hence the name JUSKY: *J*onah, *U*soffa Abdullah, *S*ammy, and *K*ing *Y*oung. They parcelled-out the chores, and agreed democratically on the name 'Jusky'. Jonah was something of a wimp, functioning rather badly in all situations; Jusky was in general a better survivor than Jonah. (Indeed, the subtitle of the article describing the Jonah/Jusky case is 'Are Four Heads *Better* than One?'—italics mine.) But none of Jonah's family had the depth of complexity that BI and BIV, and to some extent also Sally, possessed. It is easier to regard Usoffa Abdullah as a *facet* of Jonah than to think of BIV in that light, just because of BIV's *overall* competence, and her vulnerability to the inconsistencies with which normal people struggle daily. However: just as with Miss Beauchamp's family, each of Jonah's family regarded the other personalities as 'other', as not being him or her.

So I would suggest that (to the extent that the reader agrees with me that BI, BIV, and Sally are each personalities which might be, and indeed were, accepted as a 'real person' by anybody who had met only one of them), that each is as much, or as little, a 'self' as are we: in other words, as you or me.

[9] A. M. Ludwig *et al.*, 'The Objective Study of a Multiple Personality; Or, Are Four Heads Better than One?', *Archives of General Psychiatry* **26** (1972).

tudes, dress-sense, religious convictions, competences, which encourage one to believe that the modern tests would have endorsed his distinctions. Finally, it is really very easy to spot and discount his biases and presuppositions. For instance, he rejected BIV as 'the real' Miss Beauchamp because—crudely—she was insufficiently feminine by the canons of turn-of-the-century Boston society.

Kathleen V. Wilkes

What, then, *is* 'a self'? It is possible to argue that BI and BIV were different *people*. (An unwelcome conclusion, true.) Each was multi-faceted, and could grow and develop. Each had a sense of her own self-identity, which treated the others *as* 'others'. Each had some 'unity of consciousness' (remembering what she did on a previous occasion, and engaging in planning for the future), and each was—as are we all—motivated by non-conscious phenomena. (Trivial example: both BI and BIV might independently be affected by subliminal advertising.) Like the rest of us, each engaged in a variety of levels of reflection and representation. Both dreamt (Sally, interestingly, claimed never to sleep). All were regarded, by Prince as by their friends, as moral agents and as objects of moral concern. The problems here can and should be described in terms of 'persons' and 'personalities'; again, adding 'a self' adds nothing interesting either to the understanding or to the explanation of this condition.

4. The Bare Self

Let us try a wholly different tack, in the attempt to make sense of the self. It is a tack peculiarly difficult to pursue, because it rests on the vaguest (albeit often the most strongly held) of intuitions. I shall attempt to introduce it with a range of examples.

Consider: disembodied survival after death; reincarnation; 'if I were you'; 'I might have lived in the eighteenth century'; I might have been born a year earlier than I actually was'; 'I might have been Chinese' (substitute another nationality if you *are* Chinese); 'I might have had different parents'; 'I might not have been N.N.' (insert your own name). All these suggest that there is something—some *thing*—which transcends each, and perhaps all, of the properties true of the person as he or she actually, in the real world, is. What can this be but the self? Certainly it cannot be the personality.

What assists such thoughts is that certainly any one of us might have *very few* of the properties we now possess. There is a possible world in which you, he, and I were dropped on our heads a few hours after birth, and spent the rest of our lives with the cognitive capacities roughly equivalent, let us suppose, to those of a chicken. Few would doubt that such maimed individuals, in that possible world, are you, he, me—simply because of the evident truth of the counterfactual 'I might have been dropped on my head by my mother's midwife'.

Consider now the example from the list above that is most appealing, simply because it seems to make the smallest demands upon our imaginative capacities. That is: 'I might have been born a year earlier than 19XX' (insert the year in which you were actually born). Whatever we

242

think of essentialism, the question must and should arise: 'how could I distinguish that possibility from the possibility that I might never have existed, but my parents might have had a boy or girl baby (substitute your own sex) one year before 19XX?' Only, it seems, by some 'self-spark', which either glows in that 19XX-1 baby or does not, a self-spark which is somehow, uniquely, *me*.

We can ask the same question, of course, with all the other examples listed above; but with these other cases our intuitions—however strong in the 'one year older' instance—might start to falter. It is not surprising that we find it easy to imagine being one year older; after all, a child born to your parents one year before 19XX is likely to have *many* properties in common with you—just because the gene pool would be restricted by the genes of those two parents. We all have many features in common with our siblings. But could you be an eighteenth century individual, a Chinese, a reincarnated self, a disembodied self . . .? Our intuitions start to waver, and to diverge radically. Certainly we cannot appeal to them to settle the question (it is very misleading to claim that 'imaginable' entails 'possible', for many reasons, the chief of which is that we cannot, often, be certain that we *have* imagined P rather than Q—in this case, imagining a world in which I exist, only one year older, rather than a world in which I don't).

The moral seems to be that *if* one has faith in what I have called a 'self-spark', then one will be able to make sense of all the examples above; but would then be open to the challenge to say something about this spark. And since, I claim, the spark is a matter of faith rather than of reason, then it is a claim which cannot be rationally defended: a claim with which philosophy can do nothing.

5. Conclusion

The notion of a self has no philosophical utility, either as an *explanandum* in its own right, or as an *explanans*.

Sartre and Our Identity as Individuals

İLHAM DİLMAN

1. Identity: 'Sameness of Person' and 'Authenticity of Self'

The question about 'identity' under consideration in this paper is different from the one discussed in some of the other papers—for instance by Geoffrey Madell and Lars Herzberg. That question arises from the fact that human beings change in appearance and behaviour in the course of their life. By and large we have no trouble in recognizing them but we may wonder what it is that remains the same in them or about them so that we recognize them, address them by the same name, respond to them as to someone we know. What is it for a person to be the same person through these changes? By virtue of what do we call them by the same name?

The question I am concerned with is different. It is related, however, to the question about multiple personality discussed in another paper at this conference.[1] Thus suppose that someone calls herself Sally in the mornings and Emma in the afternoons, displays two different personalities and has very different memories which show little overlap. We may wonder: Who is she really? Is she simply Sally and Emma alternately, or is Emma no more than a personality that comes over her and possesses her, as this may happen through hypnotic suggestion? Or is this the case with both Sally and Emma so that she is the person she would become if and when she stops being Sally and Emma and has a chance to 'come to herself' in learning to meet people without acting these parts—if 'parts' are what they are?

This is nearer to my question which concerns the identity of a person as an *individual*. The other question about 'personal identity', I said, is related to the fact that people *change* in the course of their lives in ways in which the various objects and artefacts in our surroundings by and large do not—although there are, of course, interesting exceptions. My question, on the other hand, is related to the fact that human beings *act parts*, in different ways, and are sometimes so caught up in them that, as we say, they no longer know who they are, can no longer tell apart what is real from what is a part. Apparently this was true of the actor Kean whom Sartre has portrayed in a play by that name.

[1] 'Human Beings' held at Lampeter, 2–5 July 1990.

The problem which a person in such a predicament may have is a *personal* one, it concerns him as an individual. He need not be an actor like Kean but may be an adolescent, faced with the problem of growing up, of differentiating himself from his parents, of not becoming just a copy of his school mates, of disengaging from patterns laid down for him by others, of deciding what he wants, learning to think for himself and act on his own behalf, in short of being a person in his own right. Otherwise in *what* he is he would not be *himself: who* he is.

Or he may be an adult who has failed to make anything of his life, one who cannot call his life his own. He has never taken a stand on anything, has always towed the line. As this comes home to him it may occur to him that he has never considered the question of what he thinks about certain things or what he wants. Indeed, it may dawn on him that he has no thoughts of his own on a great many things. He may then wonder whether many of his feelings, allegiances and loyalties are genuine, whether he is himself in the things he does and takes as defining him—his profession, his occupations, his interests, his relationships as father, husband, employer, worker, etc. Am I the person I take myself to be? Are the things I take to be me really me? When I respond to other people's expectations of me, when I go along with what those who know and work with me take for granted in me, am I being myself? If not, then who am I?

No one can tell a person in this predicament who he is—as someone may tell me the man at the door is the plumber or my long lost friend who has greatly changed since we last knew each other. For his predicament is not one of ignorance, and he is searching for his *identity*, for his own *reality* as a person, as Peer Gynt was in Ibsen's play when his past began to catch up with him: a past in which he had squandered himself. He is seeking to *be* himself—we may also say 'to know himself', but this does not mean 'to know what he is like'.

What does it mean then? What does it mean 'to be himself', 'to find who he is'? This is our *philosophical* question. In what sense is what he has been evading 'real'? In what sense has he been 'evading' it in being what he has been like? Where is what he has been evading to be found and 'found' in what sense? In what sense is what he is said to have failed to be 'himself'? Does that imply that there is a 'self' that is *him* but with which he fails to *coincide* in the way he is?

On such a view the self which I have not found is thought of as something that *can*, though it may not, be clearly visible to a friend who knows me well. All I have to do to find it and be myself is to see what he sees and follow its lead; give it expression. In short, the self I have failed to be pre-exists my finding it, and discovering it is a matter of coming to apprehend it in my introspective search. This could be characterized as the *objectivist* view of the self. Its logical attraction is such that many of those who rightly wish to reject it also reject the way of speaking of which it gives an analysis. For they cannot see how else to take it; they are themselves wedded to the objectivist picture of the self.

Impatient with such language they may ask me: 'what is this *self* that you are talking about, filling our ears with? does it not smell of philosophy? is it not a metaphysical notion?' My answer to them is two-fold: First, yes, the self, as the objectivist conceives of it, is a metaphysical notion. Like the philosopher's 'soul' it has been given prominence in attempts to solve various philosophical problems. Both are artificial constructs, suspect in their intelligibility, and if we could clear the problems which create the need for such constructions they would become redundant. However, secondly, this is not to say that when a person is said not to have been himself, or to be searching for himself, we are indulging in metaphysics. The self in question here is 'what a person is searching for when he asks "who am I?"'; it is 'what the person is who is himself'. This is not a circular definition, it invites us to pay attention to the use of these expressions.

It is in this language that we shall find the sense of 'self' in question. No doubt this is no everyday language, not a language of the markets. But it is a living language all the same, one that engages with our life, the life in which some people find it difficult to be themselves in their relationships, in their work, in their moral responses, and are troubled by it, or evade doing so to such an extent that when this comes home to them they say that they no longer know who they are. This is not the language of metaphysics.

To be sure not everyone speaks it. Someone who has not felt the need to use such language may not see much sense in it. He may only see there the mystification of metaphysics. Having little sense of the problems with which it engages, and so of the work it does in contexts in which such problems arise, it may seem to him indistinguishable from the language of metaphysics—lifeless, artificial, abstract, inflated, and at best only seemingly intelligible.

2. Sartre's Rejection of the Objectivist View

Sartre, in contrast, has a lively sense of its reality. Indeed, for him the fact that some people have a use for such language, that they are served well by it, illuminates the character of human existence—by contrast with the existence of things and animals. He expresses this by saying that lifeless things and speechless animals inevitably 'coincide with themselves': all there is to them is what they are. Whereas the distinct individuality or identity of a human being is *not* to be found in what he *is*. It is not something given to him externally; he has himself something to do with who he is. Furthermore, if it is something that he can himself *be,* then it is something he can *fail* to be. Animals and lifeless things, in contrast, are simply what they are and that is an end of it. They can only exist, very much in the sense in which Russell analysed what it means to say that something exists. As Sartre puts it, they cannot exist *for* themselves.

With human beings, Sartre argues, the instantiation of predicates, however many, does not exhaust or, indeed, capture their existence. The view which a person takes of his own existence shapes his mode of existence. Its character is logically dependent on the way he thinks of it—which is not to say that he cannot be deceived. Thus when Sartre characterizes man as a being who exists *for* himself ('*pour-soi*') he means that man is a being who is conscious of himself. However, we should not on this account confuse him with Descartes. For although Descartes too distinguishes man from speechless animals and lifeless things and does so in terms of man's possession of consciousness, and even acknowledges the 'active' role of thought in human life ('activity of the soul'), he nevertheless falls squarely within the 'objectivist' camp—takes what I called an 'objectivist view' of the self. Whereas Sartre, not only rejects Cartesian dualism and Descartes' account of consciousness, he actually brings in reference to consciousness to reject the objectivist view. In his emphasis on man's capacity to become conscious of his own existence in the way he feels and the conception he forms of it, the consciousness in question is conceived of as *constitutive* of his being and not merely as a form of *cognition* as in Descartes.

This consciousness, Sartre argues, can be 'pre-reflective', as when a person feels shame for what he has done, or 'reflective', as when he wonders whether he has acted out of genuine conviction or pure conformity. For instance, in my shame not ony do I *know* the badness of what I have done as it reflects on me, I *live* it and in living it I *am* it. That is my shame is not merely a state of my being, nor is it a mere form of objective apprehension. The fact that I feel ashamed of what I did is an expression of where I stand with regard to it, of what counts for me and in what way. In the shame I feel I take responsibility for what I did. The reality of this badness takes shape in my shame. It is in my shame that this badness becomes real for me—or, as Sartre would say, my shame carries the conviction of this badness.[2] In my acknowledgement of it I make it my own. Where I dissociate myself from my own bad deeds, bad in the light of my own values, I turn away from *myself* and am diminished. Whereas in the shame I feel I come to myself, I become more of who I am and so more genuine. Wherever I am, I am more *there.* More of me is there in what I feel and go on to do, also there is

---

[2] See Sartre, *Esquisse d'une Theorie des Emotions* (Paris: Hermann, 1948).

more of me for other people to come in contact with in their transactions with me.[3]

Reflective consciousness is where I take stock of myself, reflect on the character and genuineness of my actions. A situation in which I find myself, for instance, may seriously raise the question for me of what it is I want. To reflect on this involves reflecting on the significance which certain things have for me. As I become clear about this I will come to feel in certain ways about these things, perhaps differently from the way I felt before, or perhaps I will have genuine feelings towards them for the first time. In this way I will come to know what I want in respects relevant to the situation in question.

Thus there are *internal connections* between my conception of the significance which things have for me *and* the self to which I come and so my mode of existence. To work this out is to reject the objectivist view of the self. Sartre is right to want to reject it, but in the way he does so he falls into serious confusions. I want to concern myself with some of these now.

3. Sartre's Ontology: Being and Nothingness

As we have seen, it is in the way that he contrasts human existence with the existence of animals and lifeless things that Sartre rejects the objectivist view. A thing or animal is defined by the properties or characteristics it happens to have. This is not true in the case of a human being. The inclinations which are 'his' in the weak sense may not be 'his' in the strong sense: he may not own or endorse them. When he does, it is not they which make him the person he is, but rather *he* who makes them his.

Only in what is his in the strong sense is a person himself—in his beliefs and projects for instance. They are his in the strong sense in that he *holds* those beliefs, he *forms* his projects, he *makes* the promises and commitments he makes, he *maintains* his allegiances, he *dedicates* himself to their object. He is not just saddled with them. To be free of his pains he may take an analgesic: he is a by-stander to the way it works. Where he is uneasy in his convictions, doubtful about his projects, however, he re-examines their object, reconsiders his objectives. 'What I *believe* (we could say) is what *I* believe.'

Sartre is concerned here with the differences between what makes a person the person he is, that is himself, and what makes an object the

---

[3] See Dilman, 'Our Knowledge of Other People', in İlham Dilman (ed.), *Philosophy and Life, Essays on John Wisdom* (The Netherlands: Martinus Nijhoff, 1984).

individual thing it is, and clearly this is a difference in 'grammar', or 'ontology' as Sartre would say. He expresses this difference by saying that a person never coincides with what he is. Who a person is, whether he is himself or not, is not to be found in what he is like but in his relation to it. This relation is not something external to him: it is a matter of where or how he, himself, stands with regard to the attributes his acquaintances find in him. This is subject to assessment and revision by him. Hence the self that a person comes to when he becomes himself is not something fixed, given independently of such a relation. Its reality is not independent of what constitutes his coming to it, his finding it.

Clearly Sartre does not wish to say that a person can never be 'at one with himself' in the sense in which this is understood colloquially. On the contrary his point is that being oneself is not to be understood in terms of coinciding with what one is like, or a self that one already is—independently of where one stands and what sense one makes of things. Yet in conjunction with other things he says he ends up by saying that a person can never be himself in what he is like: in *being* anything he is inevitably in 'bad faith'. He can only be himself in his non-being or nothingness: in jettisoning all his attributes, his positive being.

Thus Sartre turns a grammatical insight into a metaphysical dogma. He drives a wedge between 'what a person is like' and 'who he is' and freezes them into a metaphysical dichotomy—as Plato did with appearance and reality.[4] And so just as in Plato what is real is to be found in turning away from 'the objects of sense', in Sartre 'who one is' or one's authentic identity is to be found by jettisoning everything that gives one a positive being.

Sartre claims, rightly, that a man whose being is determined internally is largely his convictions, intentions, projects and commitments for the future. These are not states of the man or of his mind as in Descartes. And when a person has the kind of 'solidity' or 'integrity' one finds in someone genuine and one trusts him or relies on his word this is not because he is made a certain way or has some inner structure that makes him reliable—*in the way* that a bridge that is constructed a certain way can be trusted to take a certain weight. Sartre would say that here the man *is* his word or promise, and the promise fills no space in the present, so to speak, it has no volume—in the way that a spasm of pain or a pang of hunger does. He speaks of its 'non-being' in the sense in which Wittgenstein describes it as lacking 'genuine duration' (*Zettel*, secs. 81–82).

[4] See Dilman, *Philosophy and the Philosophic Life, a Study in Plato's Phaedo*, Chapter 3 (London: Macmillan, forthcoming).

In short, then, what this man *is*, namely his promise, is 'nothing'. His being, that in which he is who he is, is not anything that he *is*: it does not consist in his being in any state or in his having any positive attributes, in the way that ice, for instance, is a state of water and has the attribute of solidity. Even when he fails to be himself in the way he exists and so is 'in bad faith', his relation to what he is like, a relation which gives him a positive being, is still not a state in which he is. And the failure itself, which lies in his taking up that relation, is *his* failure. It is not something he is saddled with: it is he who takes up that relation. Sartre thus speaks of bad faith as a project.

What Sartre says, if my analysis of it is right, is clearly concerned with questions of 'grammar' or 'ontology': the 'nothingness' of which he speaks is understood by him to characterize human existence as such, mediated, as he insists, by consciousness. He confuses matters, however, when he adds that it is of the essence of a conscious being 'to be what it is not, and not to be what it is'. I understand him to be saying that the only way we can assume any 'positive being', be anything, is by being false ('bad faith'); and the only way in which we can be who we are, that is ourselves, is by refusing to take on any 'positive being'.

Sartre is thinking of the way people identify themselves with attributes that fix them in a definite posture or trajectory of movement which removes the necessity to make decisions at critical junctures of their lives. Certainly there are peope who do so and Sartre has given us sensitive portraits of them. But this is a *contingent* matter and could not be made into the content of an analysis of what it *means* to have personal attributes. It is true that people who freeze themseves into such definite postures evade the necessity of taking critical decisions. It is the way our identity is shaped by such decisions that Sartre has in mind when he speaks of our *ontological* non-being or nothingness. But this ought to be distinguished from the *contingent* non-being of a person who has failed to make anything of himself, who has never stood for anything and himself lacks the conviction of being a person in his own right.

Sartre, however, runs the two together. He thus makes it seem that something that characterizes human existence as such is something which each human being, in so far as he is aware of it in himself, finds disturbing and attempts to escape—in vain. His metaphysical story is that our inevitable non-being launches those who take cognizance of it into a search for being which is doomed to failure from the start: the moment we become anything we become false. He thus represents human existence as suspended between the vertigo of non-being and the inauthenticity of being.

I will try to 'untell' this story, but before I do so I want to consider briefly how Sartre tells it.

İlham Dilman

4. The Falseness of our Positive Being: From the Ontological to the Contingent.

Garcin, in *Huis Clos* ('closed sitting' or 'in camera') is portrayed as having been a deserter who has betrayed the trust his comrades had put in him. He asks himself: Does that make me a coward? Is that what I am? Sartre's ontological reflections have convinced him that the answer to this question *must* be in the negative.

This conclusion would be clearer if we rephrased the words 'he is not a coward' as 'a coward is not what he *is*', putting the emphasis on the second 'is'. For Sartre is commenting on the *is* in judgments like 'he is a coward'. He is saying that cowardice does not form part of Garcin's being *in the way* that hardness, for instance, enters into the being of a stone. In that case Sartre's conclusion is clearly one that Wittgenstein would have described as 'grammatical'.

But if so, what bearing could it have on Garcin's individual predicament? He has committed a cowardly act and feels this reflects on *him*; he feels demeaned and diminished by it. Yet it is over and done with, so how can what he has done be undone? Sartre's view is that this predicament is fictitious and the product of bad faith: one's past deeds reflect on one's present identity only in so far as one identifies oneself with them. Such identification is a form of 'objectification' which others push one into. In reality there is nothing to be undone, except what is the product of bad faith. Ines, a fellow prisoner in the same hell and predicament, will not let Garcin escape the label which his actions have attracted. Sartre suggests that Garcin is a coward *only insofar as* he is branded one and himself accepts the label. Such a label is always what other people pin on one.

To refuse to wear it one has to be strong and independent; one has to recognize that how one has been in the past does not commit one in any way for the future. Only one's promises and intentions do so and this is something one undertakes: commitment is not a yoke, it is an expression of will, sustained by the person himself through the passage of time. There is nothing to carry the person in his resolve, no underlying process that supports or is itself the resolve: the resolve carries itself. In short, to *be* anything, in this case a coward, is to be in bad faith: it is to allow oneself to be gelled into a fixed posture, to become a prisoner of the past. The play is supposed to provide an analysis of how this happens.

Obviously, as an analysis of what it means to think of oneself as or call someone else a coward this is inadequate and, indeed, crude. Being a coward is not the same thing as being branded a coward and oneself accepting the label. Nor is the shame that one feels for having acted in a cowardly way an expression of servility to other people's thought. At least it need not be so. In one's shame one accepts responsibility for one's past actions—given one's values. To do so is not to be confused or deluded. Indeed a person who acknowledges no such responsibility has hardly got a past, or a will to commit for the future: he has neither a distinct identity, nor is he a human agent in the full sense.

Garcin certainly has something real to come to terms with and Ines stands in his way: she will not permit him to come to terms with his past so that he can forgive himself. She confirms him in the thought that he is branded. Certainly he has to be strong to stand up to it. But more important than this: he has to be able to forgive himself for what he did in the past. That, indeed, cannot be undone, but he can change his relation to it. Forgiving himself, which is not the same thing as forgetting what he has done, is doing just that. If he can do this his relation to Ines will change inevitably and she will no longer be able to hold him in ransom over his past.

To *be* a coward is to lack what it takes to stand up to danger, to overcome one's fear. In logic or grammar it is like 'being irresponsible, fickle, false or in bad faith'. I agree with Sartre that if one can call these *failures*, they are failures of the *self*—they are not like physical afflictions. But my point is that if one can *be* in bad faith then so can one *be* a coward. Sartre might say: '*being* in bad faith is being in *bad faith*'. All right. So a man who is in bad faith is not himself. Likewise one might say: '*being* a coward is being a *coward*.' In so far as one is a coward, that is, one has not come to oneself, achieved the kind of inner unity that enables a person to face danger for something or someone he cares for. If it is for *this* reason that Sartre says, 'no one *is*, or can be, a coward or in bad faith', then it does not follow that in *this* sense 'no one can be *anything*—e.g. courageous'.

Sartre's original claim was: 'no one can be anything, for instance a coward, *in the way* that a stone is hard or glass is transparent—*in itself*'. But its sense has imperceptibly shifted to become, 'no one who is himself can be a coward' or 'no one can be a coward in *himself*'. It follows that a person who discovers that he is a coward discovers at the same time that he is not himself. At an extreme not only does he come to see that what he has imagined himself to be (e.g. brave) was an illusion or deception, but also that he has not stood for anything—that being part of being a coward. And if he has never stood for anything then he is 'nothing'. But this is no longer the *ontological* nothingness of which Sartre speaks in *L'Etre et le Néant*.

Thus in *Le Sursis* ('the reprieve') Pierre reflects:

'A coward, I would never have believed. Such a coward that it makes you cry.' It had taken one day for him to discover his real being; without the threats of a war he would never have known . . . It's not

İlham Dilman

fair, he thought, there are thousands of people, perhaps millions, who have lived in happier times and who have never come to know their limits: they have had the benefit of the doubt. Alfred de Vigny was perhaps a coward. And Musset? . . . And yet me, he murmured while stamping his foot. She would never have known, she would have continued to look at me with her air of adoration . . . But she does know now. She knows. The bitch, she holds me.

What Pierre discovers is not Sartre's ontological 'truth' that he does not have the solidity of an object, but that he does not have the solidity or integrity of a person. He discovers this in discovering that he is a coward. Could he have made such a discovery in discovering that he is brave—in discovering a courage in himself he never suspected he had? It is hardly an accident that Sartre takes cowardice as his example.

When a person's character collapses in the way in which Pierre's does he loses 'the conviction of his own existence'. What falls away in this kind of 'extreme situation'[5] may be false, as Sartre suggests it was in Pierre's case. But it need not be: what normally holds a person together may no longer do so in a situation which tests his limits. His familiar ways of behaving desert him, he loses his sense of his own identity. In his new behaviour and feelings he can no longer recognize himself, yet at the same time his previously familiar behaviour no longer seems to him his own. Consequently he no longer knows where he stands, who he is. The self which had seemed solid to him now seems never to have existed, never to have been real. This is an experience of the dissolution of self and so has been described as an experience of non-being. In the midst of such an experience one cannot believe one has ever existed as oneself, that there is a self that one is.

In Pierre's case the dissolution is that of a *false* self. What it reveals is a void: where he had thought he had existed Pierre finds nothing. Sartre seems to think that this is the nothingness that he has argued characterizes human existence as such—what I called our 'ontological nothingness'. He also suggests that what slips from a person in such a situation of crisis is inevitably a sham. Consequently he gives the impression that between being reduced to such nothingness and the kind of existence in which a person's solidity is an evasion there is no other mode of existence.

The truth is that, whatever his mistress may think of him, the war tests Pierre's limits, his integrity, as it did those of Garcin. This has nothing to do with ontology. They are both found wanting in courage, and this is something each wants to come to terms with. This calls for courage—the courage to face guilt and personal failure. To find such

[5] See Bruno Bettleheim, *The Informed Heart* (New York: The Free Press of Glencoe, 1962).

courage is already to be on the way towards greater integrity. The courage does not, of course, exist before one finds it. If one's failure matters enough to one, the way one cares about it and the inner work in which one engages may rebuild one's confidence, so that one is able to go on with what, previously, one would have abandoned.

The solidity one finds in such courage is perfectly genuine and it comes from the convictions of which it is an expression. It is those convictions which give one unity, enable one to stand firm, not to put first considerations of one's safety and of one's appearance to other people. One is necessarily at one with one's courage.

Cowardice, in contrast, is always an expression of self-betrayal and one is never solid in it. If Garcin did not care for the people he left without protection, if they had not been his comrades, if he had recognized no bond of obligation to them, there would have been no act of betrayal and Garcin would not have thought of himself as a coward. But the reverse of this being the case Garcin will inevitably have gone against something that is part of him, part of what he stood for, and in doing so he will have let himself down. For a person who is aware of his lack of courage, his cowardice is something he has to contend with when he has to act—like one's weak will, bad temper, or impulsiveness. One's courage, on the other hand, lies at the very source of one's freedom and autonomy.

I am arguing that the 'nothingness' to which Pierre feels reduced in recognizing his cowardice and the 'nothingness' of courage, so to speak, are not the same thing. In the first we have an expression of the kind of loss of self suffered by Pierre. The 'nothingness' of courage, on the other hand, is the nothingness of any human being in so far as he is who he is in the sense he makes of the things that enter his life and, through them, of himself—of the things to which he responds and of his responses to them. Sartre's claim, we have seen, is that he is who he is in his *understanding* of those things and not, as in the case of a stone or a horse, in what is *given* in him, determined externally, independently of what he makes of them. There is nothing that he *is* in *this* sense, nothing that is not subject to his appraisal and reappraisal. This is the sense in which he is *inevitably* 'nothing', and it is the same as 'the nothingness of courage', 'the nothingness of our projects, intentions and commitments'. For none of these are 'states' which happen to characterize the way we are, accidents of our fate.

Thus Pierre's nothingness, his cowardice, is a *contingent* matter. Sartre insists he could be otherwise and holds him responsible for his bad faith. In contrast, the nothingness which characterizes human existence as such is something *from which no one can escape*. It is no contingent matter.

İlham Dilman

5. Between Non-being and False Identity: Untelling Sartre's Story

So far we have seen how Sartre constructs a metaphysical story 'based' on his ontological perceptions. I have criticized some of the conclusions that form part of this story. I want now to try to 'untell' this story.

Sartre, we have seen, argues that since human existence is characterized by a lack of positive being, human beings will tend to aspire to the existence of things. But in following this aspiration they will fall into bad faith. The café waiter Sartre depicts in *L'Etre et le Néant* is someone who yields to such a desire. For in his attempt to 'coincide with' being a waiter he seeks the security and solidity of things. Sartre means that he lets being a waiter determine how he sees things and what he does, so that he does not have to make up his own mind about the significance of things he has to respond to and about his attitude towards them.

> Just look at the lizards—they bask in the sun
>   and scuttle about with no worries at all.
> How well they obey the Creator's behest,
>   each fulfilling his special immutable role.
> They are *themselves*, through thick and through thin—
>   *themselves*, as they were at his first order 'Be!'.

This is Peer Gynt, in Ibsen's play, contemplating the existence of things with a positively Sartrean envy. Gynt, in the play, has never been himself. Sartre's waiter emulates, as nearly as he can, the lizard's mode of existence: 'fulfilling his special immutable role'. The danger he thus evades is being answerable for who he is, and for what he thinks and does. He prefers this to be something externally determined, ready made.

'There is no doubt [Sartre writes] that I *am* in a sense a café waiter—otherwise could I not just as well call myself a diplomat or a reporter?' But only 'in a sense' and not 'really': 'the waiter in the café [Sartre writes] cannot be immediately a café waiter in the sense that this inkwell is an inkwell, or the glass a glass'. This is a comment on the *sense* in which the waiter, or anyone else, *is* what he is. But from this Sartre draws a conclusion which is unwarranted: the inkwell is an inkwell *in itself*, but the waiter cannot be a waiter *in himself*.

> It is precisely this person who I have to be [in order to be a waiter] and who I am not . . . I cannot be he [the waiter], I can only play *at being* him . . . In vain do I fulfil the functions of a café waiter. I can be he only in the neutralized mode, as the actor is Hamlet.

In other words Sartre concludes that the waiter—any waiter—is necessarily not himself, is in bad faith. In being anything he is 'play acting'.

There is no other way for me to be the person I am. Yet without that I am nothing. I am, therefore, either Kafka's 'complete citizen' or his 'shipwreck'. Kafka says: 'I am concealed by my profession, etc.'. Sartre says: what my profession, etc., conceal is my nothingness. Here is what Kafka writes in his *Diaries* 1910–13:

> The truth, naturally, lies in this . . . For whoever appears as a complete citizen, that is, travels over the sea in a ship with foam before him and wake behind, that is, with much effect round about, quite different from the man in the waves on a few planks of wood that even bump against and submerge each other—he, this gentleman and citizen, is in no lesser danger. For he and his property are not one, but two, and whoever destroys the connection destroys him at the same time. In this respect we and our acquaintances are indeed unknowable, for we are entirely concealed: I, for instance, am now concealed by my profession, by my imagined or actual sufferings, by literary inclinations, etc., etc. But it is just I who feel my depth too often and much too strongly to be able to be even only half way satisfied. (p. 25)

Kafka's passage is pregnant with various meanings and is susceptible of other interpretations. So let us return to Sartre's waiter and the metaphysical story he builds around his portrait of him. In what he is, we have seen, he tries to emulate the substantiality of things wherein they coincide with themselves so that no room is left for him to have to assume responsibility for who he is. The coincidence is precisely the absence of such logical space. In *The Sane Society* Erich Fromm writes:

> If things could speak, a typewriter would answer the question 'Who are you?' by saying 'I am a typewriter' . . . If you ask a man 'Who are you?', he answers 'I am a manufacturer', 'I am a clerk', 'I am a doctor', or 'I am a married man', 'I am a father of two kids', and his answer has pretty much the same meaning as that of the speaking *thing* would have. (p. 142)

The question Fromm has in mind is the question I mentioned at the beginning of this paper: 'Who am I?' It cannot be asked in the third person. Fromm's point is that the person who speaks like a 'speaking thing' has lost his understanding of the first-person question.

Sartre's waiter is in just such a condition. He thinks of himself as a waiter in *this* way, he tries to make this thought true in his life, to put it into practice in his actions. What he wants and tries to realize is to *be* a waiter, and not, for instance, to earn a living in serving in a café. If I may put it this way: what he is thus does not grow out of what he does, but rather, conversely, what he does is directed at realizing what he

İlham Dilman

wants to be. He must, therefore, bring it into being by imitation, enactment or play-acting. This is *the only way* in which what he wants *can* be realized: 'I can be he only . . . by mechanically making the *typical gestures* of my state and by aiming at myself as an imaginary café waiter through those gestures taken as an "analogue".' Hence what he is is something he takes on, imposes on himself; it does not grow out of his occupation, interests, relationships. No wonder he cannot be himself, have an authentic existence.

In some ways Sartre's waiter is like a child who wants to be an engine driver. He is attracted by the glamour he finds in being an engine driver. He may not become an engine driver when he grows up, but if he does, hopefully this will be so because of the love of engines he develops in the meantime. This transforms his original desire. Sartre's waiter is like such a child *before* his desire has been transformed. What he does is in the service of his desire to be a particular kind of person. What makes that attractive to him is not the glamour he finds there but the security it offers him.

I agree with Sartre that someone who wants to be what he is in *this* way—say a hero as in Conrad's 'Lord Jim' or a 'Napoleon' in the case of a madman—will *inevitably* have an inauthentic existence, not be himself in what he is. But I would *contrast* Sartre's waiter with someone who is a café waiter because, through circumstances, that has become what he makes his living at, or someone who becomes an engine driver because of his love of engines. There need be nothing inauthentic about such a person, no bad faith need be involved in his being what he is.

Sartre, however, dismisses such a contrast; indeed he does not even countenance it. His argument, briefly, is as follows. The reason why the waiter needs to be what he is is not just something particular to him, some vulnerability or insecurity that has its source in his personal development and so rooted in his psychology. No, it has its source in something that characterizes human existence *as such* and which he, therefore, shares with the rest of mankind, namely his 'ontological insecurity', as it has come to be called, rooted in the 'nothingness' of human existence.

This, I have argued, is an unwarranted philosophical presupposition which rests on confusing two different senses of 'nothingness'. A person who doubts his own existence will certainly lack a sense of security. But the 'nothingness' which Sartre claims characterizes human existence is not, or at any rate need not be, a source of insecurity. As we have seen, when Sartre speaks of 'nothingness' he has in mind the projects and commitments which, as he argues, lie at the heart of human existence. To form the projects and undertake the commitments which shape one's identity involve *responsibility*, and it is this which Sartre claims we seek to evade. It is certainly understandable that people should wish and seek to shun such responsibility. Misquoting T. S. Eliot we could say that 'human kind cannot bear very much responsibility'. All the same the fact remains that there are people who are prepared and willing to shoulder such responsibility. Indeed, far from being an impossibility, this is something we have to learn in learning to be ourselves.

The notion of 'ontological insecurity' is thus the kind of metaphysical construction responsible for the idea that anyone who is anything cannot be himself, and that we are, therefore, all inevitably in bad faith in that we are like Sartre's waiter. Hence the idea that Sartre's waiter and Roquentin, whose case I shall consider in the next section of this paper, exemplify the two poles of human existence: we are either what we are and, therefore, in bad faith, or we have nothing we can call our own and lack all positive being.

I have tried to indicate how one may come to think of the way Sartre's waiter is a waiter as being *paradigmatic* of the way anyone is anything. Once one is led to think this, everything one sees around one will seem to confirm it. We may think, for instance, of the thousands of people who take themselves seriously in what they do (what Sartre calls 'l'ésprit du sérieux'), whose self-esteem depends on their doing so, and whose voice is inseparable from the voice of their profession, their social status and position—Kafka's 'complete citizen'. The identity they develop in their occupations and social relations stand in the way of their being themselves. This is what Erich Fromm writes about in several of his books: the way in which in a society which measures the worth of everything by its market value, people package themselves as commodities and come to think of themselves as such—that is come to measure themselves by standards of worth external to themselves. The difference, in the case of Sartre, is that this phenomenon is made out to be rooted in our *ontology*—it is not seen as merely social or psychological and, therefore, contingent. Consequently it is represented as inescapable. Sartre concludes that since no one can be who he is in what he is (a metaphysical claim *par excellence*), to be authentic a person must dissociate himself from everything that he is ('radical divestment') and content himself with being nothing.

I have criticized the premise of this argument and exposed the source of the necessity in what it claims. I *can* be myself in my profession, my occupations, my relationships. Whether or not I am myself in these things is a matter of my relationship to them—what I make of them, how I see myself in relation to them. I *need not* be a philospher in the way that Sartre's waiter is a waiter. I can find my own voice in philosophy; I need not make the voice of philosophy—the furrowed brows, the hesitant manner, the jargon, the 'rationality'—my voice.

Further, far from this being impossible, I can *only* be myself in something or other; I have to find my voice in something. Indeed, apart from the language I learn to speak, the traditions in which I learn to think, I can neither speak nor think, nor paint or sing either. I cannot have any voice that could be mine.

Having thus rejected the premise of Sartre's argument, namely that no one can be who he is in what he is, the way is open for the rejection of his conclusion, namely that to be oneself one has to have the courage to be nothing, to dispense with everything which (as Sartre sees it) is an encroachment on one's freedom. Now, it goes without saying that to be who I am, myself, I have to detach myself from what makes me false: finding myself involves jettisoning that. I agree with Sartre that this calls for an ability to tolerate the spiritual vacuum which such detachment is bound to leave within one. But this is a clearing of the way towards more genuine forms of commitment and relationship. To pursue it as an end in the way Roquentin does in Sartre's first novel *La Nausée* ('nausea') is suicidal. It is to this that I wish to turn now.

6. Human Non-being and Genuine Identity

The nothingness which Sartre's early hero is portrayed as attempting to attain and remain faithful to is the nothingness of a person who has no conviction in his own existence—as is the nothingness which confronts Pierre when he discovers that what he believed himself to be was false or sham. Sartre, however, does not see this.

But one may wonder how such a lack of conviction is possible: did not Descartes establish incontrovertibly that a person cannot doubt his own existence—in the way he cannot doubt that he is alive and conscious? Certainly. But this does not mean that he cannot doubt or lack conviction of his own existence *as a real person*. That conviction, however, when present, is not something that occupies any space in a person's consciousness. He lives it, it characterizes his mode of existence or being. What it adds up to is an absence of doubt. When such a doubt is in a person's life we may say that he lacks conviction of his own existence. It is not too difficult to understand why we speak this way.

The person of whom we say this is one who does not believe in the things he does and lives for. He is not in them or behind them or, as in the case of Roquentin, he is detached from them. Consequently, he cannot take himself seriously, or he takes a cynical view of human actions. He does not see why he should stand up to anyone, nor why anybody should consider him. Indeed, he cannot believe that he counts for something or matters to anyone. He lacks 'a conviction of his own existence' in the sense that he cannot find himself in the only place where any person comes into being and so is to be found, namely in his life and actions. Or, as in the case of Roquentin, he makes it his profession to separate himself from them. He, therefore, feels himself not to exist as a person and, as such, to be *nothing:* he finds nothing where *he* should be. Thus in his feelings he appears to himself as lacking 'substance' or reality. His life, in the weak sense, is not his life, in the strong sense. Given that he has no other life, he is not himself. He feels himself to be nothing in so far as he makes no difference to anyone, matters to no one, is not noticed when in the presence of others and not missed by them in his absence.

But there is no question as to whether he may be mistaken. There is no distinction here between 'believing' and 'being'. A person who cannot believe in himself is not himself. It is true that a person's belief in himself may be false. But that only means that he does not really believe in himself and that appearances to the contrary are deceptive. He needs convincing and his belief is an attempt to do so. It is not a natural expression of his being himself, not a conviction he lives. That is what makes it false.

Roquentin is the opposite of such a person. Far from wishing to evade any such doubts, he attempts to live his nothingness. That is what makes him a hero for Sartre. But what is the nothingness he attempts to live? Is it something he *finds* in himself or something he *brings about* by disengaging from those things in which people find themselves. Sartre sees little difference since he takes identity to be a delusion. For him Roquentin is someone who faces what most people run away from, namely his own inevitable non-being.

Thus Sartre represents him as moving towards greater authenticity by denuding himself of his identity, of everything he is or could be. When the novel opens we find him already having separated himself from his profession, broken his family bonds, and detached himself from most social relationships. His one intimate relationship is built around leave taking. In stages he jettisons his habits, possessions, and even convictions, that is everything that gives a person roots and the means of acting and understanding things. Not surprisingly, Roquentin's inward journey, in intention towards greater freedom and authenticity, in fact progressively destroys any possibility of his realizing what he is aiming at. It takes him to the limits beyond which sense and order, the possibility of acting and understanding disappear, unity of will and cohesion of self disintegrate, and the possibility of freedom and authenticity recedes. Indeed, we find Roquentin approaching the limits of sanity. This is the inner contradiction within his project and the blame lies with the philosophical ideas which inspire it.

Sartre nevertheless portrays him as a person who deliberately and with courage rejects all pretensions and consolations and in his own life

İlham Dilman

tries to eschew all the lies he sees in the lives of other people. He sees Roquentin as heroically true to himself, or at least struggling to maintain a life that is illuminated by such an ideal. In this respect one may think of him as a modern example of the Socratic philosopher who makes 'dying his profession'. But there is a big difference between them which is philosophically crucial. The purificatory denudation pursued by the Socratic philosopher is not absolute as in Roquentin's case. The self to which he seeks progressively to die is only a part, aspect or dimension of the person. However it is described, one can always ask of what the Socratic philosopher seeks to divest himself, what it is contrasted with: the self in which sense? as opposed to what?

As both Socrates and Jesus recognized, it takes special strength and courage for a person to discard much of what holds us mortals together. Surely, whatever it is that a person finds this strength in must be something he makes his own, and this is the very opposite of disengagement or divestment. If a person is to be able to embark on and carry out such a feat of divestment he has to be *himself* in what he believes. He cannot also jettison the beliefs in which he is himself. Being himself in them is the very opposite, indeed, the antithesis of the kind of nothingness toward which Roquentin is represented as journeying in *La Nausée*.

So even if it were possible for someone to deliberately embark on carrying out as radical a policy of self-denudation as Roquentin's, it is not possible for him to do so without undermining himself just where he is most required to be himself in order to carry it out. Indeed, it is in this respect that Roquentin's programme of 'radical divestment' on an 'existential' or personal plane is reminiscent of Descartes' method of 'absolute doubt' on an intellectual plane. Wittgenstein in *On Certainty* showed how much what Descartes rejects is needed for the very possibility of doubting, that it is not possible to doubt in a complete vacuum: there is much we come to accept before we are able to doubt. Similarly one can argue that the very possibility of self-criticism and self-renunciation presupposes the reality of a self, founded in certain beliefs and relationships: one needs to be oneself before one can begin to discard aspects of oneself.

Roquentin, therefore, in so far as he is a credible character, is someone whose hold on himself is tenuous. The disengagement he undergoes is something he *suffers*. What is heroic in him is the way he tries to come to terms with this process by trying to own it, by converting it into something he wills. In so far as he is himself in it, however, the nothingness he encounters in himself is a hole *he* is digging, and it finally engulfs him. That is he is someone who is cutting the very branch on which he sits.

262

Still it is not clear that what Roquentin divests himself of is false. His case is very different from Ibsen's Peer Gynt who peels off different phases and aspects of his life in which he has not been himself, like the layers of an onion, to find nothing at the centre. He has not been himself in the life he led, at every turn he has assumed false identities, very much like Sartre's waiter. What he finds is that he has squandered the opportunity to be himself, wasted his life. Roquentin, in contrast, has not lived a false life, since he has hardly lived at all. His relation to what he divests himself of is ambivalent, his hold on it tenuous. That is what makes him diametrically opposed to Sartre's waiter or Kafka's 'complete citizen'.

But he, Roquentin, does not represent the ideal or terminus towards which Kafka's 'complete citizen' or Ibsen's Peer Gynt would be moving in the divestment of their false identities. Take one such kind of example to be found in the case of patients in psycho-analysis who give up their defences as they find sufficient confidence in their relationship with the analyst to be themselves in it. This is, of course, a gradual process, counterbalanced at each stage by what the patient learns. As the analysis progresses the patient is able to put into effect in his life what he learns in the analysis. He finds he is able to be himself to a greater degree in his family, marriage, social relationships and work. The divestment is thus the negative part of a positive process of learning to be himself.

In those more exceptional cases where patients in analysis are people who in their early childhood suffered extreme neglect, rejection and emotional deprivation, the analysis may bring them to re-experience the dependency, insignificance and ineffectiveness which they once felt and have never outgrown because they have run away from it. What they come to realize in this experience is that they have never existed as a person.

But there is nothing final about this *nothingness* which has been covered up by the assumption of false identities. Their renunciation, however excruciating, should in theory open up the way to the formation of more genuine relationships and commitments. Whether or not it does so in practice is up to the person himself, the patient. But certainly for him to be able to give up the aloofness and arrogance which have so far protected him and to abandon himself to the dependency and helplessness which then engulf him calls for trust—trust that he will not be pushed around, ignored or exploited as he once was, that he will meet with a caring response in the analyst. It is such *trust* which will enable him, if things go well, to grow out of his dependency and make something of himself, to become a person in his own right. This is what gives substance and reality to the self and is the antithesis of the

İlham Dilman

nothingness which is contingent on the particular life and early relationships of a person.

So, first, the nothingness which in Sartre's philosophy characterizes
human existence as such is not something that excludes the possibility
of genuine identity for the individual. Secondly, there is nothing final
about the nothingness that is contingent on a person's life and circumstances. A person who has never been someone in his own right *can*
learn to build a life in which he is himself. What is false has to be shed;
but the idea that the true self will then be found waiting on the wings so
to speak is a misconception which belongs to the objectivist view of the
self. No, the true self will emerge, grow *in* the person's life as he makes
of it something more genuine—primarily in his commitments and
undertakings.

7. Conclusion

We started with Sartre's rejection of the objectivist view of the self. We
saw how his extravagant language, borrowed from philosophy, leads
him to the conclusion that we cannot be ourselves in *what* we are. His
analysis of that is crude and defective in a way which I tried to indicate.

As for what it means to be oneself, to come to oneself, I emphasized
how much this is a matter of learning to make sense of things, developing convictions, forming allegiances, attachments. I say more about
this elsewhere.[6] As I put it there: one participates in one's own development—the development in which one becomes oneself, with an identity
of one's own. Sartre, however, goes too far and, indeed, falls into
confusion when he suggests that we create ourselves, invent our values.
His notion of 'radical choice' is, I believe, as confused as his idea of
'radical divestment' which I criticized. Indeed, it is a weakness of his
existentialism that in rightly wishing to bring out the importance and
responsibility of the individual in the moral beliefs he holds and in what
he makes of himself, Sartre does not pay sufficient attention to the role
of what comes to the individual from outside. He does not make enough
of the debt the individual owes to the society to which he belongs for
who he is and what he believes, indeed for everything that is original to
him—his ideas, his decisions, his gifts, his art.

Having said this, however, his rejection of objectivism, especially in
psychology, though he is by no means a pioneer here, is something that
needs serious appreciation. I have tried to give it such appreciation in
the context of the philosophical question concerning what I called 'our
identity as individuals'.

[6] See Dilman, 'Self-knowledge and the Reality of Good and Evil', in
Raimond Gaita (ed.) *Value and Understanding* (London: Routledge, 1990)
and 'Self-knowledge and the Possibility of Change', in Mary Bochover (ed.),
Rules, Rituals and Responsibility (Illinois: Open Court, forthcoming).

264

Bibliography

Allison, R., *Mind in Many Pieces* (New York: Rawson, Wade, 1980)

Aldridge-Morris, Ray, *Multiple Personality: an Exercise in Deception* (London: Lawrence Erlbaum, 1989)

Armstrong, A. H., *Enneads* (London: Loeb Classical Library, Heinemann, 1988), vol. 7

Baier, Annette, *Postures of the Mind: Essays on Mind and Morals* (Minneapolis: University of Minnesota Press, 1985)

Beardsmore, R. W., 'The Limits of Imagination', *The British Journal of Aesthetics 20*, No. 2 (Spring 1980), 99–114

Berger, John, 'Why Look at Animals?', *About Looking* (New York: Pantheon, 1980)

Berne, E., *Games People Play* (New York: Grove Press, 1964)

Bettleheim, Bruno, *The Informed Heart* (New York: The Free Press of Glencoe, 1962)

Blake, William, *Collected Works*, G. Keynes (ed.) (Oxford: Clarendon Press, 1966)

Brennan, Andrew, 'Fragmented Selves and the Problem of Ownership', *Proceedings of the Aristotelian Society LXXXX* (1989–90), 143–158

Brink, David, 'Externalist Moral Realism', *Southern Journal of Philosophy 24*, Supplement (1986), 23–41

Brodkey, Harold, 'Reflections: Family', *The New Yorker* (November 23), 1987

Cavell, Stanley, *The Claim of Reason* (Oxford: Clarendon Press, 1979)

Cherry, Christopher, 'The Inward and the Outward', in D. Copp and J. J. MacIntosh (eds.), *New Essays in the Philosophy of Mind* (Calgary: University Press, 1985), 175–193

Cherry, Christopher, 'When is Fantasising Morally Bad?', *Philosophical Investigations III*, No. 2 (April 1988), 112–132

Cherry, Christopher, 'The Possibility of Computers Becoming Persons. A Response to Dolby', *Social Epistemology 3*, No. 4 (December 1989), 337–348

Churchland, Patricia S., 'Replies to Critics', *Inquiry 29* (1986), 241–272

Clark, Stephen R. L., *From Athens to Jerusalem* (Oxford: Clarendon Press, 1984)

Clark, Stephen R. L., 'Is Humanity a Natural Kind?', in Tim Ingold (ed.), *What is an Animal?* (London: Unwin Hyman, 1988), 17–34

Clark, Stephen R. L., 'Reason as Daimon', in Christopher Gill (ed.), *The Person and the Human Mind* (Oxford: Clarendon Press, 1990), 187–206

Clark, Stephen R. L., 'On wishing there were unicorns', *Proceedings of the Aristotelian Society LXXXX* (1989–90), 247–265

Clarke, S. G. and Simpson, E. (eds.), *Anti-Theory in Ethics and Moral Conservatism* (Albany: State University of New York Press, 1989)

Code, Alan, 'Aristotle: Essence and Accident', in R. E. Grandy and R. Warner (eds.), *Philosophical Grounds of Rationality* (Oxford: Clarendon Press, 1986)

Bibliography

Conrad, Joseph, 'The Nigger of the *Narcissus*' (Harmondsworth: Penguin, 1963)

Conze, Edward, *Thirty Years of Buddhist Studies* (Oxford: Clarendon Press, 1967)

Cory, C. E., 'Patience Worth', *Psychological Review 26* (1919)

Cory, C. E., 'Spanish Maria', *Journal of Abnormal Psychology 14* (1920)

Crabtree, A., *Multiple Man* (Eastbourne: Holt, Rinehart and Winston, 1985)

Dancy, Jonathan, 'Ethical Particularism and Morally Relevant Properties', *Mind 92* (1983), 530–547

Davidson, Donald, *Essays on Actions and Events* (Oxford: Clarendon Press, 1980)

Davidson, Donald, 'A Coherence Theory of Truth and Knowledge', in E. LePore (ed.), *Truth and Interpretation* (Oxford: Blackwell, 1986)

Davidson, Donald, 'What is Present to the Mind?', in J. Brandl and W. Gombocz (eds.), *The Mind of Donald Davidson* (Amsterdam: Rodolphi, 1989)

Dennett, Daniel C., *Brainstorms* (Hassocks: Harvester Press, 1979)

Dennett, Daniel C., *The Intentional Stance* (Cambridge, Mass.: MIT Press, 1987)

Descartes, Réné, *Philosophical Works,* trans. Elizabeth S. Haldane and G. R. T. Ross (Cambridge: Cambridge University Press, 1975)

Diamond, Cora, 'Eating Meat and Eating People', *Philosophy 53* (1978), 465–479

Diamond, Cora, 'Rules: Looking in the Right Place', in D. Z. Phillips and Peter Winch (eds.), *Wittgenstein: Attention to Particulars* (Houndmills and London: Macmillan, 1989)

Dick, Philip K., *Blade Runner* (London: Grafton, 1987)

Dickens, Charles, *Our Mutual Friend* (London: Chapman and Hall, 1901)

Dickens, Charles, *A Christmas Carol*, in *Christmas Boc :s* (London: Chapman and Hall, 1901)

Dickens, Charles, *Bleak House* (London: Chapman and Hall, 1901)

Diels, H. and Kranz, W. (eds.), *Die Fragmente der Vorsokratiker* (Dublin and Zurich: Weidmann, 1968)

Dilman, İlham, 'Our Knowledge of Other People', in İlham Dilman (ed.), *Philosophy and Life, Essays on John Wisdom* (The Netherlands: Martinus Nijhoff, 1984)

Dilman, İlham, 'Self-knowledge and the Reality of Good and Evil', in Raimond Gaita (ed.), *Value and Understanding* (London: Routledge, 1990)

Dilman, İlham, 'Self-knowledge and the Possibility of Change', in Mary Bochover (ed.), *Rules, Rituals and Responsibility* (Illinois: Open Court, forthcoming)

Dilman, İlham, *Philosophy and the Philosophic Life, a Study in Plato's Phaedo* (London: Macmillan, forthcoming)

Dolby, R. G. A., 'The Possibility of Computers Becoming Persons', *Social Epistemology 3,* No. 4 (December 1989), 321–336

Dostoyevsky, Fyodor, *The Brothers Karamazov,* trans. David Magarshack (Harmondsworth: Penguin, 1958)

Dunne, J. S., *The City of Gods* (London: Sheldon Press, 1974)

Eco, U., *Foucault's Pendulum* (London: Secker and Warburg, 1989)

Eliot, T. S., 'Tradition and the Individual Talent', in D. Lodge (ed.), *Twentieth Century Literary Criticism* (London: Longman, 1972)

Evans, C. O., *The Subject of Consciousness* (London: Allen and Unwin, 1970)

Evans, G., *The Varieties of Reference* (Oxford: Clarendon Press, 1982)

Feinberg, Joel, 'The Rights of Animals and Unborn Generations', in W. T. Blackstone (ed.), *Philosophy and Environmental Crisis* (Athens, Georgia: University of Georgia Press, 1974)

Feinberg, Joel, 'Abortion', in Tom Regan (ed.), *Matters of Life and Death* (New York: Random House, 1986)

Frede, Michael, *Essays in Ancient Philosophy* (Oxford: Clarendon Press, 1987)

Freud, Sigmund, *Art and Literature* (London: Penguin, 1985)

Gaita, Raimond, *Good and Evil: An Absolute Conception* (London: Macmillan, 1990)

Geach, P., *Logic Matters* (Oxford: Blackwell, 1973)

Geach, P., *Providence and Evil* (Cambridge: Cambridge University Press, 1977)

Geschwind, N., 'The Development of the Brain and the Evolution of Language', in C. I. J. M. Stuart (ed.), *Monograph Series on Language and Linguistics,* (Washington: Georgetown University Press, 1964). Reprinted in Geschwind, N., *Selected Papers on Language and the Brain, Boston Studies in the Philosophy of Science 16* (Dordrecht-Holland: Reidel, 1974)

Gill, Christopher (ed.), *The Person and the Human Mind* (Oxford: Clarendon Press, 1990)

Gold, Joseph, *Charles Dickens: Radical Moralist* (Minneapolis: University of Minnesota Press, 1972)

Guin, Wyman, *Beyond Bedlam* (London: Sphere Books, 1973)

Guignon, Charles B., *Heidegger and the Problem of Knowledge* (Indianapolis: Hackett, 1983)

Haldane, J., 'Folk Psychology and the Explanation of Human Behaviour', *Proceedings of the Aristotelian Society, Supplementary Volume 62* (1988), 223–254

Haldane, J., 'A Glimpse of Eternity?', *The Modern Churchman XXX,* No. 3 (1988)

Haldane, J., 'Brentano's Problem', *Grazer Philosophische Studien 35* (1989)

Haldane, J., 'Mind/World Identity Theory and the Anti-realist Challenge', in J. Haldane and C. Wright (eds.), *Realism, Reason and Projection* (Oxford: Oxford University Press, 1992)

Haldane, J., 'Putnam on Intentionality', *Philosophy and Phenomenological Research 52* (1992)

Hanfling, Oswald, 'Criteria, Conventions and Other Minds', in Stuart Shanker (ed.), *Critical Essays on Wittgenstein* (London: Croom Helm, 1986)

Hawthorn, J., *Multiple Personality and the Disintegration of Literary Character* (London: Edward Arnold, 1983)

Heidegger, Martin, *Sein und Zeit* (1927), trans. John Macquarrie and Edward Robinson as *Being and Time* (London: SCM Press, 1962)

Bibliography

Heidegger, Martin, *The Metaphysical Foundations of Logic,* trans. Michael Heim (Bloomington: Indiana University Press, 1984)

Heidegger, Martin, *The Essence of Reasons,* trans. Terrence Malick (Evanston: Northwestern University Press, 1969)

Hobson, Robert, 'The Curse in the Dead Man's Eye', *Changes 2* (1984), 40–44

Hoffmann, E. T. A., *Tales of Hoffmann* (London: Penguin, 1988)

Holland, R. F., 'The Miraculous', in *Against Empiricism* (Oxford: Blackwell, 1980)

Holtzman, Steven H. and Leich, Christopher M. (eds.), *Wittgenstein: To Follow a Rule* (London: Routledge and Kegan Paul, 1981)

Hume, David, *A Treatise of Human Nature,* ed. L. A. Selby- Bigge (Oxford: Clarendon Press, 1978)

Hume, David, *Enquiries Concerning Human Understanding and the Principles of Morals*, ed. L. A. Selby-Bigge (Oxford: Oxford University Press, 1975)

Hume, David, *The Letters of David Hume,* ed. J. Y. T. Greig (Oxford: Clarendon Press, 1969)

Husserl, E., *Logical Investigations* (London: Routledge, 1970)

Isaacs, Susan, *Intellectual Growth in Young Children* (London: Routledge, 1930)

The Gospel according to John, trans. Raymond E. Brown (New York: Doubleday, 1966)

Johnson, W. E., *Logic* (Cambridge: Cambridge University Press, 1924)

Johnston, Mark, 'Human Beings', *Journal of Philosophy 84,* No. 2 (February 1987), 59–83

Kafka, Franz, *Metamorphosis and Other Stories* (Harmondsworth: Penguin, 1961)

Kerr, Fergus, *Theology After Wittgenstein* (Oxford: Blackwell, 1987)

Keyes, Daniel, *The Minds of Billy Milligan* (New York: Random House, 1981)

Koch, S., 'Psychology as Science', in S. C. Brown (ed.), *Philosophy of Psychology* (London: Macmillan, 1974)

Lawrence, D. H., *Phoenix* (Harmondsworth: Penguin, 1980)

Lewis, I. M., *Ecstatic Religion* (Harmondsworth: Penguin, 1971)

Locke, John, *An Essay Concerning Human Understanding,* ed. P. H. Nidditch (Oxford: Clarendon Press, 1975)

Lovibond, Sabina, *Realism and Imagination in Ethics* (Minneapolis: University of Minnesota Press, 1983)

Lowe, E. J, 'Substance', in G. H. R. Parkinson (ed.), *An Encyclopaedia of Philosophy* (London: Routledge, 1988)

Lowe, E. J., *Kinds of Being: A Study of Individuation, Identity and the Logic of Sortal Terms* (Oxford: Blackwell, 1989)

Lowe, E. J., 'Impredicative Identity Criteria and Davidson's Criterion of Event Identity', *Analysis 49* (1989), 178–181

Lowe, E. J., Review of Harold W. Noonan *Personal Identity, Mind 99* (1990), 477–479

Ludwig, A. M. *et al.,* 'The Objective Study of a Multiple Personality; Or, are Four Heads Better than One?', *Archives of General Psychiatry 26* (1972)

Lycan, G., *Consciousness* (Cambridge, Mass.: Bradford Books, 1987)

Madell, Geoffrey, *The Identity of the Self* (Edinburgh: Edinburgh University Press, 1981)

Madell, Geoffrey, *Mind and Materialism* (Edinburgh: Edinburgh University Press, 1988)

McCabe, H., *God Matters* (London: Chapman, 1987)

McDougall, W., 'The Case of Sally Beauchamp', *Proceedings of the Society for Psychical Research 19* (1905–7), 410–431

McDougal, W., *Outline of Abnormal Psychology* (London: Methuen, 1926)

McDowell, John, 'Non-cognitivism and Rule-following', in Steven H. Holtzman and Christopher M. Leich (eds.), *Wittgenstein: To Follow a Rule* (London: Routledge and Kegan Paul, 1981)

McGinn, C., 'An *a priori* Argument for Realism', *Journal of Philosophy 76*, No. 3 (March 1979)

McGinn, C., 'Can We Solve the Mind-Body Problem?', *Mind 98*, No. 391 (July 1989), 349–366

MacIntyre, Alasdair, *After Virtue* (Notre Dame: University of Notre Dame Press, 1981)

McNaughton, David, *Moral Vision: An Introduction to Ethics* (Oxford: Blackwell, 1988)

Margolis, Joseph, *Dracula the Man: An Essay on the Logic of Individuation*

Mellor, H., 'I and Now', *Proceedings of the Aristotelian Society 89* (1988–89), 79–94

Merlan, Philip, *Monopsychism Mysticism Metaconsciousness* (The Hague: Nijhoff, 1963)

Midgley, Mary, *Beast and Man* (Hassocks: Harvester Press, 1978)

Midgley, Mary, *Animals and Why They Matter* (Harmondsworth: Penguin, 1983)

Midgley, Mary, *Wickedness* (London: Routledge and Kegan Paul, 1984)

Mondin, B., *St Thomas Aquinas' Philosophy in the Commentary on the Sentences* (The Hague: Nijhoff, 1975)

Morris, T. V., *Understanding Identity Statements* (Aberdeen: Aberdeen University Press, 1984)

Morris, T. V., *The Logic of God Incarnate* (Ithaca: Cornell University Press, 1986)

Murphy, Jeffrie, *Retribution, Justice and Therapy* (Dordrecht: Reidel, 1977)

Nagel, Thomas, 'Subject and Object', in *Mortal Questions* (Cambridge: Cambridge University Press, 1981)

Nash, R. H., *The Light of Knowledge* (Lexington: University Press of Kentucky, 1969)

Noonan, Harold, *Personal Identity* (London: Routledge, 1989)

O'Connor, Flannery, *Mystery and Manners* (New York: Farrar, Straus and Giroux, 1970)

Palmer, G. E. H., Sherrard, P. and Ware, K. (eds.), *Philokalia* (London: Faber and Faber, 1979)

Parfit, Derek, 'Personal Identity', *Philosophical Review 80* (1971)

Parfit, Derek, *Reasons and Persons* (Oxford: Clarendon Press, 1984)

Paton, H. J., *The Categorical Imperative* (London: Hutchinson, 1953)

Bibliography

Peacocke, Christopher, *Sense and Content: Experience, Thought and their Relations* (Oxford: Clarendon Press, 1983)

Perry, J., 'The Problem of the Essential Indexical', *Nous 13* (1979)

Philo, *Collected Works*, trans F. H. Colson, G. H. Whitaker, *et al.* (London: Loeb Classical Library, Heinemann, 1929)

Plath, Sylvia, *The Bell Jar* (London: Faber, 1966)

Plotinus, *Enneads,* trans. Stephen MacKenna (London: Faber and Faber, 1956)

Plato, *Timaeus* (Harmondsworth Middlesex: Penguin, 1965)

Potts, T. C., *Conscience in Mediaeval Philosophy* (Cambridge: Cambridge University Press, 1980)

Price, Anne, *Interview with the Vampire* (London: Futura, 1977)

Prince, M., *The Dissociation of a Personality* (London: Longmans, Greene and Co., 1905)

Putnam, Hilary, *Reality and Representation* (Cambridge, Mass.: MIT Press, 1988)

Radford, Colin, 'Life, Flesh and Animate Behaviour: A Reappraisal of the Argument from Analogy', *Philosophical Investigations 4,* No. 4 (Fall 1981), 59–60

Rawls, John, *A Theory of Justice* (Cambridge: Harvard University Press, 1971)

Richardson, John, *Existential Epistemology: A Heideggerian Critique of the Cartesian Project* (Oxford: Clarendon Press, 1986)

Robinson, H. M., 'Aristotelian Dualism', in J. Annas (ed.), *Oxford Studies in Ancient Philosophy,* vol. I (Oxford: Clarendon Press, 1983)

Rorty, Richard, *Contingency, Irony and Solidarity* (Cambridge: Cambridge University Press, 1989)

Rousseau, J. J., *Reveries of the Solitary Walker* (Aylesbury: Penguin, 1981)

Ryle, Gilbert, Review of *Sein und Zeit, Mind 38* (1929); reprinted in Gilbert Ryle, *Collected Papers,* vol. 1 (London: Hutchinson, 1971)

Sacks, Oliver, *The Man Who Mistook his Wife for a Hat* (London: Pan, 1986)

Sangarakshita, *Survey of Buddhism* (London: Tharpa Publications, 1987)

Sartre, Jean-Paul, *Esquisse d'une Théorie des Emotions* (Paris: Hermann, 1948)

Sartre, Jean-Paul, *L'Etre et le Néant* (Paris: Gallimard, 1943)

Sartre, Jean-Paul, *Huis Clos* (Paris: Gallimard, 1945)

Sartre, Jean-Paul, *La Nausée* (Paris: Gallimard, 1938)

Sartre, Jean-Paul, *Le Sursis* (Paris: Gallimard, 1945)

Searle, John, 'Is the Brain's Mind a Computer Program?', *Scientific American 262,* No. 1 (January 1990), 20–25

Shoemaker, S. and Swinburne, R., *Personal Identity* (Oxford: Blackwell, 1984)

Sidis, B. and Goodhart, S. P., *Multiple Personality* (New York: Appleton and Co, 1909)

Singer, Peter, *Animal Liberation* (New York: New York Review, 1975)

Singer, Peter, 'Animals and the Value of Life', in Tom Regan (ed.), *Matters of Life and Death* (New York: Random House, 1986)

Smith, J. C. and Hogan, Brian, *Criminal Law* (London: Butterworths, 1973)

Snowdon, P. F., 'Persons, Animals and Ourselves', in Christopher Gill (ed.), *The Person and the Human Mind* (Oxford: Clarendon Press, 1990)

Spanos, N. P., Weekes, J. R. and Bertrand, L. D., *Journal of Abnormal Psychology 94* (1985), 362–376

Stapledon, Olaf, *Last Men in London* (Harmondsworth: Penguin, 1972)

Strawson, P. F., *Individuals: An Essay in Descriptive Metaphysics* (London: Methuen, 1959)

Suzuki, D. T. (ed.), *Manual of Zen Buddhism* (New York: Grove Press, 1960)

Taylor, Charles, *Sources of the Self* (Cambridge: Cambridge University Press, 1989)

Thigpen, Corbett, and Cleckley, Harvey M., 'A Case of Multiple Personality', *Journal of Abnormal and Social Psychology 49* (1954), 135–51; reprinted in I. G. Sarason (ed.), *Contemporary Research in Personality* (Princeton: Van Nostrad, 1962)

Thigpen, Corbett, and Cleckley, Harvey M., *The Three Faces of Eve* (London: Secker and Warburg, 1957)

Thomas Aquinas, *Commentary on the Sentences*

Thomas Aquinas, *Summa Theologica*, trans. Fathers of the English Dominican Province (London: Washbourne, 1912)

Tooley, Michael, 'Abortion and Infanticide', in Peter Singer (ed.), *Applied Ethics* (Oxford: Oxford University Press, 1986)

Tournier, M., *Gilles and Jeanne* (London: Minerva, 1988)

Turnbull, Colin, *The Mountain People* (New York: Simon and Schuster, 1972)

Warren, Mary Anne, 'On the Moral and Legal Status of Abortion', in Joel Feinberg (ed.), *The Problem of Abortion* (Belmont: Wadsworth, 1984)

Weschler, Lawrence, 'A Reporter at Large: The Great Exception', *The New Yorker* (April 3 and April 10), 1989

Wiggins, David, *Sameness and Substance* (Oxford: Blackwell, 1980)

Wiggins, David, 'The Person as Object of Science, as Subject of Experience, and as Locus of Value', in A. Peacocke and G. Gillett (eds.), *Persons and Personality* (Oxford: Blackwell, 1987)

Wilkerson, T. E., 'Natural Kinds', *Philosophy 63,* No. 243 (January 1988), 29–42

Wilkes, Kathleen V., *Real People: Personal Identity without Thought Experiments* (Oxford: Clarendon Press, 1988)

Wilkes, Kathleen V., '—, Yishi, Duh, Um, and Consciousness', in A. Marcel and E. Bisiach (eds.), *Consciousness in Contemporary Science* (Oxford: Clarendon Press, 1988)

Williams, Bernard, 'Personal Identity and Individuation', in *Problems of the Self* (Cambridge: Cambridge University Press, 1973)

Williams, Bernard, *Descartes: The Project of Pure Enquiry* (Harmondsworth: Penguin, 1978)

Williams, Bernard, 'Descartes's Use of Skepticism', in Myles Burnyeat (ed.), *The Skeptical Tradition* (Berkeley, Los Angeles, London: The University of California Press, 1983)

Bibliography

Winch, Peter, 'Ceasing to Exist', in *Trying to Make Sense* (Oxford: Blackwell, 1987)

Wittgenstein, Ludwig, *Philosophical Investigations,* ed. G. E. M. Anscombe and R. Rhees, trans. G. E. M. Anscombe (Oxford: Blackwell, 1958)

Wittgenstein, Ludwig, *Zettel,* ed. G. E. M. Anscombe and G. H. von Wright, trans. G. E. M. Anscombe (Oxford: Blackwell, 1967)

Wittgenstein, Ludwig, *On Certainty,* ed. G. E. M. Anscombe and G. H. von Wright, trans. Denis Paul and G. E. M. Anscombe (Oxford: Blackwell, 1969)

Wittgenstein, Ludwig, *Remarks on the Philosophy of Psychology* vol. II, ed. G. H. von Wright and Heikki Nyman, trans C. G. Luckhardt and M. A. E. Aue (Oxford: Blackwell, 1980)

Notes on Contributors

Christopher Cherry is Reader in Moral Philosophy at the University of Kent. He has made numerous contributions to books and journals in a wide variety of philosophical fields, including moral and social philosophy, philosophy of language, philosophy of mind and philosophy of history. He is a regular contributor to *Philosophy* and takes a defiant interest in parapsychology, on which he has written extensively.

Stephen R. L. Clark is Professor of Philosophy at Liverpool University. His most recent publication is *A Parliament of Souls*. Other writings include *Aristotle's Man, The Moral Status of Animals, The Nature of the Beast, From Athens to Jerusalem, The Mysteries of Religion* and *Civil Peace and Sacred Order*.

David Cockburn is Lecturer in Philosophy at St David's University College, Lampeter. He is the author of *Other Human Beings*.

Cora Diamond is Professor of Philosophy at the University of Virginia. She has taught at the University of Aberdeen, the University of Sussex and the University College of Swansea. She is the editor of *Wittgenstein's Lectures on the Foundations of Mathematics, Cambridge, 1939* and the author of articles on Wittgenstein, Frege and ethics, some of which are collected in a forthcoming volume from Bradford Books.

İlham Dilman is Professor of Philosophy at the University College of Swansea. He is the author of many papers in philosophical journals and books. His books include three on Freud—*Freud and Human Nature, Freud and the Mind* and *Freud, Insight and Change*.

Raimond Gaita is Lecturer in Philosophy at King's College, University of London. He is author of *Good and Evil: an Absolute Conception*, and editor of *Value and Understanding: Essays for Peter Winch*.

John Haldane is Reader in Moral Philosophy at the University of St Andrews. He has published widely in such journals as *Analysis, Inquiry, Philosophical Papers, Philosophical Review, Philosophy, Philosophy and Phenomenological Research, Proceedings of the Aristotelian Society*, and *Ratio* and has co-edited several volumes including *Mind, Causation and Action*, and *Reality, Reason and Projection*.

Oswald Hanfling is Reader in Philosophy at the Open University. He is the author of *Logical Positivism, The Quest for Meaning* and *Wittgens-*

Notes on Contributors

tein's Later Philosophy, and editor and part-author of *Philosophical Aesthetics: An Introduction*.

Lars Hertzberg is Professor of Philosophy at Abo Academy, Finland. He has contributed articles to *Philosophical Investigations, Inquiry* and *Proceedings of the Aristotelian Society*.

Fergus Kerr, who is a friar of the Order of Preachers, teaches philosophy at the Roman Catholic seminary in Edinburgh. He is the author of *Theology after Wittgenstein*.

Jonathan Lowe is Senior Lecturer in Philosophy at the University of Durham. He specialises in metaphysics, logic and the philosophy of mind, and has contributed to various journals, including *Analysis, Mind, Philosophy, Philosophical Quarterly, American Philosophical Quarterly*, and *Journal of Philosophy*. He is the author of *Kinds of Being: A Study of Individuation, Identity and the Logic of Sortal Terms*.

Geoffrey Madell is Senior Lecturer in Philosophy at the University of Edinburgh. He is the author of *The Identity of the Self* and *Mind and Materialism*, and of articles in *Mind, Philosophy, Inquiry* and *Analysis*. He is at present working on a book on emotion.

David McNaughton is Lecturer in Philosophy at the University of Keele. He has several times been a visiting member of faculty at the University of Georgia, most recently in 1989–90. He is the author of *Moral Vision: An Introduction to Ethics* and is currently working on Butler's ethics and on the concept of agent-relative reasons.

Paul Snowdon is a Fellow of Exeter College, Oxford. He has twice held visiting posts at Williams College Mass., U.S.A. He has published articles on perception, philosophy of mind and personal identity.

Kathleen Wilkes was educated at Oxford, Princeton, and Cambridge. She is at present Fellow and Tutor in Philosophy at St Hilda's College, Oxford. She is the author of *Physicalism* and *Real People*. Her published articles are mainly in the fields of the philosophy of science, the philosophy of mind, and ancient philosophy.

Index

Radford, Colin, 17
rape, 53, 56–7
rationality, 35–6, 39–40, 42–4, 83, 164
Rawls, John, 52
'ready-at-hand', 186
reductionism, 89
relativism, 192–4
res cogitans, 165–70
retarded, 52–7, 72–6, 79–81, 83–4, 85–6
role-playing, 217–18
Rorty, Richard, 36–9, 48–50, 53–4, 56, 58, 130
Ryle, Gilbert, 185, 187
The Sandman, 11–15

Sartre, Jean-Paul, 247–64
   Esquisse d'une Théorie des Emotions, 248
   L'Etre et le Néant, 253, 256–9
   Huis Clos, 252–5
   La Nausée, 260–3
   Le Sursis, 253–5
scepticism, 105–6, 157–63, 170–1, 173–4, 179–80, 196–7
Scrooge, 42–3, 49–51
self, 7–9, 213–33, 235–43, 245–64
self-knowledge, 246–7
sense, 148–9
shame, 248, 252–3
Singer, Peter, 52
solidarity, 49–50, 55, 58–9, 84
species-bias, 4–5, 52, 81, 90–1, 95, 97

Strawson, P. F., 87, 98
substance, 87–8
substance/attribute relation, 208–9

theology, 174–8, 180–4, 189
Thigpen, Corbett and Cleckley, Harvey M., 215–21
thinking (reasoning), 157–71
Thomas Aquinas, 199, 208–10
thought experiments, 6, 27–8, 31–4, 118–25, 136–40, 147–8, 151
The Time Machine, 148
Tomlinson, H. M., 40–1
Tooley, Michael, 3–4
transcendence, 175–80
Transfiguration, 207

unity of consciousness, 236–9

Wiggens, David, 90, 93–4, 115n
Wilkes, Kathleen, 117–22, 138–41, 147–51, 153–4, 213–14, 218, 221, 230
Williams, Bernard, 113–14, 123–5, 136–8, 167–9
Wittgenstein, Ludwig, 14n, 17–19, 25–6, 29, 32, 34, 60–2, 170n, 179, 191, 196, 250, 252, 262
world, 182–4
wordless subject, 173–8, 181–4, 186, 197–8

zoological taxonomies, 90–5

Zwingli, 175